OUR CULTURAL CANCER AND ITS CURE

HOWARD A. SLAATTE

UNIVERSITY
PRESS OF
AMERICA

Lanham • New York • London

Copyright © 1995 by
University Press of America,® Inc.
4720 Boston Way
Lanham, Maryland 20706

3 Henrietta Street
London WC2E 8LU England

Library of Congress Cataloging-in-Publication Data

Slaatte, Howard Alexander.
Our cultural cancer and its cure / Howard A. Slaatte.
p.   cm.
1. United States—Civilization—1970–   2. United States—Moral
conditions.   I. Title.
E169.12.S5643   1995   973.92—dc20   94–38335 CIP

ISBN 0–8191–9787–4 (cloth : alk. paper)

Contents

Contents

Preface

There is much to be said about what we herein refer to as our cultural cancer and its cure. This book is written as a down-to-earth philosophy of the overall problem and its answer. Much of it is written relative to the weaknesses in American education and the intellectually dyspeptic extremisms that contribute to cultural decline.

In this respect the relationships between the sciences and humanities are basic to most of the appraisals involved. In too many circles there is an intellectual imbalance, which prevents our society from being healthy. Without a popular awareness of how our scientific and technological means must be related to our axiological ends, our culture will remain out of kilter or cancerous.

People need to learn how to relate clever means to respectable norms. This cannot be realized if their education and religion do not vitally prepare them for it. Unless the public grows in philosophical shrewdness, the weaknesses in our culture can hardly be overcome, because what happens socially in this respect must spring from the grassroots of our society. This goes back to the individual and how and what he or she thinks. If technology is superb in our times, that is all the more reason for our values being made superb. Much more attention has been given in education and society to the former than to the latter. This in itself is a strong factor in our intellectual anemia basic to our cultural cancer.

Peculiar to this project is the fact that, unlike most writings related to the subject, about twice as much attention is being given herein to the prescriptions as to the diagnoses, to the answers as to the problems. This is a much-needed emphasis, for so often the criticisms of our culture are stressed with little or no solutions. Also peculiar to this work is the re-examining of our scientific methods, especially as related to our psychologies and the philosophical implications thereof. In addition are the grounds and sources as well as criticisms of our cultural values at their best. Related to the latter are both the importance and weak points of contemporary religions.

Another feature of this project is a number of epistemological factors clarified relative to how we know what we know with special regard for how the scientific method relates to the scientist himself and to the interpreter of all things from within his existence. Though the project refers to ideas from theoretical philosophy, it is still related to specific problems in education, society and everyday life. Thus theory is not left ethereal but brought closer-to-home, as it were.

Most of the book can be called original, so it is not heavily documented for that reason. The last chapter is an exception in that it is based on my study of Viktor Frankl in *Analecta Frankliana*, a book of lectures given at the World Congress of Logotherapy at San Diego University. Much of what I have to say about R.W. Sperry's psychobiology is based on several of his articles and my communications with him over the past decade. Being specialized in psychology, philosophy and theology, the writer does not hesitate to address critical issues in these areas and hopes to stimulate others in education to re-think them.

The writer expects some negative reactions from pragmatic people who look primarily for techniques to solve our problems. They are apt to think that the author should write like a social scientist in this respect rather than as a philosopher. Let's be frank about it. Our American and Western societies have methods and techniques galore, but our people in general have failed to allow principles to motivate them and orient their methods properly. For a down-to-earth examination of this problem, the reader need but read Chapter 18 in which this issue relates to literature and creativity in the arts. Today, for instance, we have many artists who have techniques, abilities and styles linked with moral debauchery, and they even have the gall to expect the federal government to monetarily support their works. Is it enough to be clever in terms of "how" and ill-advised or unversed in the principles which should inspire good art and all aesthetics?

As this book suggests in various contexts relative to both our cultural cancer and its cure, we must place our philosophical and religious principles ahead of our methodologies, lest the latter continue to betray this generation by failing to keep our students and the general public sensitive to our best values, ends and goals. It is not enough merely to look for *how* to solve problems. We must have sound motivations for whatever we undertake, not unrelated to *why*. This demands serious reconsideration of what gives us our ends, purposes and goals. Seldom do people whose minds and hearts are clear about these matters need specifications of how to fulfill them. "How to" and "why" questions are faced up to. Here is where America and the West in general are weakest today. Another anticipated case in point is where President Reagan went wrong in stressing more police action in our cities; though not entirely wrong, it proved to be a weak solution, for it was not integrated with clarified moral expectations of the people.

Again, let it be said that the social scientist or his approach is of little consequence apart from ethical principles applied from within the personal consciousness of people and the social conscience based thereupon. Ethical principles come to us neither automatically nor coincidentally. They are given most people by role models, who have sound moral principles. These are not merely social precedents but willingly accepted philosophical and/or religious teachings. Too few public school teachers and political leaders know what such teachings are based on today. Thus our younger generations are weak in ethical understanding. Enlargements of this issue are made in several chapters which follow.

In Part II various intellectual problems are deliberately posed for the intelligentsia of today to confront and all teachers in particular to contemplate. If solutions are to be found in today's world, they and all of us must learn the art of shrewd philosophical thinking. But if we insist on "how to" solutions, let us take note that they must first be based on the intellectual solutions discussed in Part II, which are essential to the so-called cure of our cultural cancer. Clear thinking and dialectical acuity are essential to these solutions. Leaders coming through our school systems must reckon with these issues if they are to lead us in the right directions.

The educational parallel to our cultural problems is that more techniques do not supersede sound curricula. Our underlying problem, in plain language, is the lack of sound thinking. Our leaders are poor thinkers. Until this is remedied, little else will matter. So, reader, do not expect this philosopher to stress methodological solutions without the underlying philosophical principles. Pragmatic answers have a place if, and only if, they are underwritten by sound principles, which look with respect to absolutes — and more often than not these absolute ideals are based on the Absolute as religiously revealed. If this is rejected, the least we can do is consider philosophical possibilities related thereto.

In addition, I must express my thanks to Dr. Mervin Tyson of Marshall University for his editorial suggestions; also to Dr. Jim Bell of the University of South Florida for his encouraging appraisal of the manuscript. I am still a debtor.

Part I

Diagnoses of Our Cultural Cancer

Chapter 1

The Symptoms of
Our Cultural Cancer

There is a serious cancer eating away at the fiber of our American and Western culture. A main feature of this disease is one of social uniformity or conformism. Recognizing this, Arnold Toynbee, noted historian, blames it on "the schism in the soul" of modern man. Symptomatically, this is due to our distorted sense of values and increased meaninglessness of life on the part of myriads, if not millions, of people, who fail to be integrated, purposive and creative persons. The problem socially is that we have developed a sick lifestyle that demands change.

In a recent interview, Alexander Solzhenitsyn, noted Russian writer, declared that for the past 70 years Russia has been destroying everything including its moral basis. In fact, he also observed that the moral life of the West has declined for an even longer period.

I wrote to Raisa Gorbachev about my recent book on a Russian Christian philosopher and sent her a copy. I also said that her husband's critique of contemporary Russian culture in his book *Perestroika* could readily apply in all its details to the United States. Just recently one of our great states passed a law asserting that schools cannot teach morality. Good or bad, the fact is that our public school teachers and most college faculty members know little about ethics, because they have not studied it. Our typical colleges of education and many colleges of liberal arts have weak curricular requirements relative to the humanities, especially philosophy and religion basic to morals. Such ignorance is moving our society toward extreme relativism and nihilism, which support moral debauchery. Solzhenitsyn even sees it as paganism.

It is for such cultural weaknesses that Arnold Toynbee stated after many works on history that we are now living in "the eleventh hour of Western civilization." How can this be the case? Weakened culture and education are directly tributary to this decadence and, he says, it is time for a change in the direction of recovering our moral and religious values. Conformism is the result of this moral decline. At this point, Toynbee is joined by such varied interpreters of modern history as Sorokin the sociologist, Whitehead the philosopher, and Tillich the theologian. What Solzhenitsyn says relates to this cultural decline:

> There is technical progress, but this is not the same thing as the progress of humanity as such. In every civilization this process is very complex. In Western civilization — which used to be called Western-Christian but now might better be called Western-Pagan — along with the development of intellectual life and science, there has been a loss of the serious moral basis of society.

A bit more specific, the Russian writer adds this to his appraisal of the West:

> . . . there has been a sweeping away of duties and an expansion of rights. But we have two lungs. You can't breathe with just one lung and not with the other. We must avail ourselves of rights and duties in equal measure. And if this is not established by the law, if the law does not oblige us to do that, then we have to control ourselves. When Western society was established, it was based on the idea that each individual limited his own behavior. Everyone understood what he could do and what he could not do. The law itself did not restrain people. Since, then, the only thing we have been developing is rights, rights, rights, at the expense of duty.

What is the reason for this cultural debilitation? Our society has found it necessary to add more laws to more laws, a major sign that people either refuse to observe moral principle from within their consciousness or are morally too weak in their understanding to recognize them. They either do not care or they fail to see the seriousness of moral decisions. Without what the Johanine Jesus speaks of as "the new birth," men "do not see the Kingdom of God," the latter being the composite of all virtues. When our leaders in government and education "do not see" these absolute principles, we slip as a society into the mucks and quicksands of relativism that suck us under as a civilization. No civilization can become or remain healthy or alive without the cultural values, which guide it from within. Laws are from without. We need moral sensitivity from within. Mandates are no substitute for character.

Solzhenitsyn is correct when he says we of the West plead for rights but neglect our duties. I should like to ask: Just exactly what do we base our rights upon? Many of our current leaders fail to answer let alone even ask the question. Do rights just happen? Are they self-evident? Hardly. Are they merely products of self-assertion? Far from it. And what about our duties? On what are they based? Surely not just social conformity. What makes our social mores respectable when at their best? Can our educational endeavors merely look the other way when such issues are confronted? It's being done, hence our education is on the side of our cultural nemesis, a cancer defeating us from within.

The glaring contemporary fact is that a third or more of our college freshmen are not prepared for college. Often this is related to a failure or plain unwillingness to concede the need in their high school days. Beneath it is an intellectual laziness and disinterest. Much of it is due to a failure to see the relevance of their education to their personal lives and practical goals. Lack of interest is intensified by not being led to interrelate one discipline with another. This is an academic anemia of a philosophical type, for education is more than a collection of information. It is insight based on correlated thought. Often teachers and educational theorists are at fault. In a discussion, one college educationalist said to me, "It is not important that our students can write well as long as they can speak well." Also, so-called progressive education led by John Dewey has neglected old-fashioned memory work in spelling, for instance, since to him it is only based on "learning by association." I have observed personally even graduate students who were products of such schools, whose spelling was atrocious if not pathetic.

Dewey's one-sided stress on social adjustment, but a step removed from biological adjustment to one's environment, has done much to promote social conformity without intellectual maturity. This fails to make for more than socially and economically adjusted personalities who are resourceful, self-disciplined, responsible, and creative persons of character, who seek more than self-gratification of the lesser values. Wisdom as an end-in-itself is not even thought of. Only what "works" expeditiously is respected. The once-common drive to help elevate the world is totally missing. A "what's in it for me" attitude is the primary mood. Getting dominates the role of giving and serving. Hence, President Kennedy was more than provocative when he said especially to younger Americans, "Ask not what your country can do for you but what you can do for your country."

So, educators and other leaders of society, just whose side are you on? Are you steeped in the means which are unconcerned about the ends? When technology is unrelated to sound moral ends it only hastens our pace to the pits of decadence. Can we afford to disrelate science and technology from our values? To do so is to view them as ends-in-themselves regardless of their consequences to men. This is a major malady of our culture and social destiny. Thus the sciences and humanities must become a working team. At present few of our schools make them so. The logical result is the derogation of our civilization as relativism, nihilism and paganism go unstopped due to the failure to help students to see where our values and principles come from. We need to wake up to this before what Toynbee calls our civilization's "eleventh hour" slips into "the twelfth." Nuclear powers from without are not our only threat; our cultural cancer from within is as big a threat, if not bigger.

As individualistic in its approach as the pragmatic educational psychology of today may be, it is not producing creative non-conformists but a "follow the crowd" sycophantic set of conformists. This is really personal defeat helping to obscure individualism through quick adaptations to an industrialized society which keeps the individual next to anonymous or irrelevant. Not fostering a creative individuality it merely stifles it. This is an erroneous individualism, if any at all, for it is geared to the social and economic system of our day. It fails to preserve genuine existential individualism such as that expressed by Kierkegaard, who specified "the crowd is untruth." It reduces one to a false self. The latter type of individualism is not that of a mere socioeconomic unit of society but that of a *person* of wholeness, uniqueness, commitment, and fulfillment to what is called "authentic existence." It is based on far more than workable ideas as focused on vocational education. It elevates the individual to see and be committed to more than materialistic values. Quantitative adjustments are at least supplemented by integration, lest education merely be training with social experiences thrown in. As a college student put it within my hearing, "Boy, in high school we sure had a ball!" A principal said to me that he had to turn a study hall into a recreation period.

It is not enough for the educator to say that our school system is sound, because it caters to the democratic majority. We must ask: Are we really helping the average student to realize his potential? Why is it that millions of Americans are "suckered in" by the electronic evangelists of the sensational type. Frankly, we have so many dumb American people who are weak thinkers and who cater to emotionalism of all sorts, both religious and secular. TV exposition of sex and violence also makes them vulnerable and symptomatic of our cultural cancer. The result is many of our citizens are led to material success comparable to a castle while culturally still living in a dog kennel, as Kierkegaard would put it.

Speaking of the degeneration of our society, we must overtly concede that it relates strongly to a degraded sex ethics. Our media make us well aware of the problems of abortion and unwed mothers, but more should be said about the many unwed fathers. They represent one of the most irresponsible types of behavior rampant in our world today. Often teenage women with children assume that marriage, even if coerced by their pregnancies, is the means to security. But what about the fathers who run out on them? Today 90% of our ghetto children have fatherless homes. Is it not true that this reprehensible practice should be stopped? The out-of-wedlock pregnancies are rapidly increasing, but the fathers involved are quite literally going into hiding, a truly immoral practice all too common today. With barely a farewell to their sex partners, they are simply saying to themselves, "It's not my problem," then they play the field again and perpetuate the evil.

Meanwhile the pregnant young women have tremendous burdens and decisions to make often relative to whether they should abort or give their offsprings up for adoption or have them live with the grandparents. Just as young men must learn to play the game by the rules in sports or be discredited or penalized in one way or another, so they must learn to play by the social rules of morality relative to sex conduct. If not they should be designated openly. The same for the young women, who too often make sex a kind of trap. But at the moment we are stressing the young men who walk away from the problem whether trapped or self-made. These unwed fathers are usually very selfish, doing nothing to support their partners and offsprings financially. Often the women remain poor even if they have part-time work. The problem is most common in areas where young women must resort to government relief. Often this is taken advantage of, more relief being granted with more illegitimate offsprings. Yet such practices do much in many cases to weaken, if not destroy, their self-image and confidence as they face the future. Psychologically and domestically the women have more to lose than the men. Yet they are often held to be blameless victims of an economic system. Perhaps it is time for the U.S. to observe what Holland and Sweden have done upon rejecting the welfare system as tributary to the lowering of the incentive to work. Welfare dependents in most cases need to be shown that they can work their way out of such dependency. President Lyndon Johnson began such a trend, but it was squelched when later administrations took over.

Part of the problem is that many of the men directly or indirectly involved in these matters have been jailed. If not already killed, most young men from our ghettos are in jail. Hence, a big reason why U.S. is No. 1 in the number of incarcerations; formerly it was third. As specialists on prisons and prison reform Colson and Eckerd claim that our prison population is growing 10 times faster than our general population, nearly a million in all today. One common notion relative to the prison problem is that we should release habitual and violent offenders to society. This is foolish. It would be far better to release the non-violent first-time offenders. In addition overly accommodating facilities need not be granted inmates. Work should be expected of all, especially those anticipating early release. Too much ease provided offenders invites repeated performances.

Even if a man hardly knows a woman with whom he had had sex relations, he should be held responsible if she becomes pregnant. Socially he should be regarded as diabolical, and it should become more common for unwed fathers to be identified, if not "blackballed." The problem, as we all know, is intensified today by the rampant transmission of AIDS, mainly through sexual contacts. Perhaps more workshops on AIDS will help somewhat in the coming decades, the same for drug abuse and alcoholism dealt with in another chapter. But many young men need more than scientific information. They need a stronger moral conscience that leads to more self-control and respect for others directly or indirectly involved. But whence this moral sensitivity? Are our schools fostering it? Are our churches doing a good enough job? It remains questionable. Until a reversal is achieved whole segments of our society will remain in trouble. The degeneration of sex ethics in this generation is most symptomatic of our cultural cancer and is not unrelated to the deficient philosophies of our people and our failure to offset them in our schools with higher brands of thought. Much of this denigration of morality is related to peer pressure. How can it be curtailed except as our youth learn to respect the values which prevent such conformism basic to our cultural cancer?

It is quite obvious to most people that race prejudice is one of the basic problems of American society. The major tensions in Los Angeles in April 1992, preceded by the Watts dispute of 1965, are vivid signs of this social phenomenon, which is ripping the country apart. Similar explosive calamities have occurred in other parts of the U.S., including Detroit, Miami, Newark, and other cities. Bigotry among both the whites and the blacks trigger such tensions. Most leaders try to prevent such outbursts, but often lesser motivated, self-centered individuals ignore the social consequences of their rebellious to violent response to things which do not appeal to them. Debauchery of all sorts then follow.

When Rodney King resisted the L.A. police, he angered them, perhaps understandably, but they had absolutely no reason to literally beat him up. This lit the fuse of mob reactions, many being overdone by causing innocent people to be killed, maimed or robbed. As foul as these reactions were, we are reminded that the Kerner Commission, appointed by President Johnson to examine racial conflicts back in 1967 observed that police abuse was often an underlying cause, since they symbolized primarily the power structure of the white community. Yet police actions were and are but a fraction of the total pattern of social abuses, mainly in urban America today.

The racial problem is intensified by the poverty of the ghettos and the related issues previously discussed. The main cause of deaths of young blacks between 25 and 35 years of age is homicide within their own ranks. Gang warfare runs rampant. Unemployment among black youth is now about 50%. Such phenomena in the context of discouraging economic conditions and segregation make the blacks extra sensitive, when whites do not have such problems so extensively. Few blacks have managed to develop their own businesses, while Koreans and Vietnamese citizens near them seem to do quite well. Jealousy naturally sets in like another social virus causing more social tension. White people have a hard time understanding the ghetto environment and how white-controlled properties and businesses are usually involved.

The Afro-Americans have made strides in labor, education and politics, but many are still depressed if not oppressed. Drug-dealers and the pernicious evils perpetrated by them are of no help simply giving to youths and young adults short-cuts to economic gains and promoting disassociations from their schools and families. The work ethic discussed below is commonly missing. Lawless, violent reactions such as seen in Los Angeles make for thievery and disrespect for the property of others. This only intensifies the race problem and makes the black community a lower type of citizenry in the eyes of the world.

But it is a mistake to think, as Reagan did, that these problems are settled merely by the enforcement of the law. He was wrong, as one editor put it, to dismantle the social agencies, not the least of which was the federal housing programs. Giving more authority to the police was of little help, if any, for it was not a preventive measure focused on the socioeconomic roots of the problem. The cure for this aspect of our cultural cancer must call for more than local treatment. It is a national problem. Not enough to call out the National Guard and increase our police forces. We must work from the other end, the grass roots of society. We must provide a nationally sponsored set of labor opportunities much like those of the depression years — the CCC, W.P.A., and P.W.A. Jobs must be available to everyone, not just some or even most of our citizens. Combined educationally with a renewed work ethic and social conscience this can be a boon to fostering opportunities for more people and the lessening of social and economic tensions, which cause and intensify the race problem.

Though during the L.A. riot the media so much as asked us to understand and excuse the violent reactions to the Rodney King case, we cannot look the other way about the looting, arson, and murders that followed. It all amounted to the worst criminal actions and social anarchy. King himself really invited negative police response when, intoxicated, he resisted arrest after speeding and threatening others. This ignited the conflict.

But beneath the surface explosive social pressure had been mounting up. Though economic problems were very much involved, an underlying "moral rot," as one ethicist put it, was basic. The black community of south central Los Angeles lost their poise and dignity when under pressure, because their ethics had deteriorated internally. Yet this was not a single, isolated incident. It was symptomatic of society. The entire country has come to a moral crisis involving all levels of society from the most educated to the less educated and poor.

Writer Elliot Carlson has informed members of the A.A.U.P. that the head of the U.S. Civil Rights Commission, Arthur A. Fletcher, long before the L.A. eruption warned President Bush and all the governors as well as the leaders of the major parties that a racial catastrophe was in the making in 1992. But no one took seriously this warning from the noted black leader, who, also had suggested that a summit conference be called to address the underlying issues of unemployment, poor education, bad housing and crime. Fletcher is convinced that there are elements in our society which seek to "stymie black economic progress." So Fletcher has managed to support Bush's slow-coming call for "tax breaks for center-city businesses" and for "housing tenants to buy their own homes." He also makes appeals for something akin to the former G.I. Bill of Rights to help anyone to attend college. One thing that black people need to do is to join efforts to help those who need economic boosts to get better adjusted or to make fresh starts. The example of the Jews at this point is well-worth following; that of the Asian peoples as well. Social and economic team work is what it implies.

Many involved in racial tensions may feel bad, but excuses are basic to their rationalizations of wrong doings. Much of this begins in our schools, where cheating is all too common. Both school and business resumés often include lies. Suzanne Fields, a columnist, reports that "surveys show that between 40 and 50 percent of college students cheat and between 12 percent and 25 percent of all job applicants lie on their resumés." The underlying assumption is one of reaching one's objective regardless of how it's done. So-called success is not integrated with moral principle or responsibility.

The so-called I.D.I. syndrome is fundamental to the American moral crisis. Adults between 18 and 30 suffer from this, the "I deserve it" attitude, which the Josephson Institute of Ethics in California shows to be the result of 30 years of neglecting ethical restraints. Parents, teachers, and political leaders have fostered a do-your-own-thing attitude and have perpetrated the notion that you need not pay your dues to anyone. As I see it, many colleges have intensified these moral weaknesses by stressing in literature especially the atheistic existentialism of writers like Sartre and Camus. Ideals of any type are scorned and relativism, again, invited. Middle managers in business adapt this ethical rot and lie to their overseers on sales reports to make themselves look successful. Expense account paddings are common.

As hinted above, our cultural cancer with all its social blemishes and civic sores can be overcome only as we recover a deep-seated sense of moral responsibility – regardless of our circumstances. Many of our poorest people across the years have made great advances by hard work and creative achievement — not looking for excuses but making headway by sacrificial service to others. Too many today are looking for short-cuts to success and hand-outs for security without genuinely conscientious work. This makes for a sick life style and a serious soul-sickness, which destroy character.

In view of these cultural symptoms, it is understandable that crime should be on the upswing across our nation. The Gannett News Service reported in the fall of 1990 that violent crime increased by 10 percent; forcible rape, 10 percent; robbery, 9 percent; murder, 8 percent, an all-time high in big cities. The rise in violence is fostered partly by the "baby boomerang" children reaching crime-prone teen-age years. As James Fox, a criminologist of Northeastern University puts it, we can expect more crime in this decade. In 1990, New York City has had a 20 percent increase in murders, Washington, D.C. an increase of 352 murders over 1989.

Barry Krisberg of the National Council on Crime and Delinquency claims that our nation is "reaping the harvest" of its past policies, many correction facilities serving as "breeding grounds for crime," as writer Sam Meddis reports, their policies being too soft. A delinquent was asked by other youths in the present writer's former neighborhood, "How did you get away with it this time?" Came the reply, "I just gave them another sob story." Yet various social problems also lean the lower classes towards crime, poverty being a big factor along with a weakened moral sensitivity.

It appears to be a legitimate question: Is TV harming our children by competing with the best in moral values? Much of it popularizes violence and crime, even through children's cartoons and sitcoms. This makes them aggressive and more apt to fight. Many children are becoming TV addicts, the premium placed on being passive observers rather than active and creative participants. When it comes to more serious thinking, some psychologists think the attention span of youngsters is shortened. Various groups are asking for TV reforms. A recent bill before Congress required stations to present more educational material with less advertising for children. It has been reported that the average child out of high school will have watched TV thousands of hours more than he has spent in school.

U.S. News and World Report indicated November 5, 1990, that children age 2 to 11 concentrate on the tube about 26 hours a week and absorb over 520 commercials, which condition them to desire deodorants and even brassieres for 4 years olds. Many teachers believe TV is the blame for the decline in reading habits and weakens productivity and creativity. TV throws children much sooner into the adult world. A writer for *Time*, William Tynan, quotes Professor Meyrowitz, who says, "Television exposes kids to behavior that adults spent centuries trying to hide from children." It takes but little imagination to agree with this. Counterbalancing influences from families to books will be needed to make television a more temperate and serviceable media, as well as direct aid in supplemental teaching methods.

It needs to be asserted more strongly than ever that our cultural cancer cannot be cured without an intellectual and religious recovery of the best in our ethical principles and heritage. Our schools, media and homes need to work together to this end. Have they not been at fault?

The latest Kinsey Institute report refers to the U.S. as "a nation of sexual illiterates" and stresses the high cost to health and happiness of this problem. Inadequate sex education is the major cause. Less than half of our teenagers are given sex education classes, and many of these are insufficiently explicit. Such illiteracy contributes to the 12 million cases of sexually transmitted diseases each year. Educational efforts to explicate all that is involved is believed to be an important aspect of the answer to the public's sexual behavior and attitudes. Do we not need a coordinated effort here on the part of parents, schools and the media to effectuate a change for the better?

One of the specific causes of the social decadence of our time is the sensationalizing of immoral practices by the television "soap operas" and "talk shows." A few years ago I wrote to Phil Donahue, the host of one of the first and most popular of these shows. I politely tried to tell him that he was leading millions of Americans farther into the pits of moral relativism not merely by disclosing evil phenomena but by the intellectual unfairness of allowing persons to express disdainful forms of realism while not inviting specialists in ethical and religious philosophies to counter their claims with more intelligent and better informed points-of-view. The debilitating consequence of this practice is the public's growing ignorance of many moral and spiritual issues; also the aspersions cast on mature religious thinking and the undermining thereof by leading people to think all religion is hypocritical.

Other talk shows contribute to similar types of deficient thought. They include "Oprah," "Geraldo" and "Sally." Their bizarre candor is enhanced by the competition they confront. So, the more erotic and sensational the exposed people prove to be supposedly the better — while really the worse for our society. All that is respected is "how you see it or what's in it for me," since "anything goes." There is no place for moral absolutes. Opinions supersede convictions. This undermines the moral fiber of the viewers as it helps popularize many common sins and crimes. Thus television shapes and almost determines the ethics of millions of Americans as it gives party to more and more animalism. Whatever springs from biological passions and erotic, self-gratifying urges is regarded as more important.

Television is often regarded as a cohesive social force. While true in various ways, this kind of entertainment is a moral cancer threatening our cohesiveness as a people, for it applauds anything and everything coming out of our social sewers. Sound moral and spiritual values are downgraded or disregarded, and viewers are led to look the other way when it comes to the consideration of principles of most any kind. Moral sensitivities are sterilized as promoted by these money-grabbers of the entertainment world, who lack the God-given guts to stand up and be counted in favor of the best in the familial, educational and religious values that made American society both possible and great in the first place. When intellectually little is done to counter this relativism, our entertainment and educational enterprises actually foster the increases in our crime-laden society.

There are some teachers, columnists and commentators who would support what we declare here, but too many disregard all respect for absolutes or ultimate reference points in thought and society; hence, they promote the cancerous relativism which is sucking the life blood of our culture at its best. Too often the whims of our leaders in politics and education are accepted without being challenged in the light of permanent time-tested standards. Not all truth is determined or defended by a democratic majority. Standards are always essential. Take, for instance, the case of pro-choice pseudo-liberationists: On what grounds can a woman say, "I have the right to do with my body as I please." Not disallowing some exceptions for the moment, where does she get that so-called "right?" Freedom from restraint does not guarantee the freedom from duties. Today the sense of duties to others, including reverence for human life, is being undermined. Wherever the religious view of personhood is depreciated duties toward others is minimized or lost sight of.

The only moral alternative promoted by most of our schools is tolerance for the other person's ideas, since anything goes when ideals or absolutes are rejected. In attitude, if not in philosophy, the trend is to agree with Jean-Paul Sartre, the French atheistic existentialist, when he says, "There are no ideals, for there is no God to think them." The logic of this is that our society must and will slip further into the meaningless depths of relativism, any and all absolutes being scorned. The net result is moral corruption, the insidious undermining of society by a social sickness or cultural cancer destroying the soul and fiber of human character. Thus the prevalent type of culture today is post-Christian; it is almost totally secular and humanistic at best. It caters to a naturalism, which detracts from the distinctiveness of human beings and even makes civilization and history meaningless. All is absorbed in a monistic process of materialism while dissolving the particularity and worth of conscious human beings. Philosophically, the trend caters to forms of immanence while disregarding the transcendent reference springing from a vital, revealed religion. Without the latter we have no solid ground for building or re-constructing a respectable culture, which protects eternal values while making them relevant to our temporal world.

Education must play a major role in offsetting all aspects of our cultural cancer including this one. Let's now look into the problems of education itself.

Chapter 2

The Betrayal in American Education

What is wrong with education in the United States today? Not only is the rate of illiteracy rising as statistics plainly indicate, but the general quality of education among the literate is deteriorating noticeably. I do not wish to sound pontifical, but as an educator and concerned citizen I feel it is time, if not past time, to speak out. Daily I am reminded of the problem when I drive my car through the city and am struck by the many misspellings on the signs that greet me.

Some articles in prominent journals these days deplore the deterioration of American education, but few point to a remedy. Perhaps it is time for a philosopher to speak up publicly after years of restraint.

Let's face it. The fundamental problem lies at the doors of our colleges of education. Their main fault is one of stressing methodology before intellectual substance. As a British-educated professor has observed, our schools are superior on the level of the primary departments of our elementary schools but from then on they become weak in both content and discipline. The newer methodologies of a Deweyistic type apply well to enhancing the interest of the very young, but the ego-trips they open up for these youngsters cause them to be problematic for teachers from around the fourth grade and up. By the time they are in junior high school their cocky egocentricism is such that they lose respect for their elders including their teachers, not to mention their parents.

When this loss of respect for teachers is combined with a lowering of demands upon the academic content, the education system is in trouble. Teachers hesitate to expand the requirements of the content of their classes when they see that their pupils lack a resolute desire to learn anything and everything. But whence the desire to learn anything and everything? It is simply missing among the majority of our youngsters of the fourth through sixth grades and beyond.

What is the basic problem? It is this: Our colleges of education place but minimal intellectual requirements upon our prospective teachers. They teach methodology more than they demand academic substance. How so? They have a weak curriculum and fail to help prospective teachers to learn the art of dialectical thinking. The result is that such thinking fails to rub off on the pupils when they are mature enough to examine the outside world and what is involved in interpreting it. The consequence of this is that the pupils do not discover the old-fashioned excitement of learning. When such is the case, their education is to them a burden rather than a blessing. Disinterest follows on up through high school. In short, our teachers do not teach students how to think. The reason is they themselves have not been taught.

What is the basic cure? Broadly, it is the need for more liberal education. Colleges of education should be dissolved and a few of their specializations absorbed by liberal arts colleges. Specifically, no teacher should be allowed to teach on any level who lacks a liberal arts degree and, more particularly, no teacher should be allowed to teach any subject on any level who has not studied two or more courses in philosophy. Why? Because philosophy is the very hub of the academic wheel where dialectical thinking is most apparent. When teachers learn to think dialectically, they have more interest in their subjects; and when their pupils or students catch on to such thinking, they enjoy their learning experience and seldom need to be challenged or inveigled to do their studies, because they love to learn. Teachers colleges, greatly influenced by John Dewey, have literally snubbed the study of philosophy. Since 1900 our colleges in general have placed the study of philosophy in the back seat. Why? Dewey and his cohorts scorned anything to do with classical thought in favor of pragmatic matters such as vocational education. The result has been an educational system geared to our economic system. The sad consequence of this is that myriads of people have viewed education as a means for making a living rather than an art for living a life. Another consequence is that our teachers know too little about the intellectual groundwork of our culture, where it has come from, where it is, and where it may be going. One of the most ridiculous circumstances to develop in several states is the appointment of specialists in physical education to become superintendents and principals of schools.

It is reported that in 1945 the vocabulary of American children between the ages of 6 and 14 was 25,000 words; by 1990, it fell to 10,000. There were similar drops in college SAT scores, and high school drop outs rose from 25% to 75% in poorer sections and those of minorities. It is not enough for educational associations to demand more money for school programs. Colson and Eckard assert that the U.S. already spends much more per student than do Japan and Germany. As suggested above, our colleges of education are not promoting the necessary drive toward academic excellence. Their pablum must be replaced with sound scholarship and achievement tests for both our teachers and their students. Standards are kept too low. Putting it brusquely, our present educational system cannot resolve our problems, for it *is* the basic problem.

A recent 1992 poll sponsored by *Time* newsmagazine reflected that the public sees the need to revamp our educational system. Seventy-five percent of the 300,000 respondents agreed that all high school graduates should have to pass standardized national exams in mathematics, science and English. In addition 86.8% said "parents should be allowed to establish tax-free savings funds for their children's college education." Sixty-two and one-half percent called for stronger gun control laws to help cut down the crime rate. Gun-toting is becoming much too common in many schools.

Also, it is time we Americans confessed the inferiority of our colleges in general. Too much time is spent in remedial catch-up work, since our high school graduates in general are poorly prepared for advanced work, especially in the humanities and social sciences. A capable American exchange student, age 19, went to Germany and observed that a 16 year old youth in the home he stayed at was far superior to him in discussing most any conceivable subject. Among other things Europeans study foreign languages early in grade school. American educationalists say our students are not ready for languages until high school. Why are they so incapable? Surely it is not the students but the teaching. Our schools are suffering from intellectual anemia due to low aims and a low understanding of what it means to be educated. We need an understanding of other peoples' cultures as linked with their languages and philosophies. Our educational specialists are themselves too often limited intellectually failing to communicate with people in the liberal arts especially, the consequence being a replacement of substance by form and methodology. Hence, our prospective teachers usually are lacking in a sound curriculum and philosophy of education. How pathetic we must look to others when our American statesmen abroad can speak only English.

Walter Lippman may have been right when he said that the prevalent type of American education, if it continues, is destined to destroy our civilization. Most of our students graduate from college without having wrestled with the momentous intellectual and ethical issues of the past and present. Combined with fragmentation this is linked with the failure to cross-fertilize the fundamental findings of the various disciplines. Higher education contributes to our cultural undoing when it promotes specialization without integration. This academic anemia is a philosophical one, for it is philosophy's business, more than any other discipline, to communicate and interrelate the basic tenets and principles of the respective fields of inquiry. It is the difference between training and education.

Perhaps the worst toll of our educational betrayal today is being taken on the secondary level when charm school forms of personality development often go unaccompanied by creative academic achievement. The general result is a people of lower tastes, lower morals and minimal etiquette along with a lack of respect for scholarship. What Max Rafferty called "the cult of the slob" has become a reality. It is time to stop being only egalitarian about education and to begin something akin to an elitism. Democracy cannot retain a high level of culture if we fail to enhance the quality of our curriculum requirements and raise our educational standards across the board. Though we must not neglect the average student, we must expect the most from him, not the least. Spoon-feeding must not become a substitute for self-assertion. Too often the superior student must hide his superiority in order to be socially accepted. This is tragic. Thus educational conformism caters to social conformism.

Until the educational betrayal fostered directly and indirectly by our teachers colleges is curtailed. the cultural debilitation of the times cannot be stopped. We must expect all students to stretch themselves to the maximum rather than be accommodated as cultural sycophants seeking shortcuts to adulthood. The academic trend, while often pragmatically vocational, is such that our students are being returned to us as culturally stunted persons who are weak in intellectual discernment, moral responsibility, and philosophical and religious understanding. We must teach our students that in this free land we are not free from responsibility but free for it. At the turn of this century, the average college student was eager to roll up his sleeves and change things for the better. This was related to his philosophy. Today the tendency is for students merely to seek personal security and succumb to social conformity. Aiming at mere social and economic adjustment, such persons under pressure from their peers soon become subjects of social maladjustment as reflected in the increasing phenomena of moral relativism, mental illness, and the breakdown of family life. Thus, there is a direct correlation between our cultural trends and our weak educational philosophy. Until this is overtly acknowledged and acted upon, we cannot withstand the effects of the great betrayal in American education today.

It is in the face of the above-mentioned issues that we must understand why it is that the study of education or educational techniques has lost its respect as a discipline in higher education. Such specialists are seldom regarded as scholars. They are even looked upon as professional perpetrators of our academic ills, for many of which they have received legislative backing.

A conspicuous consequence of our lowered aims in education is a lowering of values held by the public. Scholars, scientists and teachers themselves often barely manage to eke out a reasonable economic existence while entertainers and athletes collect millions overnight. What does this reflect but the lowering of American value judgments. Such distortions promote and reflect our cultural cancer.

What is the cure? Though more specifications will be made in Part II, basic is a fresh appraisal of what is truly meant by the university and its goals. But with it must come a close self-examination of our educational system as such. American education in general is subject to attack mainly on the following counts: 1) The pragmatic and vocational perspectives, while having a place, have become too much the vogue under the low aim of social adjustment intemperately interpreted in economic terms. 2) The democratic concern for the masses, while not wrong, has become an intemperate, domineering concern which tends to neglect the potential of the superior student and thereby stifles the future leadership of the masses, even as it tends to keep the potential of the average at its minimum rather than maximum. Accompanying this is the overall lowering of academic standards and expectations. 3) Our educational institutions in general show little or no concerted aim, goal or mission for our country. Aside from making for a people who can adjust to their environment and vote with some degree of intelligence, there appears to be no long range goal for elevating the values and thereby the cultural quality of our people. Functionally, the departmentalization and fragmentation of curricula, especially in higher education, leads to an imbalanced understanding of things, so that the student's thought is not sufficiently organized or integrated into some semblance of wholeness, apart from which it is dubious that there can be real wisdom or true liberal education. Facts and more facts are not enough; there must be a dialectical shrewdness of insight and correlated thought on all levels. This means we must educate more toward wisdom, not merely economic success. 4) Our educational institutions also contribute to our cultural weakness by failing to impart a common set of ethical principles or concerns beyond that of respect for the democratic majority. Though this respect for democratic opinion has become a secular religion of a sort, the subterranean influence is one of enhanced relativism. Nothing is stable, ideal, or permanent, so nothing is subject to total commitment. One result is the separation of scientific findings from cultural values, a matter fundamental to the cultural crisis of our time.

In short, we cannot arrest this educational decline until the betrayal is conceded and overcome, i.e. until our teachers are taught how to think — how to think philosophically, not just atomistically; theoretically, not just factually; holistically, not just in bits and pieces. Unless this is changed for the better our students will improve little if at all.

Perhaps some more objective data will be more convincing concerning the betrayal in American education. In an address at Arizona State University our recent Secretary of Education Lauro F. Cavazos included several statistics that realistically describe American education today. I'll avoid his comments herein other than his words, "Quality is lacking." Here are the statistical facts alluded to:

1. Business and industrial leaders report that most job applicants "could not read, write or calculate well enough. . . ."
2. Only one in five 17 year olds can compose "an adequate persuasive letter."
3. Only one in 20 of our 17 year olds can read well enough to learn from literary, historical and scientific materials.
4. Only 43% of our 17 year olds know that our Constitution divides power between the federal and state governments.
5. Only 60% of them recognize the meaning of "checks and balances."
6. Twenty-five percent of our students today fail to complete high school. Less than half (11%) of them earn a diploma or equivalency by the age of 25.

7. Only 60% of Hispanic 25 year olds have a high school diploma.

8. The average Hispanic or black 9 year old is already behind in science and math by as much as 25%.

9. The National Commission on Excellence in Education recommended five years ago that "every high school student be required to study 4 years of English, 3 years of science, 3 years of math, 3 years of social studies, 2 years of foreign language and a half-year of computer study." Today only one of eight students complete this regimen.

10. Fewer than 50% take a world history course in high school. Just 17% take geography. (That was formerly in junior high.)

11. Only half of our high school juniors can handle math usually taught in junior high.

12. Our students get only a third to a half as much science as children in other advanced nations. Comparatively, our college-bound students score near the *bottom* in science and math, specifically *last* in biology out of 12 industrialized countries.

13. Our public schools in general "have overlooked moral education." (Can you guess why?) One state has even made it illegal.

14. Only 8% of students currently enrolled in teacher preparation programs are of the minority groups, while 25% of our public school children are black or Hispanic.

Yes, "Quality is lacking," as Secretary Cavazos put it. No wonder, as Morton A. Kaplan, noted editor and publisher observes, that a higher percentage of our population is becoming unfit to hold jobs, especially as most skills are required by a more sophisticated economy. Most of this "occupational unfitness," he says, is found among the minority groups. The American dream eludes most of them except in athletics and drug exchange.

Robert L. Jackson of the *Los Angeles Times* states that the performance of most of our elementary and high school students is low and not improving. Little or no progress has been made in the past two decades. As we have expressed elsewhere, they demonstrate an inability to think through problems. The Department of Education concedes this but fails to see that our teachers have the same problem. They, too, are weak thinkers, because they do not know how to think philosophically. As stated above, our colleges of education have betrayed them; too little has been expected of them intellectually. Teachers have not been required to become good philosophers who can think dialectically and creatively.

Though the democratization of American education has been helpful in elevating the masses, we have paid a big price for it. Editor Kaplan observes that not only has the teaching profession become a low paying career for mediocre students who hail mainly from teacher and agricultural colleges and who test low in Army tests, but "many of our high-school teachers," says Kaplan, "are only semi-literate." These teachers are frightened by students who ask questions or challenge pat answers. As I have observed, they are philosophically weak; in short, victims of the great betrayal.

Kaplan applauds educational districts which use television with courses taught by capable specialists and adapt the use of computers. Both the more capable and less capable students could be taught effectively, not only math and science but foreign languages. But even this approach has its problems. As Earle M. Busse of Matteson, Ill., says, "I can imagine the blank minds . . . if the batteries in their calculators go dead." We must keep in mind that every computer and calculator is dependent upon the human mind, the best such "device" ever invented and one which needs no programming. (Cf. my book, *The Creativity of Consciousness*). There is a danger that our young people will become too dependent upon calculators while losing much of their own ability to calculate. Their common weakness in math today as they enter the business world reflects this conspicuously.

An improved head-start program would be helpful. Kaplan like Bloom supports my assertion that our schools should cultivate sensitivity to moral issues. Unless this is promoted our schools will bequeath to our children a society advanced in technology but philosophically primitive in quality. The problem is upon us. A college president stated rightly at commencement exercises, "We have become a nation of technological giants but moral pygmies."

Education today also has failed students by keeping their cultural aims too low. Consequently as citizens they no longer have the ambition once popular around 1900 and before to help change the world for the better. Moulded by their society, they fail to help re-mould it. How can they when not steeped in moral and spiritual values that can elevate their motivations? With little exposure to classical thought and the humanities, they lack ambitions that surpass just "getting by." The pragmatic aims of popular education are too short-sighted as they promote an excessive egocentricism. The student then looks for every conceivable short-cut to adulthood and social status. The consequential conformism stunts him as a student and a self. This is tragic.

"Why can't I just major in my chosen field of speech," asked a college student. "Why must I study other fields?" A more philosophically astute student replied, "So that you will know what your are talking about." Techniques and methodologies of all sorts call for a total corpus of thought with which they may be enmeshed, lest academics and intellectual responsibility be depreciated. This demands the philosophical correlation and integration of specialized thought; also more concern for intellectual substance basic to the liberal arts. Cultural tastes cannot be elevated without this. European visitors to our shores often see our weaknesses represented by the typical Americans who turn to comic strips and scandal sheets before the front page news articles.

Another aspect of our society's deterioration has both moral and economic implications. It is the growing loss of what sociologists have called "the Protestant work ethic", mainly introduced by the Puritans. Many middle-aged people and many youth in their train today are not dependable workers. Much of it is related to sheer laziness and a lack of ambition to fulfill a full day's work for a full day's pay. The problem has become so pronounced that hundreds of big businessmen and industrialists are now using varieties of mechanisms, often camera-like, for the surveillance of their workers. This is another sign of an ethically weakened conscience on the part of the American people. The writer has observed first hand how some recent immigrants prove to be much more dependable and industrious workers. Often typical Americans become envious and impatient with them because of their superior productivity. The problem is not unrelated to the common practice of the withdrawal of many youth from our schools and their lack of a spiritually inspired character to want to be productive and dependable. The less our people can do constructively through personal willingness the less we can say in favor of our society. Democracy is no more successful than the character or quality of its people. But it is weakening today. Surely, this phenomenon is a basic symptom of our cultural cancer.

Many of our economic problems today relate to the loss of our work ethic. This is akin to "the schism in the soul" of our people or what Kierkegaard anticipated as "soul sickness" causing men to lack a native drive toward responsibility and achievement. Colson and Eckerd in their book, *Why America Doesn't Work* (pp. 14-25) agree with this and specify that in 1960 U.S. made 75% of all cars, the percentage dropping to 25% by 1990. Part of the problem is that the work forces fail to trust managers, who have never worked on the production line and have too little contact with workers.

Unlike the Greeks, who viewed work as a curse, most Americans of the past several generations and various ethnic groups, Protestant, Catholic and Jew, felt that their work was of consequence and mattered to God. This gave them a set of transcendent values, which made work basic to worthwhile living and enhanced their dignity. The obvious loss of this outlook has contributed to a deep spiritual malaise today. Higher education in America has not contributed much to a recovery of the work ethic, for it has snubbed ethics basic to philosophy and religion. Many educators think the study of ethics interferes with the freedom to do as we please. Thus they undermine the work ethic which made America great by ignoring the religious values basic even to our culture's conscience at its best. Consequently, we have no less than an underclass "trapped in a culture that teaches them not to work and not to hope for better than they have." (Ibid, p. 75). Children often fail to catch the dignity of responsibility and work and are too often spoiled by luxuries not achieved but given them.

Martin Luther stressed that any person can serve God in any respectable work. John Wesley vivified this when he said, "Gain all you can. Save all you can. Give all you can." He and his lay class leaders were also the main critics of child labor in the mines of northern England. The loss of this work ethic in our time has been observed even by sociologists. They and others have recognized that Americans have greatly lessened both their productivity and the quality of their workmanship. Manufacturers for quite some time have added to the problem by policies of planned obsolescence. The writer has observed for instance, that some products from toys to automobiles have been quite well made except for some deliberately weaker parts. The plan is for the product to wear out early so that new purchases must be made. I have also observed personally where businessmen have promised things like repairing a car trunk door, only to hear them reject it and emotionally put me down when expecting to have the job done after the car was paid for. What is this trend but a greedy self-concern without full respect for others? It goes with the moral decline of our times marked largely by the loss of ambition and dedicated labor.

A while back I was involved in raising funds to help meet religious needs and remedy economic problems in Chile. I learned specifically that businessmen in that country catered to workers who were evangelical Christians, because, like their Puritan forebears, they could be trusted and relied upon for a full day's work for a full day's pay. Their work ethic was an aspect of their spiritual commitment. Unlike the typical workers around them, they did not have to be checked up on by cross-checkings of bills and receipts among customers. Their work ethic was very much linked with their theistic faith and its implicit promotion of integrity.

The American labor force everywhere needs to recover such a work ethic. But how can it be done? Only as the character of our people is changed from within, there being no substitute for a theism making for "the new heart" which the prophet Jeremiah anticipated or "the new birth", which Jesus vivified, giving higher motivations for both living and dying. The result is dedicated persons who do dedicated work. What is more basic to such a recovery than the fresh realization of a strong theistic faith made relevant to the everyday life of Americans?

The needed recovery of a sound work ethic will call for more than a conscientious minority if as a society we are to cure our cultural cancer. Our schools will need to clarify and popularize the values which make ethical responsibilities meaningful to all people. The values springing from theistic commitments must be made relevant to what we mean by true Americanism. The philosophical and religious principles which once made our nation great must be recovered. College professors must study the bases of such values and clarify them for our prospective teachers and their students. Only then will our society recover its moral backbone by being nurtured by principles which motivate people to be directed toward the welfare of others, not just themselves.

A new culture of violence is veering its head, reflecting the need of higher character. Discipline is needed among our youth as based on the moral education, which once inspired our work ethic. Home and school alike must join the church in overcoming this cultural cancer.

Though a well-known problem in the United States is our increasing crime rate, our legislators tend to be sluggish about it along with our judiciary. A practical matter related to their difficulties in handling crime is the shortage of prison facilities. We need more jails and prisons in most, if not all, states. Too many criminals are getting by with light sentences, because the number of them is so great and the means of punishing them so inadequate. All too common is the practice of allowing executives of various types of business and government to be released after fines which are low in proportion to the profits they make through criminal action. To them these fines amount to business investments. What should be done more often is to imprison these executive leaders, because they detest being incarcerated, even for short periods. They would rather pay fines than have the public see them as necessary confined criminals with black marks on their records. Then, too, often people who are better off financially find it easier to meet their fines, while criminals from poorer classes must be jailed when they cannot meet such costs. In short, corruption of all types needs to be stopped, while too often the "big wigs" of business and politics are among our most serious offenders. This, too, is symptomatic of our cultural cancer.

One of the important improvements we need to universalize relative to the punitive treatment of criminals is to give prisoners the opportunity to do constructive work and be paid for it at least to some extent. Over a century and a half ago inmates paid for their confinement by honest labor. By 1990 this practice was almost eliminated, union leaders being jealous of their outputs. A major therapeutic factor was that inmates could pay back something to their victims. Such restitution enhanced their responsibility and self-esteem not unrelated to the work ethic referred to above.

As the cells of our cultural cancer multiply before our eyes, it is time for our intelligentsia to become more realistic. Responsible individualism must replace the popular egocentric type. But this cannot be realized unless our philosophy of education and life in general is reappraised and redirected. Academic standards must be raised beginning with what is expected of our prospective teachers. Without higher requirements, our classroom discussions and buzz sessions will amount to little more than shared ignorance. Truth must be viewed as both objectively based and subjectively relevant.

Conditioned by peer pressure and modern advertising, it is little wonder that a mere ho-hum attitude toward cultural values does not prevent our students from being victimized by drugs and alcohol. With superficial interest in social adjustment, they choose social acceptance over individualistic drives for self-improvement and social service. Steeped in ethical relativism if not nihilism, since guided educationally with little else, they become victims of drugs and constant entertainment. Social adjustments of this kind lead to maladjustments that smother the sense of responsibility. Character is undeveloped and the individual lacks enough inner stamina to withstand the frustration when his social acceptance is jeopardized. Often in our schools the more capable person must hide his superiority or be a victim of this trend. Thus our cultural cancer mounts up.

We must also concede that the crises of today are global in scope while man-made as products of our social priorities. Science and technology alone cannot save our civilization, for their methodologies and temporary answers are no substitute for our long-term cultural problems and the implicit principles accepted or rejected. The basic causes of our social cancer are the low moral tastes that have weakened and yet steered our social structure. These must be remedied. Decadent priorities must be replaced if we are to improve our world order rather than destroy it.

Anticipating a little of what shall be brought forth in Part II, we see some hopeful signs in the recovery of moral ideologies that are both existentially and socially relevant. Much of this is based on a new-found respect for phenomenology and the new mentalism uncovered especially by R. M. Sperry's psychobiology and the closer relationship between the sciences and ethics and religion. With such reappraisals, we can redirect our social goals and ambitions through reformed value judgments. Much will be related to the new scientific paradigms already implied offsetting the materialism and behaviorism in much modern psychology. The sciences and humanities will need to work together. Our educational programs must make this mandatory, lest the betrayal referred to dominate us in the coming generations.

Immanuel Kant believed that everyone has a moral sensitivity though also subject to abuse. He viewed moral thinking as the greatest type of knowledge. Alfred North Whitehead would concur but would say that it calls for a sensitivity to human greatness itself. Today our schools do not clarify true greatness as moral. One of the weaknesses is the failure to vivify the true heroes of our society, past and present. The youth of today have too few heroes beyond athletes and movie stars. They know too little about men and women who have sacrificed themselves for the sake of principles and the welfare of others. For instance, a generation ago the average junior high student knew about Albert Schweitzer; today college students barely hear of him and what made him great. Much the same for persons like George Washington Carver, whose science laboratory was also a place of prayer. These men represented true greatness, for they integrated their above-average expertise in the sciences with the moral and spiritual values grounded in their religious faith and experience as expressed in the arts. Our youth need to realize that the greatest models of humanity are anchored in moral convictions and expendable deeds. When this kind of heroics is made paramount in education our cultural cancer can be curtailed considerably.

Americans are usually expected to promote academic freedom, since we are presumed to be a free society or nation. But in recent decades academic freedom has too often slipped into a form of license. Upon catering to autonomy both teachers and students have allowed it to promote more and more relativism. Freedom is regarded today as a "do-your-own-thing" outlook or do as you please attitude with too little respect for traditional morals and values. Social conformism is given free rein rather than commitment to ideals. Jean-Paul Sartre endorsed this phenomenon when he said, "There are no ideals since there is no God to think them." Nothing is respected as absolute, for the humanistic notion of Protagoras has returned to the surface: "Man is the measure of all things." This makes every individual his own authority and his own god. On two occasions I asked intellectual leaders, "Are you your own god?" One some years ago, a confirmed humanist, Charles Francis Potter, flinched when he was asked the question. But another, a current teacher of classics, resolutely replied, "Yes, I am."

True academic freedom allows for varied perspectives and opinions, but it is not synonymous with the idea that truth is relative. Many today assume it means a freedom "from" rather than a freedom "for," i.e. freedom from the values which made democracy a possibility rather than freedom based on virtues which make for mutual respect and true greatness. Logical positivism is a current movement which fosters such intellectual and moral relativism. Catering to the exclusiveness of the sciences its leading spokesman, A. J. Ayer, has overtly asserted that morality is "nonsensical" since not a product of scientific methods of thought. Students who accept this view find it a boon to their forgetting about moral responsibilities. One consequence of this is the sexual debauchery practiced by more and more of them today. Ideal ends and goals are barely known or heard of in their colleges. Facts are respected in our schools as linked with specialized studies, but they are seldom integrated into philosophical schematisms which make for what both Greek philosophers and biblical prophets regarded as wisdom.

With too little help from their teachers our children and youth today can do little mentally to withstand the glaring forms of violence and sexual promiscuities thrown at them in their many hours of boob-tube entertainment. Much the same for adults, who have not learned to recognize wisdom. Self-control and family discipline elude them as sensate and sensational entertainment bombard their minds enhanced by the moral relativism rampant almost everywhere including our universities. The number one antidote to the educational viruses making for our cultural cancer is higher intellectual standards and expectations of our teachers. They must become better guides as philosopher-in-action, who do more than train our children to become echoes of their environment and better able to think critically, holistically and morally in a person-producing universe.

This development of mental maturity calls for dialectical thinking, which poses and welcomes varied points of view. The clash of ideas must be deemed an asset rather than a liability. Any dogmatic viewpoint in any field including scientific theory at times is not mature thought. It is not true to academic freedom. Yet respect for varied opinions should never be viewed as condoning relativism as truth. Even the existentialist idea that truth must be "true for me" does not imply this. It simply means that what is deemed truthful must be virtually relevant to the thinker involved. No university does its work well unless such freedom of inquiry is promoted and the exchange of thought encouraged. But to promote responsible inquiry and exchange, the university should encourage all specialists to think philosophically about their disciplines and do their best to correlate their findings with those of others. This calls for holistic thinking. Nothing facilitates such thinking better than philosophy, for without it the individual does not possess a corpus of thought essential to a wholesome and mature outlook on life. Dialogue is far better than monologue; it represents the exchange of thought basic to intellectual growth into maturity. In this respect teachers and students have an advantage over the general public, and for this they need not apologize. Even so they cannot speak freely without speaking responsibly. Academic freedom does not mean that "anything goes." It is not academic license but maturity. It functions with both respect and constraint so that a fair interplay of ideas may benefit all persons involved in the exchange.

Our industrialists are becoming envious of the Japanese business investment in America and rising Europe. It is time for our educationalists to become equally envious of Japanese educational accomplishment. The raising of standards is absolutely essential here. The pledge of President Bush to make our students top-ranking in science and mathematics will not be fulfilled until we copy Japan's 12-month school calendar. When Japanese youths finish the 12th grade today, they are almost the equivalent of our college graduates due to their year round school program. School years average 180 days in the U.S.A., 220 in West Germany and 243 in Japan. There is hope if we universalize what is done in Buena Vista, Va. where 60% of the students attend classes 220 days per year. Since 1973, the number of their students going on to college has doubled. Here we have one of the main antidotes to our cultural cancer, especially if ethical and other appeals to the humanities are included educationally so that the sense of values is not forsaken.

It appears favorable that our legislators are becoming amenable to pouring more tax money into education. But money to support techniques is no substitute for the strengthening of our educational curricula, as suggested above. But, speaking of taxes, it is time for American citizens to publicly question the ethical implications of the tax structure of their country. Consider these select tax figures given through *Time* newsmagazine in the spring of 1992. Briefly and bluntly they include these declared facts: "1. A domestic who makes $10,000 pays 7.65% of her income in Social Security and Medicare taxes. But her employer, an attorney who makes $100,000, pays just 4.9%. 2. A working mother, with one child, who earns $28,000 a year, can claim no more than $480 for child-care expenses but the employer of a $150,000 vice president who takes clients to lunch can deduct untold thousands of dollars in entertainment expenses. 3. Ronald Getty, son of the late billionaire J. Paul Getty, received $10 million tax free from his father's estate, but William Collier Carlton, a minor under the age of 14, had to pay $4,000 in taxes on $13,500 of investment income from money he received in a personal-injury case."

Are the U.S. citizens expected to condone this government-endorsed practice? Certainly not. Most of our tax monies should come from the wealthy corporations and individuals, not from the middle classes and the poor. In the next century or before will we have leaders in Washington, who will correct this blatant injustice? To balance the national budget will be a reasonable, even noble, endeavor, but only as the tax structure is kept fair in doing so. Most should be expected of those who have the most. Thus, like our culture in general our national government in particular must clean up its act concerning the tax structure, for it, too, contributes to our cultural cancer by demoralizing citizens with a near defeatism squelching the American dream.

One of the more objective signs that American education is faltering is the growing shortage of Ph.D.'s. The Associated Press reports that in the next generation industry and government will compete strongly with our schools to procure them. Early in the coming century, the United States will have an annual shortage of 7,500 doctorates in the natural sciences and engineering fields. Even sooner there will be a shortage in the humanities and social sciences. The most likely cause is the lower salaries in education today.

High percentages of our Ph.D.'s already have moved away from education into non-academic fields, mainly into industry. In 1987, this amounted to 50% relative to all fields. The Mellon Foundation has estimated that by the year 2000, there will be only eight Ph.D. applicants for every ten faculty positions in liberal arts. This will be a calamity. It will continue to weaken our students' abilities, for it will intensify the stifling of creative thought. Again what is practical and scientific will be less and less geared to our moral and axiological goals, thus threatening our culture's quality and viability.

Many of our students currently enrolled in Ph.D. programs are from foreign lands. Obviously more federal support is needed for our graduate programs, especially to inspire our home-grown students to continue their schooling. But to achieve this we will need to turn out more capable undergraduates, and this is dubious unless we strengthen our curricula all across the years and gain students who will accept the challenge of higher education. Again to do so they must be taught how to think and think well, a matter which re-raises our critique of the colleges of education, which are failing us today. Methodologies are not so much the need of the hour as philosophical acuity related to all fields of inquiry. Until this becomes almost commonplace in our schools, education can do little to curtail the cultural cancer of our time.

Chapter 3

The Stifling of Creative Thought

One of the major underlying mistakes in contemporary academia is the failure to distinguish education from training. Many of our students are not receiving an education, for they and their administrative guides only cater to training. What is the difference? some may ask. Basically, it is this: Training is usually a self-contained art of learning for pragmatic interests. Education may include such but is much more. It is the creative educement or evoking of insight into the nature of things and the correlation of what is learned in one field with what is known in another. Education, unlike training, is concerned about the correlation and integration of all thought, a much greater task. Not only becoming apprised of a variety of facts, true education seeks to guide the student toward a corpus of thought not by imposition but by illumination and discovery.

Educational specialists and administrators frequently fail to see this important distinction and, therefore, commonly mislead both students and faculty. One of the sure signs of this error is the failure to understand the basic role of philosophy, which is the core of all learning. It is the hub of the wheel of a university's spokes of specialization. It is where they meet and correlate their respective inputs, thus contributing to a holistic perspective of all learning essential to creative thinking.

Underlying this is the importance of wrestling with epistemological issues centered around the question: How do you know what you know? I've asked this question of some people who spoke with a certain cocksureness about things but only laughed at the question. What a pity! This question has been wrestled with by the leading thinkers of the

West for the past 2500 years and by thinkers in the East for several centuries as well. Unless you have tussled with various theories of knowledge, your own thinking will remain intellectually immature.

Similarly, what to you is most real, and on what grounds do you think so? Likewise, on what grounds do you believe in moral principles and values? For that matter, on what do you base your view of beauty? These are basic philosophical questions which we must have an answer for, even if not in full agreement with one another. We are not mature thinkers if we do not wrestle with such issues. They are basic to developing one's philosophy of life and understanding that of others.

One of the common causes of religious skepticism, therefore, is the inability to think dialectically about what is learned through the sciences and learned through the arts. And, how do you relate scientific understanding to the values dealt with in the humanities? Is there a scientific basis for moral values? Most ethicists doubt it. Yet we must ask: How can we really be constructive in science unless scientific findings are serviceable to human values and morals? Does not the scientist have to relate his work to what is morally serviceable to mankind? Is it right, let alone feasible, to specialize in a science without concern for its consequences to people and their societies? Is scientific enterprise an end-in-itself or a means to aiding people to achieve their higher ends, aesthetically, morally and religiously?

Dr. Sydney S. Negus of the Medical College of Virginia states that all types of knowledge and especially the sciences are "futile" unless linked, he says, with "character and reverence for God." The more a scientist knows the more humble and reverent he becomes, for he is in a position to observe some of the awesome laws of the universe, which bespeak a remarkable orderliness or design, which Einstein called "God's rule book." Where there is a design there must be a designer. If not, all is a meaningless hodgepodge or happenstance. Is nature just a mere coincidence? Isn't it remarkable how things fit together in nature like the organs of an organism? Or say, how the sexes, while distinguishable, are functionally related if not designed for each other in most forms of life?

Dr. Negus declares that there have never been laws of nature which may be declared absolute. The noted physicist Dr. Arthur H. Compton similarly says, "Natural phenomena do not obey exact laws." Hence, it is a big mistake for any student to believe only in what is presumably verifiable by science, for that fails to address the many issues of life which are more than scientific. Furthermore, the grounds for logic and mathematics are not scientifically proven. Nor are they purely rational. What proves the reason at work in proving things? Can reason prove itself by itself? Hardly. (Cf. my books, *Modern Science and the Human Condition*, Chapter 1 relative to mathematics, and *The Pertinence of the Paradox* relative to reason and existence.)

These few observations support what contemporary physicists see to be the unpredictabilities of things, especially the smallest units of matter and light. They help question the once-held Newtonian determinism in all of nature. Thus, the exactitude of the sciences is put in question. Related to the lack of absolute laws of science, Dr. Negus poses several questions from within his field of biochemistry for which there are no definite answers. With permission to quote may I cite them:

1. What keeps the temperature of a normal human body practically constant at 98.6 degrees Fahrenheit?
2. What holds the normal body content of H_2O so close to 68 percent?
3. How is the food one eats "burned" or oxidized by the body?
4. Where does the hydrochloric acid in the stomach come from?
5. A diabetic human body cannot utilize sugar properly . How does insulin remedy this situation?
6. What is the actual mechanism of blood clotting?
7. How do enzymes act in helping food to be digested?
8. Why doesn't one's stomach digest itself?
9. What makes it possible to move one's fingers?
10. What happens when sugar dissolves in water?
11. What causes a common cold?
12. How does a simple human cell function?
13. What causes holes to appear in some persons' teeth and not in others?
14. Exactly how does any one of the many vitamins act in the body?
15. How does liver extract act in increasing red blood cells in a human being?
16. What is cholesterol in the human blood for, and why in some persons does it appear in the form of gallstones but not in others?
17. What is the fundamental chemical action within the body when any one of a hundred drugs is taken?

18. What brings about the first heartbeat in a baby?
19. How do the kidneys aid in maintaining the various constituents in the blood at such constant amounts?
20. State anything that is definitely and fundamentally known about the human mind.

Often scientists specialized in a narrow field are quoted as though they had a command of a larger whole of things. Also, I have observed how some are indifferent to the moral aspects of their findings and/or applications. Clarence Darrow was "no spokesman for true scientists," says Negus, who sees most scientists as reverent toward God and finding nature the workings of a Divine Mind. Furthermore, what we often must taken on faith in daily existence is more germane to one's happiness than what is objectively known. William James said many things must be believed before they can be known. This writer had to believe it before he could hypothesize and demonstrate that a modified chemical combination could become a powerful healing agent in short order, now being taken seriously by pharmacists.

Eternal values like sacrificial love and absolute justice, especially love, supersede reason and empirical explanation. Scientific technology has not necessarily made our modern world overall a happier one. All the corruption of the contemporary world bespeaks the naturalistic failure of self-centered human conduct to make for a world of self-giving love that is typical, not atypical. Until people of our time activate their faith in God as the Spirit of sacrificial love, our culture can only further decline, for it will take more than relativistic notions to live by. Being at home in a world of scientific achievement is possible, but without faith in God and the higher principles linked with reverence for life and humanity, it is inconsequential or without purpose.

Students, do no settle merely for specialized training, lest you lack the insights of a sound education. It is not enough to glean and cite facts; they must be interrelated in a system of thought, which provokes and preserves insight. If you wish to be educated you must seek such a holistic perspective and be able to relate the parts to the whole of things or link the specialized spokes of the hub of learning, which is philosophy itself. Remember, each of us is a philosopher, an interpreter of all things, but you will remain a lame duck if you do not work at it so as to have a holistic perspective, not just piecemeal learning. Unless you strive for a holistic education and seek to preserve and promote it, you can do little to offset the cultural cancer that is weakening our society today.

One of the specific weaknesses of education in America today is scientific illiteracy. This should be comparatively easy to correct by expecting more science of our students and through better teaching. Administrative educationalists need to move with alacrity among school boards and committees to improve curricular requirements in the sciences. One of the best moves would be to demand additional courses in the philosophy of science, also the philosophy of mathematics. Teachers and their students become more enthused about their specialties when philosophical questions are raised and expected of them relative to their studies. I have had mathematicians and astronomers thank me for calling this to their attention.

But, in general the intellectual immaturities among both students and teachers lie in their failure to learn, let alone to be exposed to, the art of philosophical thinking. Much of the creative thinking done in any field comes from the more philosophically astute minds in academia and beyond. The stifling of creative thought is a sad state of affairs, for which our schools are largely to blame. Underlying this immaturity is the failure to cultivate in the minds of our youth and young adults the art of dialectical thinking, which is at the heart of philosophical and critically religious thought. Besides the awareness of facts the important question becomes: What do we do about it? How do we relate these facts to the rest of our knowledge? An Ohio State professor of chemistry in a lecture once put it brusquely like this within my hearing: "Science: So What?" A professor of astronomy, on the other hand, after his lecture, showed disgust when he was asked speculative philosophical questions about his lecture. He showed an ignorance not shown by the leading astronomers of our day, some dealt with in another chapter of this book who are among the more creative thinkers in their field. Writer Charles Krauthammer calls to our attention astronomer Robert Jastrow's astute claim that science cannot overlook the mystery of creation. In his book, "God and the Astronomers" he is quoted as saying of the scientist, "He has scaled the mountains of ignorance: He is about to conquer the highest peak: as he pulls himself over the final rock, he is greeted by a band of theologians who have been sitting there for centuries."

It appears that creative thought is being stifled in our time, much due to the failure to distinguish education from training. Too few educators are reckoning with this weakness. What has been stated might well be given further specification. In this respect, Allan Bloom's book *The Closing of the American Mind* is an intellectual examination and appraisal of the cultural decline of American society as focused on our universities and the state of education today. In general he describes how higher education has "failed democracy and impoverished the souls of today's students". Thus, Bloom, too, sees what we mean by education's involvement in our cultural cancer.

To reduce his arguments to a direct statement, Bloom recognizes, unlike most educational specialists, that the state of the university is inextricably linked with the fate of philosophy. He eventually says that our problems are such that "we need philosophy more than ever." There are many educators who fail to see this, because they fail to understand the function and role of philosophy to promote educational interpretation besides specialization. What is the student to be taught? This question is the beginning of the philosophy of education in view of the fact that the university must have goals and should "stand for something." In short, it must have visions of what an educated person is. Philosophically, it is no less than an exposure to a whole spectrum of thought, not merely to piecemeal learning, i.e. not merely tastes of specialized fields but a holistic perspective of our culture both as it is and as it ought to be. Students must learn of the great decisions and values reflected in their cultural past and find them relevant to the present. Too few professors aid the student, Bloom contends, in giving him insight into the values basic to education that supersede the mere techniques for making a living. Too much of the latter has geared the university to the economic system and has promoted careerism before wisdom as an end in itself. General education for the undergraduate has suffered greatly in our time; it is even a "fraud" says Bloom. We must recover the "core," i.e. studies that are "both synoptic and precise" to give the student the ability to correlate all that he learns. Too often the sciences are an "island" and are oblivious to this responsibility, in which case the student continues to lack a corpus of thought. Too often he graduates with a mishmash of ideas, which stifles creative thought and philosophical insight.

The most neglected area of studies is the humanities due to their being snubbed by the sciences. Often scientists fail to see that after all the scientific facts are in, they must be interpreted philosophically. Why? Because they must serve man as more than a physical specimen. The social sciences also have suffered from "the definitive ejection of man" as more than biological. Also students find the respective social sciences to be too disparate, each being presumably self-sufficient. Hence, Bloom says, ". . . the glory days of social science from the point of view of liberal education are over." But the need is still there. It may be that the current correlation of anthropology with philosophical phenomenology is a sign of new hope. "True liberal education requires that the student's whole life be radically changed by it. . ." says Bloom. Too often the students who aim at graduate professional studies are but "tourists" in the liberal arts. This writer has observed that professionals are often among the most gullible and naive about critical, ethical, political, and religious interpretations of life. They know their fields but cannot think well across disciplinary lines. Bloom states that the university that stresses specializations without guiding the student to a sense of "the whole" is grossly remiss. Scientific objectivity without respect for the role of the subjective, creative consciousness is often a cause of this. Often the sciences go their own way on their "islands" as though alien to the rest of the world and its other educational perspectives. Sciences, after all, could not exist were it not for the conscious knowing subject, whose creativity is behind it. Phenomenology supports this today, stressing the primacy of consciousness.

Democratic society today often lacks respect for tradition, while it stresses pragmatic utility. A civilization demands cultural values to guide it. More explicitly, this applies to science and technology. Unless related to human values they can be a cultural liability rather than an asset. The sciences per se are not the source of cultural values. They need to be supplemented by philosophy, yet philosophy which surveys the whole of things and interrelates the disciplines, has been "dethroned" by democracy due to the American public's inability to appreciate its distinctiveness. No wonder Europeans almost laugh at us. On the continent today even European youths can far out do out twenty-year olds intellectually. Until 1900 no American college students graduated without philosophy. John Dewey and the colleges of education have betrayed us in this respect. The practical supersedes principles.

Allen Bloom is not confident that the university of today can be reconstituted around a strong liberal education. This is because the university administrators do not contemplate or envision a possible wholeness. Yet we need it, for human nature is the same in our altered circumstances, and we face the same problems basically as in the past. But to understand our problems, "we need philosophy more than ever," Bloom contends. Not limited to the classical philosophers in this respect, Bloom strongly hails the emphases of modern philosophers like Locke, Rousseau, Kant, and Hegel. They have been strong influences upon modern education and culture, but too few students and professors know this. As the university goes, so goes our society. Since the university neglects philosophical wholeness, the same for our culture and people.

One of the main failures of our universities is that of not clarifying the values upon which our culture is based. The consequence is an "anything goes" relativism that threatens our civilization, especially when forces like materialism undermine our sensitivity to a higher composite viewpoint. Bloom senses after a life-time of teaching that we need to start afresh with the question: "What is man?" At Southern Methodist University, an interdisciplinary approach to this question made it the most popular course on the campus. It is not unrelated to the existential question: "Who am I?" Essential to autonomy and individuality such issues are basic to a civilized society no matter how technically adept.

Popularly, the only thing that unifies students today is their "allegiance to equality," says Bloom. The relativity of truth is thought to be a "condition of a free society," and this has replaced the once-held seat of unity in our inalienable rights and classical ideals. Bloom states of students today, "The danger they have been taught to fear from absolutism (or ideals) is not to error but intolerance." Thus you must never be sure you are right about anything — as though this "openness" were essential to democracy. One consequence of this is "the changed understanding of what it means to be an American." But if we in our diversity have no common goals or rights can our social contract subsist? Do we not need principles to guide us?

The new relativism or openness stems from Mill and Dewey, who taught us only to look to what was new, workable or "progressive." The principles and virtues of our intellectual forebears and the founding fathers overtly become passé. Bloom states of this: "The natural soul was replaced with an artificial one." Lost sight of is the fact that the Constitution is more than rules of government but an implied moral order. Fortunately, the civil rights movement helped curtail both overt and hidden hostilities to the morals implicit in the Declaration of Independence and Constitution.

Bloom rightly states of today's relativism, "Thus what is advertised as a great opening is a great closing of the American minds." The failure to require the study of religion and philosophy, he says, has made much of our social education "demagogic intention." There is a failure to recognize that even non-Western societies are ethnocentric, because they have certain principles — which is no grounds for assuming that our scientific approach to them is superior or makes our cultural relativism better. Bloom sees that we must re-recognize platonically that there is a "nature" that gives "standards" by which to evaluate both ourselves and other cultures. "That is why philosophy, not history or anthropology is the most important human science," he states. It poses the basic issues. (Currently, anthropology students in a few of our more alert universities are expected to first study philosophy, especially phenomenology.) History and cultural studies do not prove that values or cultures are relative. Though prejudices of all sorts need to be challenged, there is no grounds for wiping them out unless they are replaced by something more stable, i.e. something better for guiding students' lives. On the other hand, many students and teachers today are ready to doubt everything before they believe anything. This is say that as philosophers of sorts (which they are), they lack philosophical grounding in basic principles and standards for points of reference. The result is a mishmash of opinions which lack foundations for good thinking and argumentation.

All this implies that our schools are not doing their job. Instead of turning out creative thinkers they are but pragmatic sycophants of their society conditioned by the very relativism that is sucking us under and which some thinkers, including the writer, believe may be the downfall of Western society. Even our best students know little about the unity of our heritage, both familial and religious as well as political. Traditions and absolute virtues have become superfluous. Specialization for "success" is the new idolatry. Their homes are commonly divided and lack what was once deemed "spiritually rich" as based on a unity of beliefs and values. "So there is less soil in which university teaching can take root. . . ." says Bloom. Intellectual shallowness and social conformity are taking their toll. Thus the educational situation today is indeed critical, because values are being undermined by neglect with nothing to replace them. "How to" learning is not related to "why?" Pragmatic quantity is replacing intellectual and moral quality. The stifling of creative thought is the net result. Fundamental to this is the neglect of man and as a conscious subject, not merely an object.

As provocative as Bloom proves to be, he may be criticized for a type of Platonic elitism. How can his Great Books approach be made relevant to science students and others in pragmatic types of study? My reply is that all students must learn to dialecticize through required studies in philosophy even as more should be expected of incoming students respecting the basic skills. Colleges of education must either be radically improved or dissolved, for, as implied above, our teachers on secondary levels are poorly prepared intellectually and expect too little. One need on the college level is for issue-oriented studies in every division if not department. Furthermore, students need to be introduced to Eastern types of thought, not just the Western brands, especially as our contemporary world shrinks and peoples encounter one another more than ever before. But without philosophical frames of reference all cultures and values are apt to be regarded alike with an equal claim to truth, the result being more relativism, not less. Though a cultural viewpoint may well be taken in the classroom, a good teacher should allow it to be questioned so as to be tributary to the dialectical growth process of student minds.

Bloom may be a bit too skeptical with regard to the "democratization" of the university causing a loss of academic focus, vision and mission. Though the implied dualism appears to be a weakness, it does not demand an either/or perspective. Can we not recover or discover a both/and approach to education, which interrelates what Aristotle saw to be the theoretical and the practical? Speculative thought can be interrelated with the practical studies, ethics and political science being cases in point. This both/and paradox can be the holistic remedy for much pernicious relativism. Without such an adjustment, Bloom may be accused of a retreat from much modern thought. The strong points in both historical and contemporary thought must not be dichotomized but interrelated. When this is the case, both theoretical humanistic studies and the scientific studies can become working teams all the more relevant to the student's area of concentration. Without this kind of correlated cerebration, our schools will continue to stifle creative thought and only spread our cultural cancer, the main feature of which is relativism. One major consequence of this is "the changed understanding of what it means to be an American," but if we in our diversity have no common goals or rights can our social contract subsist?

While the studies of the classics may be important to the recovery of the vitality of liberal education through a meeting with the minds of great thinkers whose values were more than relativistic, we must interrelate their principles with our modern practicalities. Here is where Bloom could strengthen his position by correlating the strength of elitist thinking with those of a democratic cross-section. Some critics say we must place the burden of education on strengthening elementary and secondary education. Not all wrong, may I ask: How can this be done unless we strengthen the curriculum of our prospective teachers on such levels? Do we not need more intellectual disciplines in our teachers colleges? Are they not turning out weak thinkers who are versed in methods but not substance? All college students need a "common core," as Bloom puts it, but also an interdisciplinary perspective hardly possible without philosophical insight and shrewdness. A so-called democracy in education can still have its place, but it cannot avoid a cultural anarchy without strengthening the more therapeutical moral and humanistic studies. Only then can values guide our sciences and technologies with direction and purpose. Some scientists I have known have rejected any such responsibilities, but more and more are coming to recognize the cruciality of this matter.

Issue-oriented studies are then kept alive and essential to a stronger college education. Specialists in medicine and business have come to see this. Medical specialists are parking their pride and beginning to listen to the Ph.D.'s, especially in ethics and psychosomatics. Social scientists are also beginning to heed philosophers, notably in phenomenology, so as to regard the social phenomena dealt with as based on the activities of *conscious*, moral beings, whatever their types of culture and social problems.

Educational administrators need to recognize these factors, lest our colleges continue to fail us. It may be pertinent, yet debatable, just what courses we should prune. One thing seems sure, we must retain those which promote dialectical thinking. In this case, there is no substitute for philosophy. Here Bloom is surely right. Philosophy is also essential to intellectual maturity, for by it a focus is given to the varieties and specializations of thought, whereby a superficial relativism is overcome. Everyone is a philosopher — either slovenly or shrewd. Is not guidance needed here? Democratization in education can be retained, yet it must not overlook this, if we are to remain educationally alert, nor do we need to betray the meaning of democracy with its multifaceted approaches to culture and education. It may very well be that true academic excellence must correlate these approaches, the theoretical and the practical. Is it not the case that our Constitution in principle really opens up this perspective? Unity and diversity are both basic to the principles behind our republic.

Yet we must assert that an imbalanced educational democratization has contributed even more to our cultural relativism. The danger implied is that students will be prone to think that any system of beliefs is as good as any other. This openness makes for mutual respect but in itself makes for a weak, spineless type of thinking, almost an "anything goes" attitude adding to the pernicious relativism that has already infiltrated modern Western education. As Richard T.W. Arthur has observed as a teacher in Canada and the United States, when students think truth is mere opinion they have little to support their arguments, a matter of strong intellectual and ethical implications. Thus Arthur agrees with

Bloom, as does this writer, that philosophy is the main discipline, which offsets relativism as our "educational malaise." It educationally preserves the idealistic and religious values, which heal this illness. Bloom rightly sees that our inalienable rights are more than a mere humanistic concoction, since they appeal to a human dignity linked four times to God in the Declaration of Independence. Unless respect for this is recovered, our democratic styles of education will sever itself entirely from the more aristocratic quality, which the humanities must preserve if liberal education is to be true to itself. Not an either/or matter, this is a both/and paradox.

Accepting these qualifications we need not settle for Plato's assumption that education is for the few, but we can make sure that education for the many is far more than a collection of facts and information making for a mere stew of ideas. A qualitative curriculum need not make for a classism if every specialization is given a strong liberal context, that of a kind which makes for dialectical exchange and challenges the student to make intellectual commitments, which enhance his philosophical development. This is essential to an education designed for living a life while not disrelated from making a living. Here the search for wisdom and creative thought remain the basic goal of education, as it always has been at its best. Not an elitism as strong as Bloom's, this claim, nevertheless, keeps the specializations and classes of men in vital communication and the higher values more relevant to all, for the theoretical studies are interlaced with the practical.

One important way to foster this is to have philosophical courses related to every specialization including math and medicine. Bloom's strong points need not spell a retreat from the modern sciences while he, too, attacks contemporary relativism. Nor do they need to be an intellectual monopoly but rather an intellectual crucible provocative of the most mature types of thought, for we cannot afford to disrelate the theoretical from the practical in our time. Our students remain stunted until they understand and apply these factors, for education is more than information and training. Their professors must lead the way and not be so unenlightened about the holistic and qualitative studies of philosophy and religion, if we are to overcome our cultural cancer in our time.

Chapter 4

The Bane of Secular Humanism

Secular humanism is the bane of modern culture, the number one intellectual force leading to the threat of our civilization. Immediately, the question arises: How can this be the case?

The question is legitimate, and there are also legitimate aspects of its answer. First of all, secular humanism contributes directly to the moral relativism of this age. This is because it denies an absolute, either philosophic or religious. It settles only for empirical relativisms that give no stable undergirding to our values, morals and systems of justice. Claiming to believe in democracy as a working ideal, it negates any *absolute* ideals to which people may look in instrumenting the very functions of democracy itself. It is caught in a vortex of moral relativism.

If there is no absolute to look to, there is no standard by which men are to be guided or by which to judge the changing mores of their society. The best they can come up with is an empirical ethic based on the trial-and-error of experience, the height of which has been achieved theoretically by John Dewey and the net result of which is education's promotion of the relativism of our age — something to be eschewed by all who would defray the moral bankruptcy of this epoch.

Though secular humanists may be more right than wrong about castigating the ethical authoritarianism of fundamentalism, especially when linked with politics, they are more wrong than right about their inability to come up with any *permanent* values. As humanism in general has done since the Renaissance, the secular humanists have borrowed the dignity of man from religion but have given it no real undergirding. (Some professed humanists like B. F. Skinner have even denied man's dignity, reducing him to a mere animal at best.)

Usually appealing to human "reason," humanists fail to see the deficiencies of reason and how it is a mere instrument of experience. As a tool, it is not a tribunal and can give no special dignity to the toolmaker unless it has a tie-in with what Heidegger and Tillich call the "Being of our existence" — which calls for a more than relativistic instrumentalism, recognizing God as the awesomeness of our being or the "Ground of our being." As Tillich says, "Looking at God, we see that we do not have him as the object of our knowledge but that He has us as the subject of our existence. "

Human dignity to be effectuated must be based on more than the trial and error of social relationships. It must be based on a mutual respect for persons that is anchored in the Absolute Other. No one has honor or dignity except as it is accorded him by an Other. Man's dignity is not "a given" but it is *given*. He must answer to an Other. His relativistic pursuits have no meaning except as they look to the Absolute beyond all relativism. Religion sees the Absolute Other as the subject-Being or "I Am," the supreme Person of God that is the "is" of our existence. Scientific naturalism can provide us with no related dignity, as Behaviorism concedes.

Secular humanism usually respects the love ethic derived from religion, but, again, it gives it no undergirding. As a psychologist, Eric Fromm is a case in point, for he has stressed the need of Agápe or self-giving love but only as something to copy, empirically. He has given it no motivation or re-motivation, no real incentive from within, no true character. Christianity sees Agápe as something that is intrinsic to the divine Absolute, as revealed by Christ and anticipated by the major prophets of Israel, and as something inspirationally *re-motivating* from within a person's inmost self. It is not a product of mere trial-and-error socializing but a product of encounter with the revealed Absolute and is an out-going concern for others that does not come naturally. Man is naturally self-centered; Agápe is divinely sacrificial and benevolent with no thought of reward when true to itself. Fromm has not recognized this psychologically.

Secular humanism is usually superficial in its optimism about man. It commonly sees man as self-sufficient and, therefore, his own savior in that it relies solely on human achievements of intellectual, cultural, and technological types to solve all problems. Its biggest folly is that it fails to see that man's biggest problem is himself. It fails to reckon with what Martin Heidegger called man's Gefallenheit or "fall from being" into inauthentic existence or what Paul Tillich called man's "estrangement" from the "ground of his being;" both are forms of separation from the Absolute. In this respect, secular humanism is unrealistic about man in general and this age in particular. It closes its eyes to the realism of twentieth century history. In their prejudice against religion as based on revealed principles that supersede intellectual relativisms, secular humanists often castigate religion as non-scientific. Nothing could be farther from the truth. Long lists of historical and modern scientists with religious convictions could be made, from Galileo to Pascal, from Einstein to Arthur H. Comptom. Many scientists have recognized that revealed principles are not the enemy of science — surely not in the hands of today's major theologians — but a supplement thereof. Higher criticism in modern biblical studies is the most scientific approach to religious literature ever taken.

Many humanists, when put on the spot, say that religion is a human invention and God a projection of man. To them God is created in man's image not vise versa. The consequence of this is that man is superior to God. As I once said to Charles Frances Potter in a discussion relative to his definition of humanism in the Oxford Dictionary, "You, sir, are your own god." He had no reply. Later he admitted we gave him a hard time. How vain can *we* get?

Not all humanism is secular, however. One can be a religious humanist, too, which is to say that while man can achieve much through his native endowments, he can be truly fulfilled as a man only in relation to the divine Absolute that gives him the mystery of life both as a beginning and as a destiny. Without respect for this or something akin to it, our culture slips downward in its relativistic whirlpool and man walks on a treadmill of meaninglessness, which is to say his achievements lack an ultimate orientation and consequence. Religious existentialists beginning with Soren Kierkegaard see this alternative to humanistic relativism centering in "the Moment" of faith-conditioned encounter with the Absolute, which re-motivates and re-orientates all of life giving it a meaningful existence and destiny.

The mystery of beginning(s) cannot be accounted for by science. Creation is a legitimate claim as contemporary astronomers like Gold, Bondi and Hoyle attest — though it must not be literalized with the fundamentalists. Science, including evolution, can only deal with nature's processes, not its source and not its goal. Religious humanism sees evolution as a divine process linked with creation as the mystery of beginning(s).

Secular humanism is a threat to our culture and civilization, because it leaves man lifting himself by his own bootstraps and does not give answer to man's deep-seated yearning or ultimate concern. Borrowing human dignity from religion, it gives it no real basis. Projecting human goals, it gives them no foundation. Presupposing moral principles based on experience, it gives them no permanence or stability. Thus, secular humanism is the bane of our culture today. Must our universities be accomplices to such cultural degradation?

Thinkers as noted as Whitehead, Schweitzer and Sorokin, despite their different specializations, basically concur with Arnold Toynbee that "we have now come to the eleventh hour of Western civilization" and in the face of humanistic relativism "we must pray for a reprieve," lest what Sorokin describes as our "sensate culture" fail to be balanced up by an "ideological culture' of moral and religious values and our civilization go down like twenty-one civilizations before us. Our "challenge," says Toynbee, is moral and religious in nature. Obviously, the secular humanist is not helping much to meet the challenge.

As a long-standing humanistic philosopher at the University of Wisconsin, Max Otto eventually expressed strong misgivings about the trends of thinking in this age. He confessed the need to respect "the awesome and mysterious." Seeing how science is exploited for wrong moral ends, he said that "science cannot supply me with a program of life" and that "without that program science may be our undoing." Therefore, he said, science and religion must become a working team or "inseparable" endeavors. In other words, secular humanism is deficient. Similarly, Bertrand Russell as a positivist eventually saw the problem and wrote, "We must get back to the Christian ethic." Such an ethic does not come naturally, for it is based upon Agápe, a self-giving love that cannot be turned on and off like a TV switch. It calls for a remotivation from within that springs from a reverence for the Divine Absolute beyond all our relativisms and appropriated by a "total self-commitment" of faith, "the Wager" referred to by Pascal that Divine sacrificial Love is a revealed truth, not a humanistic invention.

One of the issues returning to the forefront these days is the revived resistance to the teaching of evolution in our schools. Perhaps the chief scene of this resurgence is the State of California, where fundamentalists are going to court, because high school teachers are teaching evolution without giving equal time to the belief in the divine creation.

A court battle shaped up a few years ago in Sacramento reminiscent of the Scopes "monkey trial" in Tennessee decades ago. It is contended in reply to the fundamentalists that the state has the right to decide between the two theories. The fundamentalists are saying that the teaching of evolution violates some children's religious rights, and one of their spokesmen has stated that the state's policy is even "hostile to religion."

The thrust of the fundamentalists is that the state illegally prohibits the teaching of biblical accounts of creation as supported by science from their perspective. Kelly Segraves of the Creation-Science Research Center in San Diego contends that *both* the creationist view and the Darwinian theory are scientific about the appearance of life forms. The California textbooks concur with Charles Darwin, who theorized that living forms evolved from a common stock through natural selection. The creationists, on the other hand, claim to have scientific evidence that God created the world and all forms of life in six days.

As a teacher of both philosophy and theology for over twenty-five years, I have been tempted to dismiss the current resurgence of this issue with an air of impatience, if not disgust. Isn't this a long-since dead issue? I have thought. For me it is, and for most philosophers and theologians, who have not been reluctant to employ critical methods of intellectual honesty with respect to both science and religion, including the Bible. In short, there is a profound sense in which the issue of evolution versus creation is out-of-date for most better-educated people. Yet not altogether. On what grounds can this be said?

For at least a century and a quarter since Darwin set forth his evolutionary hypothesis, many leading thinkers in religious philosophy have managed to blend or synthesize the views of evolution and creation. One of the first Americans to do this was John Fiske. Others in philosophy and theology took their cue from him. In time the keynote idea became this: Evolution is not an anti-religious theory, for it is very probably the method God used to create the various forms of life. In addition, what matters where we came from as human beings? Most significant is the fact that we are here as men of rational and moral sensitivities. We have arrived as persons in a person-producing universe. Many philosophers and theologians have viewed this teleologically, i.e., an end in nature is being fulfilled. Witness the evolution of the human brain; it is hardly accidental. Furthermore, where there is design, there is Designer; where there is direction and fulfillment, there is purpose.

One advantage of this view is that it delivers us from a naive fundamentalistic view of God as a giant Santa Claus on Cloud 9, who creates all things almost at once in a magical fashion. It respects what the sciences have observed, while it also respects the mystery of beginnings. A totally naturalistic explanation or theory of how things have developed does not account for either the first cause or the purpose of nature's processes. Even the Big Bang theory of astronomers, that the universe began in an explosion that resulted in planets including the earth, cannot rule out the mystery of the cause behind the unformed gases suddenly giving rise to formed planets. There is no reason to overlook the mystery of the beginnings of either planets or forms of life. In principle that mystery is divine to many thinkers, lest it be sheer happenstance without purpose in a meaningless world. The fundamentalist attack on evolution has re-aroused the reaction of the "secular humanists" of our time. Recently a small body of that designation issued a statement attacking the fundamentalists for not only teaching the creation theory but for their legalistic ethics. What they most fear is the set-back of intellectual freedom, human rights, and scientific progress. However, the secular humanists seem to have their own problems even as they create some for others. Among them is B. F. Skinner, the behavioristic psychologist, who denies the very reality of consciousness and moral freedom of men. It is dubious that he can rightfully espouse the main tenets of any brand of humanism. Also among them is Brand Blanshard of Yale, a philosopher, who sees the absurdity of Skinner's denial of consciousness. Obviously, the secular humanists have their own inconsistencies and intellectual schizophrenia.

One thing that we must be open-minded about, however, is the fact that the California fundamentalists are appealing to what to them is more than a dogmatic claim, since they claim a scientific view of creationism. I have perused one of their books by Dr. Henry M. Morris. Though I think the little book is one-sided, I find it fairly impressive. If men of this type can make a valid case for creationism as a truly "scientific" theory, it might warrant more respect in the science classrooms than it has received. But until the day comes when scientists themselves can accept creationism as scientific, it does not warrant such respect. This is not to say that creationism is to be ruled out altogether, but it is to say that as yet it leaves a lot to be desired in order to be ruled in. To be ruled in it must be validated as a scientific theory, not merely as a religious dogma. A religious belief per se has little or no warrant in a science course — unless it be a concession to the scholastic doctrine of orderliness of nature, a view from religious philosophy that scientists have had to take for granted since the beginning of modern science.

Though creationism, as the typical fundamentalists view it, is a naive position, based on the literalized view of the Genesis story, the spirit of the theory has its good points in that it tries to avoid the notion of the secular humanists that this is a meaningless universe. Recognizing in its way that life is a mystery is to its credit and implies that human reason does not have all the answers. But it were far better to accept the more liberal religious theory that evolution and creationism are not antithetical but may be viewed as two perspectives of the basic phenomena involved in the beginning and development of life forms. I for one hold to this position. Religiously, God may well have used evolution as a creative methodology. Witness the evolution of the human brain and body.

One thing that the secular humanists must answer for is much of the intellectual skepticism of our day relating to the relativism of morals and values. They claim to be against authoritarian forms of morality while espousing the sufficiency of human reason. As a specialist in ethics, existentialism, philosophy of science as well as philosophy of religion, I must say that human reason per se cannot give us any certitude of anything absolute in the field of morals. As Arnold Toynbee, Alfred North Whitehead and Peterim Sorokim have all observed, if the door is closed to all forms of religious respect for the Absolute we will continue to decline as a culture into the pits of relativism and skepticism; the best in our mores will disappear and our sensate trends will not be offset. No scientific theory of morality can be devised, as the positivists like A. J. Ayer, a confessed secular humanist, has himself said. What, then, have the secular humanists to offer us respecting a morally based society? Little or nothing.

I think it important that the issue posed between the fundamentalists and secular humanists is a legitimate one; it is even crucial. The cardinal issue is that they are both right and both wrong at key points. The basic answer is one of ballast between the good points of each, some clues to which are proffered above as focused on a pro-religious view of evolution. There is nothing that prevents the major findings of the sciences from having a religious orientation. The basic issue is not an either/or dichotomy but a both/and paradox that allows us to think both religiously and scientifically from different vantage points. In the more liberal religious context referred to above adjustments can be made so that both perspectives, when adapted, can be tributary to meaning and thus help inhibit the spread of our cultural cancer.

But more must be said about the bane of secular humanism. We have begun to see that the relativism of our age is largely a betrayal of philosophical and especially religious absolutes respected in the main until recent generations. This kind of sloppy thinking has been spread by our schools and made popular in almost every neighborhood. It is reported that a 1992 poll showed that 67 percent of the American people believed that no truth is absolute. Both classical philosophers and biblical prophets are ignored by such thinking. Ignorance thereof is directly involved. The precedent for this was set by John Dewey, perhaps the greatest influence upon the twentieth century school moms of America, who scorned matters of classical vintage in favor of pragmatic things that "work" to one's interests. The suspension of idealisms and religious absolutes contributed educationally to relativisms made synonymous with secular humanism.

Combined with the atheistic existentialism of Sartre and his cohorts, this brand of thinking has caused many supposedly educated people to lose respect for the divine Absolute, which Kierkegaard, Berdyaev, Tillich, Buber, and Marcel as religious existentialists conceded to surpass human reason's finitude and to keep alive respect for spiritually revealed truths from beyond our empirical and rationalistic theories. Here is the one source of absolutistic thinking which sees an alternative to all the "deconstructionism" in modern education, which negates the meanings in history and past philosophical, religious and political literature. Much of this decadent thought is perpetrated by religious skepticism and is promoted by the literary license of many modern novels and movies. (Cf. Chapter 18 for the philosophical issues entailed.) Where standards are lacking restraints are ignored and civic values derived from the past are made to appear of no consequence. The skepticisms and relativisms implied can be overcome only by commitments to the Absolute on its own faith-conditioned terms, not ours.

Many in the legal professions need to recognize that without respect for the divine Absolute or God there is very little ground for the laws which ban most crimes, for there is little that warrants regard for the human person. Such thinking at a time when we have far more lawyers than ever before caters to the return to Nietzsche's Übermensch or "Superman" concept which gives free rein to those in power at the expense of the weak. Besides bureaucratic power the gun often becomes the presumed sign of those in power.

The cultural strong point of respect for the Absolute is that it offsets the naturalistic and humanistic notions that man is the center of the universe or, logically, his own god. Today naturalism breeds pseudo-mystical worship of a pantheistic system of nature related to the bizarre cults of our time. All earthly creatures are regarded materially alike, and man loses his uniqueness. Though ecology must be respected, often its enthusiasts are more concerned about animals than their fellow men. When respect for the *imago dei* is lost, man's distinctiveness is jeopardized. On the other hand, when men are viewed as their own masters, who can develop a Utopian world through their brilliant specializations, since neither defective by original sin or existentially fallen condition, people are prone to accept Rousseau's superficial optimism that men are naturally good and it is their institutions that are at fault. Many social scientists accept this philosophy and thus minimize the moral responsibility of the human individual. Social institutions and environment are deemed the cause of our weaknesses and failures. But who, may we ask, corrupted our institutions?

An educational consequence of this point-of-view is that social workers and others minimize the responsibility of criminals and delinquents, many of whom have had comparatively good or wholesome backgrounds. When criminals are led to blame society due to their social conditionings, they fail often to see the center of their problem in their own egos — what St. Paul spoke of as "the flesh," not the body but the egocentric predicament. The more outstanding psychiatrists like Karl and William Menninger and others to be dealt with below see this often more clearly than the humanistic teachers and leaders of today. The extreme liberalism of the latter often is stretched to the point where many of our judges look the other way giving little responsibility to delinquents and criminals. The spiritual core of human consciousness is overlooked. Economic oppression and racism, while not to be disregarded, are too often scapegoats for weaklings in character. When released from prison or the court systems, they often go back to society only to perpetuate the crimes they have already committed. Commonly the attitude becomes this: "If society is the cause of my downfall or mistakes, there is nothing to be done about it." Moral responsibility is suspended.

In the face of the trends of our society it must be asserted that the humanistic myth of man-made Utopia is erroneous, for it leads to the suspension of human consciences at their best. The positive reduction in crime through religious convictions will be dealt with below.

Until the consciences of our people are given a restored sensitivity as inspired by spiritual values our humanistic relativisms remain sterile of moral integrity for the average persons on the street. Meanwhile humanists may borrow human dignity and integrity from religion but will fail to give it foundation. They cannot quell the underlying virus of our cultural cancer. Secular humanism remains, then, a bane rather than a blessing.

Chapter 5

The Need of
Ethical Theism

Recently, a professed atheist called me on the phone looking for someone in the university to confirm his views. When I indicated that he had approached the wrong man, he quickly monopolized the conversation with a tirade against religion. When I finally managed to get a word in edgewise, I started to say, "Your basic problem is. . . ." Immediately he cut me off with, "I have no problem," whereupon he hung up the receiver.

The fact remains that the atheist does have a problem, a very serious one at that. It centers about what I herein call "the peril of atheism." What does this imply? Basically, it is the position that ours is an absurd world and a meaningless human existence steeped in relativism. This gives birth to a "do-your-own-thing" philosophy and a "you make yourself " on your own terms perspective. Jean-Paul Sartre took such a position and renounced all absolute principles as epitomized in his statement, "There are no ideals, for there is no God to think them." Without an Absolute to look to, persons who hold to such positions logically invite an anarchy of personal and social relationships, however hard they try to disguise the matter, precisely because they rule out ideals or absolute principles as they rule out God. This being the case, the world is absurd and total relativism implicit within it intellectually and socially, as Sartre averred. Even human conscience has no absolute undergirdings like the Ten Commandments, for instance, or Kant's Categorical Imperative, since it is as relativistic as the social culture that conditions it, thus a mere by-product of its environment. But Sartre's view of a relativistic conscience is to be criticized since it is really socially parasitical as it feeds off of the ethical philosophies and religions of other people, who hold to moral absolutes of one kind or another. Without the moral conditioning of other people, persons of the Sartrean point-of-view, logically speaking, would be a menace to society.

It may very well be that without the Absolute to look to our culture would be doomed to total relativism, if not ethical and axiological nihilism. In the face of such a Nietzschean possibility, even cultural tendency today, Arnold Toynbee, upon completing his eight-volume *Study of History*, not only said we are now living in "the eleventh hour of Western civilization," but added that we must "pray for a reprieve" to recover our moral and spiritual sensitivities if we are to meet our type of cultural "challenge." If we fail to do so, we will bite the dust of the ages much like twenty-one civilizations before us. All civilizations, says, Toynbee, have had various types of challenges to meet; ours is the first of its type and we are not doing well in meeting our challenge.

But some thinkers still contend that scientific empiricism may be the answer even ethically. One of our distinguished Nobel prize winners in physiology, Dr. Roger W. Sperry of California Tech, is sensitive to this matter and has begun to try to come up with an 'ought' from a scientific 'is.' I feel for him, but as I have reminded him in our correspondence and in my book, *The Creativity of Consciousness*, he may not be able to improve upon John Dewey's ethical empiricism, which still ends up with a relative set of social values, since he disregards the Absolute. To seek an ethical "ought" from an empirical 'is' is to be guilty of what G.E. Moore of Cambridge rightly called a "naturalistic fallacy." It cannot be done, though I, too, wish it could. This problem of ethics is intensified philosophically by the fact that we can shoot holes through every system of ethics perpetrated in the West since Plato. (See my book, *A Critical Survey of Ethics.*)

But just what do we mean by the Absolute? Basically, it is the indefinable principle beyond all relativism or what Kierkegaard, the systematizer of existentialism, spoke of as the Unconditioned, which supersedes all that is conditioned. Yet, to try to define it is presumptuous, because a definition presupposes the adequacy of that by which you define it, namely your finite reason. A finite reason cannot probe the Infinite, the Absolute or the Unconditioned, what Paul Tillich called "Being as such," because it qualitatively transcends that reason and the finite concepts it entertains. For human reason to presume to do justice to Absolute Being is like the child who says he is going to empty the ocean with his sandpail.

God is another name for the eternal Absolute that eludes all finite and temporal categories of thought and experience. Though to attempt to express it admittedly takes some thought, it is inadequate or insufficient thought, i.e., it is as deficient as the finger someone mistakenly identifies with the moon toward which it is pointing. Our limited concepts in this respect are functional but not definitive. This implies that divine truth, that which is related to or revealed by the Absolute, is neither innate nor self-attained by human reason and/or social experience. For a person to be aware of the Absolute is to realize that he is transcended by it. Only by an existential encounter with it through its self-disclosure, known faithwise as the Word of revealed truth which penetrates consciousness, can one know a meaningful existence and destiny. This is experienced through an either/or commitment of trust, when the Transcendent Absolute unveils itself as the Subject-Being of all being or what Moses encountered in the wilderness as the great "I AM" or Yahweh (Jehovah). Kierkegaard referred to such an awareness as "the Moment," by which he meant the intensive instant of encounter with the Absolute, a moment conditioned by faith and that reorientates all of one's life and opens up a good will, the only good. The inspiration of an authentic good will is based upon the existential encounter, not on one's relative conscience and social conditionings that merely reflect one's environment. This is especially the case when one comes to understand that the Absolute qualitatively transcends human thought forms and impulses and, as the highest level of reality, is synonymous with the Spirit of Love. The N. T. Apostle John saw this and wrote, "God is Love," meaning not acquisitive love but sacrificial, expendable or self-giving love. Such love (Agápe) is the greatest type of reality. It is the Spirit and is personal in nature not unlike the "I AM" of Subject-Being who confronted Moses and, for Christians, was personified in Jesus Christ.

Were Sartre tuned in to the present discussion he would say that he did not understand it. Why? The Answer is that the only absolute he considered was not the truly transcendent and self-contained Absolute, because the absolute being that he rejected was a product of his own finite reasoning. He dismissed the truly Unconditioned Absolute when he dismissed the finite "proofs" for God that classical and modern philosophers, prior to Kierkegaard, had perpetrated. Like Kierkegaard and Heidegger, Jean-Paul Sartre saw the inadequacies of such finite projections, but, unlike them, he failed-to realize that the true Absolute is transcendent of all the rational and empirical machinations of philosophers. Even Heidegger, Sartre's teacher, came to the point of recognizing that the Sein of Dasein or the "isness" of one's concrete existence is the Holy. One's consciousness of it is related to the awesome Liebnizian question: Why something rather than nothing? Upon legitimately dismissing the finite "proven" gods of the philosophers Sartre missed the Absolute that supersedes them. He failed to understand what Martin Luther meant when he said, "Let God be God." This meant: Let God be God on his own terms of Absolute Being, and do not confuse the true God with the Platonic-to-empirical projections of either finite thought or finite beings. Kierkegaard saw that finite reason was deficient and must despair of defining the divine Absolute that transcends human finitude. Yet such despair is not all bad, for it opens up a personal and intellectual honesty that allows the Absolute to break through to one's faith-conditioned consciousness in the encounter of the Moment. Such despair is parallel to the Socratic ignorance conditional to wisdom. During World War II, it was expressed in the saying, "There are no atheists in fox holes." Why? Because all artificial securities are dropped in such a moment and an encounter with the Unconditioned occurs as one lets God be God on his own terms.

If the rational arguments for God were adequate, there would be no need for faith in the Absolute. Reason would be our common denominator. As Paul Tillich realized, the divine Absolute is "Being as such" or that which transcends all other forms of being that reason conceives. Without faith in the Absolute, religion would be totally reduced to philosophy or what one makes of things intellectually on his own and without respect for the Absolute's self-disclosure that qualitatively transcends finite notions. Faith is trustful commitment to the Absolute Subject, not merely assent to the intellectual object supposedly proven by reason. In this context, the French physicist Blaise Pascal likened such faith to a wager; it is betting your life on God, the unconditioned Absolute, not merely on one's projected ideal concept or argument. To bet on the Absolute enables one to have implicit standards of life like righteousness and love, i.e. revealed, not invented, "ideals" and principles conveyed by the self-unveiling of God in the faith-subsumed encounter. Such a wager opens up moral responsibilities that supersede all social relativisms of finite thought. Included is the dignity of man accorded one by an Other. Dignity or honor is not self-concocted; it must be granted us. It was this that the blacks of Birmingham appealed to when they resisted local laws that detracted from their dignity. Without the accordance of dignity by an Other there may be no such thing at all. The humanist, including Sartre, merely borrows the dignity of man from religion but gives it no undergirding, since for him all values are relative. Sensitive to this problem culturally, Benjamin Franklin said, "Think where we would be without religion!"

Though Bertrand Russell did very little, if anything, to provide it, he eventually said, "We must get back to the Christian ethic." As true as this may be, we must ask what ethical philosophy approaches the matter today save that of a pro-Kantian type, since it provides for the Golden Rule. But, as pragmatists and existentialists have pointed out, even the moral idealism of Kant with its sense of duty may be put in question philosophically and a social relativism of experience allowed to displace it. If relativism is held to be legitimate, then where are we at ethically today? It would appear that the only alternative to nihilism is Kierkegaard's view that "faith is an absolute relation to the Absolute." Not geared to a mere part of a man such faith is "total self-commitment." But to what? To the Unconditioned Absolute on its terms, not ours.

The peril of atheism is that it fails to see such an alternative and thereby fails to respect the higher divine attributes and virtues that are associated religiously with the Absolute. The faith-conditioned person, who sees it, understands the Moment of encounter, existentially, because he also understands what Kierkegaard meant when he said, "Truth is subjectivity," — not subjectivism, mind you, but the subjective relevance of the confronted Absolute to the existing self's consciousness in the Moment. Ethically, when identified with the Christly "I Am," this inspires a good will, which is the very opposite of relativism and a person's being buffeted about by a socially conditioned set of ideas. Again the peril of atheism is that it has no absolute values by which to live and die; hence, a life of meaninglessness in an absurd world, quite as Sartre depicted in his plays. Such a condition is one of a tragic egocentricism that provides no real basis for respecting one's fellow men. Sartre tries to have a reason for respecting others, but it is only that we are all human and in the same boat. This is of minimal significance ethically, if any at all, because it gives no grounds for not joining Nietzsche in the search of power over others. In addition, though Sartre condemns the coward, he has no real basis for so doing, for the coward's relative conscience may be just as reliable as his. Thus, it is apparent that an atheistic relativism makes for a deficient culture with no ultimate values or principles for guiding the choices of either self or society. Also caught in the entangling nets of a present-tense relativism, it fails to provide a hope for the future.

The essence of a vital religion, however, is grounded in a profound reverence for the Absolute that makes for virtue. In setting the pace for what became Western philosophy Plato seemed to be groping for such an Absolute in his projection of Being, but he missed it. It is no wonder that the Princeton Platonist, Paul Elmer More, should eventually give up on Plato's version of Being, saying "It is hard to love a valid inference." Yet Plato at least sensed that Being was Good and embraced the virtues. In a higher sense, religiously, it was realized through prophets like Hosea and Jesus that the Goodness is Love, the personal Spirit of benevolence that modified the spirit of the person who encounters the Absolute Good, faithwise. It was for this reason that Roger W. Babson, the note statistician, could say to hundreds of American service clubs, "Not a single benevolent institution on this continent was founded by other than a praying man or woman or the son or daughter thereof." Indeed, as Franklin said, "Where would we be without religion?" The peril of atheism is that it has no alternative to its banal relativism. With its do-your-own-thing philosophy, it gives inspiration or precedent to no ultimate standards and no source of meaning. Consequently, it does very little to promote benevolent institutions while frequently attacking those we have. In view of this, our basic cultural need today is that of an ethical theism.

Does this imply that the atheist is necessarily an immoral person? It does not, for he/she may be copying a society with social mores that condition his/her conscience and moral conduct. However, what does this do to individuals but make them mere echoes of their environment. At best they merely respond to what society expects of them lest they pay an inconvenient price such as an embarrassment, a fine or sentence. This implies that as persons they are unprincipled from within. Their personal characters are dependent upon the moral principles and convictions of other people whose philosophical and/or religious convictions have effectuated the mores and laws of their society.

To have a parasitical conscience is to be much like a robot conditioned, in the final analysis, by outside forces — in this case moral forces. This means that such persons would be a menace to their society were it not for other peoples' moral and religious convictions that condition them. What does this amount to but making them spineless conformists without any built-in convictions of their own to subscribe to. They are at best mere sycophants of society. A dangerous ethical relativism is herein implied, and the atheist is no more moral than his acceptance of society's standards allow him to be. Subscribing to the notion of Nietzsche that "God is dead" because "we have killed him," the atheist might with consistent thinking subscribe to power over other people as his goal of self-realization, which was the logic of Nietzsche's Superman theory adapted by the Nazis under Hitler. Why? Because he has no permanent principles to guide him. The trial and error of an egotistical power-seeking is his logically "legitimate" alternative.

But most atheists do not go as far as Nietzsche. Their chosen alternative is to duplicate what society popularly subscribes to. Surely, that is better than nothing, but it only makes them carbon copies of the ethics that others have perpetuated and helped ingrain in the customs of society. Again, if it were not for other people's convictions they would be promoters of moral indolence, if not anarchy. Not having principles of their own, the conscience is completely relative, so that it has nothing stable to look to, as Sartre conceded. It looks only to their relative conscience and the thought-to-be relative standards of their society, which to them are here today and gone tomorrow. Logically, such thinking is a poison to our society, because it contributes not only to the loss or lowering of our cultural values but to their trial-and-error relativism or morals that have no character.

One of the chief marks of such social deterioration lies with our legislators and the legal profession today. Most of them examine and manipulate laws without studying deeply the ethical principles behind those laws as based on philosophical and/or religious insight. The consequence is that the laws are regarded as only devices for clever manipulation. Another mark of our cultural decadence is the excessive relativism that has rapidly crept into Western sex ethics. Related is the break-down of the family. Thousands of homes are breaking apart at the seams. Too few boundaries are given to the children, who grow up, therefore, with not only low aims but a feeling of being uncared for. Low self-esteem is the result. They realize that without parental guidelines they are not really loved.

Atheism and the loss of moral and spiritual values and ideals have contributed to the crisis of Western civilization. Sorokin of Harvard said from his sociological perspective that we have slipped down to a "sensate culture," which can be salvaged only as ethical ideologies balance it up. Without people looking to a divine Absolute, our society slips down the plank of cultural relativism, and we will be next to follow the twenty-one civilizations to collapse. Toynbee says, "We must pray for a reprieve." This means a serious recovery and re-orientation of our theistic values through what Kierkegaard meant when he said, "Faith is an absolute relation to the Absolute." More than a set of concepts, it is an encounter with Yahweh-God, the eternal Spirit-Person especially revealed through Moses' encounter with the great "I AM," known also through Jesus Christ as the Spirit of Agápe or ultimate Being identified with sacrificial love. This is the opposite of the atheistic relativism, which at its best is secular humanism, the bane of our culture today. It is highly dubious that a humanistic relativism can save our society. Only a theistic religion can do so, for it alone can preserve the absolute values needed at the grass-roots of our society. It alone can give and preserve the dignity of man, for it looks to "the Other" who grants us dignity and honor as well as purpose and destiny. Human dignity is not a product of mere self-assertion and is not self-evident. It is a given accepted by faith. Thus we need a high regard for ethical theism, lest the relativism basic to our cultural cancer be given free rein in the next century to undermine Western civilization from within.

As hinted above one of the major weaknesses in American Society today is the loss of what has been known as "the Protestant work ethic." Once made a popular practice on our shores, it was brought to this country mainly by the Puritans to whom all forms of creative labor were expressions of their divinely inspired vocations. Not altogether new it became basic to the theism and new life clarified by the Reformers. Luther, for instance, was the first to clarify and stress that any person's work, if respectable, could be a form of service to God. This did much to inspire people to do conscientious work every day. Calvin did much to popularize what became basic to free enterprise not unrelated to this work ethic. John Wesley, leader of the evangelical awakening of the 18th century, accentuated the implications of a similar ethics. History shows that this movement elevated thousands of people from the lowest in cultural and economic ranks to some of the most virtuous and accomplished in the British Isles of that day. Subsequent generations have still felt the impact. Secular humanism can point to nothing like this.

Chapter 6

The Faults Within
Our Religions

Much good can still be said about our mainline middle class churches; however, we must ask: What are their faults? This question is being asked realistically and reflects what is weak in their ranks. Why are they slipping numerically? Why are their ranks thinning? We must face the issue and not look the other way. There are, in my opinion, four important matters that explain the statistical losses. Let's be frank about them.

First, our preachers are at fault because they fail to preach sufficiently for commitment. In the kind of churches composed of middle class people, the most numerous in the land, we need to put people "on the spot" with either/or decisions for Christ or what the prophets taught. We need to preach and teach what Kierkegaard meant by "total-self commitment." Such a faith is not merely emotional consent or even doctrinal assent; it is the whole person's involvement in the "I-Thou" encounter, as Buber said. Our people need to accept and declare such a faith and let the world know whose side they are on. I have lived and worked in nine different states and sat at the feet of dozens of preachers. I must say that lack of preaching for commitment is the basic weakness in general, while where the church is strongest preaching for commitment is strongest.

Second, the next weakness is the neglect of expository biblical preaching or something close to it. Our people do not only want to hear what the preacher has to say but what the Bible has to say. Of course, these are not totally alien to each other, but our preaching needs more of a "thus saith the Lord" dimension to it. There is nothing like the Bible to verify this. I am reminded of a preacher who told Dr. Stanley R. Hopper of Drew University School of Theology that he was "all preached out' and was about to leave the ministry. Dr. Hopper said to him, "Try preaching a few biblical sermons." The man wrote Dr. Hopper awhile later and said, "I see what you mean. I'm staying in!"

Third, our preaching needs to have more doctrinal precision and exposition. Our people need to learn more about the basic truths taught by the Church through the Bible, first, and its historical experiences, second. Included here are the various slants on such great doctrines as the Incarnation, grace, reconciliation, justification by faith, sanctification, and perfect love. Ministerial students should not by-pass or minimize the courses of study in college and seminary which expound on these issues. Good preaching must be doctrinal in relation to being decisive. It is not enough to substitute more liturgy or sophisticated forms of worship, albeit an evangelistic priest like John Wesley was not averse to them. We must keep the doctrinal substance alive and central in the pulpit.

Fourthly, a problem for which I lack a clear-cut answer but for which we are paying a price is this: We are compromising our pietistic ethics while improving, rightfully, our social ethics. Years ago when Christians sensed they had some sacrifices to make not only in stewardship but in their lifestyle they were more loyal.

Perhaps we are compromising too much in terms of Sunday observances, temperance, entertainment, and marriage. To be sure we are living in a faster-paced epoch, but does this mean we should forsake our "Rules of Order" or equivalents that guide our conduct. Legalism is not the answer, but constructive ethical lifestyles may be so. Should we not accept them as fresh challenges rather than passé rules of piety? We must not become legalistic to the point of judging one another, but we need to keep our expectations high. Church members need to be versed in those high expectations. I am afraid we have become too lax in our piety despite the fact that legalism is not a substitute for personal commitment. When our priests and preachers themselves, for instance, resort to alcohol, sexual diversions or divorce, something has to be dead wrong. Our ecclesiastical leaders must lead all of us back to higher expectations.

I may not have all the answers but I am convinced that these four points must be remedied if middle class churchmanship is to regain its thrust. And if it does not, what will be the alternative but continued losses in their ranks.

There are religious leaders who think the solution to such weaknesses lies in a turn to fundamentalism. This is an early 20th century movement, which is based on biblical literalism — an uncritical, dogmatic approach, which disrelates orthodox doctrines or any other kind from pro-scientific, literary and historical studies. The interpreter assumes that all that is needed in religious discourse is the citation of scriptural passages as subjectively preferred. Usually accompanying this approach is a more emotional appeal through vehement and sentimental appeals based on some preachers' self-made authority. Actually such leaders manifest an inferior faith (pistis), for they are either too fearful or too intellectually weak or unprepared to pursue courses of studies offered by schools of theology endorsed by the American Seminary Association. Such institutions have high standards and represent academic freedom while avoiding catechetical dogmatisms. Party line thinking is discouraged in favor of a variety of perspectives. Their critical methods of inquiry open up both lower and higher criticisms of the scriptures even as they interrelate biblical studies with philosophical bridgeheads for the purpose of constructing systematic theologies, which allow the church and the world to communicate. Religious and secular types of thought are thereby allowed to blend where possible in the interest of a reasonably consistent corpus of thought.

Must the Bible be defended artificially to protect its message? The answer is negative. One of the most intellectually dishonest ideas to be foisted upon the modern world is the fundamentalist notion of the verbal inerrancy of the Bible. It is an unnecessary claim artificially designed to protect the Bible's authority so that it can function like "a paper pope." Allied with the notion is the literal interpretation of the Bible based on a presumed or imposed realism. Neither the Reformers nor Wesley condoned this.

Fundamentalism is due to the failure to be honest enough to use critical intelligence when studying the Bible or to be favorable to the more scientific method applied to it for only the last two centuries. This does not overlook the fact that, though inspired, the writers left us with problems related to their language, literary techniques, thought forms, and historical and philosophical perspectives. The fundamentalists disregard "the human side of the (good) news."

The following are just a *few* problems, in brief, which fundamentalists disregard:

1. The three accounts of St. Paul's conversion in the Book of the Acts, though informative, cannot be perfectly blended or made symmetrical.

2. In Mark 6:5, it states of Jesus, "And he could there do no mighty work. . . ." (KJV) whereas Matthew 13:58 says of the same event, "And he did not many mighty works there. . . ." There is a big difference between "could not" and "did not."

3. I Chronicles 21:1 says King David conducted the first census of Israel at the behest of Satan. II Samuel 24:1 says it was of the Lord. These are two different interpretations of history — very different. The one came from the southern kingdom of Israel, the other from the northern. One fundamentalist counterargument is the idea that God was in control of Satan. If so, he is a devilish god.

4. Fundamentalists like orthodox Christians and Jews have said that Moses wrote the first five books of the Bible. Who wrote the included story of his death? Critical theology is needed.

5. It is dishonest to literalize the Book of Revelation, which is apocalyptic literature full of symbols and deliberately hidden meanings comparable to a tapestry. To impose a realistic epistemology on it is to treat the tapestry like its background or to regard the symbols as objective events. This is an imposition of realism where it does not belong.

6. Genesis consists of at least five documentary sources from different periods of Hebrew history. Edited by early rabbis to give them a semblance of symmetry, they represent different thought forms, language and names of God, even affecting the interpretation of the Lord God. The names came from different periods of Hebrew history. The two creation stories came from different periods also. There is no need to look the other way about the implicit problems. The writers wrote as human beings, not as robots telegraphed from heaven.

7. One of the most naive fundamentalist notions is that David wrote all of the Psalms. Nothing could be more unreasonable, as even casual studies of the psalms reveals. Many events and personages referred to were simply not from his time.

8. The evolution of the ethical and eschatological views in the Old Testament must be conceded. Not only was polygamy dropped eventually but Isaiah suspended the earlier idea held since King Saul that criminals should be punished to the third and fourth generations. Concepts like Sheol and Hades (later Hell) were influenced by the Zoroastrian religion from Persia and adapted later in Israel's history after the exile. In the earlier periods of the Old Testament, there was no concept of heaven.

9. In the New Testament, the various apostles have their respective perspectives and different emphases. Probably the most conspicuous tension is the big difference between St. Paul and St. James relative to the place of works in Christian faith. While a practical both/and paradox of this problem can be enunciated, a perfectly rational synthesis or unity cannot — if we are honest. Even Ephesians 6 condones slavery on a high level.

Even so, these few critical observations need not prevent us from finding the Word of God. "We have this treasure in earthen vessels." No one has an absolute interpretation of the Bible. For as interpreters we affect what we receive by what understandings we do or do not bring to it; nevertheless, the treasure is conveyed through the human vessels like electricity conveyed through an appliance. The power of truth is not identical to the vessel or appliance but conveyed through it. The divine substance has human thought forms, and it is the latter that give us problems.

The more critical approach to theology need not lead to the surrender of sound doctrine as personally and socially relevant. Rather such an approach is more appealing to the better educated, who are critically minded and question any form of dogmatism. Many such people in the past have been almost driven from the church by their uncritical, authoritarian conservative backgrounds and find it inspiring in itself that intellectual honesty and open-mindedness can blend with the study of the Bible and basic doctrine. For instance, creation and evolution are not seen to be antithetical.

Yet, unfortunately, many intellectually better balanced churches have moved too far away from forms of evangelistic effectiveness. Usually this is due to their revulsion from the high-pitched techniques of the fundamentalists. The cure for their weaknesses lies in facing up to the four points designated above. A dignified form of religion need not avoid those points, especially a variety of ways to appeal to commitments of faith akin to what Buber calls the "I-Thou" encounter and to what Kierkegaard stressed as "total-self commitment." It seems fair to declare that without these at the heart of any religion it will eventually dissipate. Combined intellectual honesty and sincere faith can be experienced as a more mature religion. But, unfortunately, too many Americans do too little to understand this. Also, too many are too immature intellectually to trust a religion that is not highly emotional. This is related to an inferior educational background that the high-pitched type of TV evangelists and others take advantage of.

Several of the sects which are offshoots of the mainline churches of Protestantism and Judaism today are especially at fault for catering to extreme forms of emotionalism. Often their leaders appeal less to peoples' intelligence than to their feelings. Not only do their leaders often fail to expose themselves to critical studies in theology but misleadingly teach false versions of the major doctrines accepted by the mainline churches for centuries. In Latin America, sects of this kind are observed even to merge with conspicuous forms of paganism. In these lands as close as Mexico, Roman Catholicism embraces demonology and exorcisms. Catholics in the USA can and should note their differences from their Mexican neighbors.

In the United States radical cults are growing in number. Withdrawing from more respectable religious teaching, self-made leaders often motivated by moneymaking attack more mature churchmanship and develop occult practices centering around their self-made but accepted authority. Satan worship and other occult practices often lead to the pseudo-religious sacrifices of people's lives and other killings. Death threats to the negligent followers are common in some cults. It has been said falsely that Jesus would destroy anyone outside the "sanctuary" of the cult. Prediction of the dates of Jesus' "second coming" are common. Usually such sects hold to a religious exclusiveness which implies that only they shall be saved. A few months ago when a noted fundamentalist announced the date of the second coming hundreds of people flocked especially to Pentecostal churches to be baptized. What was the motive but fear?

What is the big problem? It is, first, ignorance and, second, shrewd leaders taking advantage of their ignorance and that of their followers. Does not all this remind us that our education is incomplete without our colleges promoting mature studies in religion? Does it not remind us, too, that people should put little trust in lesser educated religious leaders?

Usually they are the peddlers of a high-pitched emotionalism with maximum feelings but minimal trustworthy content. Also, their presumed biblical literalism enhances their sense of authority merely by being able to quote the scriptures. Though this lends itself to dogmatism, it does not give them the urge to think clearly about all that either they bring or should bring into the interpretation. It is strange, to say the least, that so many Americans when it comes to physical health will rely only on those specializing in medical and physical knowledge but fail to do similarly with regard to their spiritual health. Again, what is the basic problem but sheer ignorance. Many of the lesser trained religious leaders even refuse to join ministerial associations willing to address various contemporary issues in society, many of which are ethical in nature. They only cooperate with those who support their unexamined dogmatisms and are afraid they may have to re-think them by questioning and dialogue with those of other perspectives. No one is more guilty of this than the professed fundamentalists. It would be unconstitutional but practical if the law could demand high scholastic standards of any and all religious leaders. How pathetic it is that they do not accept such standards freely.

Many of our Protestant seminary graduates today go into the pastorate with an imbalanced theology which is strong on social ethics but weak in doctrinal substance. This is not all bad for we need to be made sensitive to our social inconsistencies. But until pastors become stronger in making the redemptive message of the Bible clearer and more personally relevant, their congregations will be ill nourished. Pulpit counseling and rhetoric are not enough. Though social issues like civil rights, feminism and environmentalism should not be forsaken, they must not dominate the church's themes, for ethics demand a doctrinal base, first, and a faith-commitment, second. Little good can be done about any ethical issue until people are inspired by divine Love, something which comes about only through what Kierkegaard spoke of as "total-self commitment" to God's Word.

Furthermore, many social activists do not understand or sense the need of the redemptive doctrines. Steeped in their social ethics, they think the world can be radically improved only by informing people of our moral, social, economic, and political problems. This is an imbalanced emphasis parallel to that of the "social gospel" popular in the early decades of the century. Educationally much-needed, its leaders often neglected the need of the people to be spiritually re-motivated from within. The head replaced the heart, as it were.

The need and meaning of personal salvation as biblically based has often been ridiculed by the secularists in our universities, often more by insinuation than clear argument. Doctrinal clarification is much needed today. Consequently, in a major denomination, only about 55 percent of those confirmed are still active. It lost over a million members between 1970 and 1987, one-fourth of its total. Similar losses are reported by another major denomination. Accordingly, church school enrollments have dropped noticeably. Unfortunately, many more women allowed into the ministry have caused members to sense the emasculation of religion; its toll will increase if biblical language is neutered.

Relative to the first denomination referred to, many people have revolted against the doctrine of predestination. In the other major body, the problem is due to not clarifying sufficiently the relevance of divine Grace to one's personal life and how to *find* it so, mostly the latter. While the fundamentalist emphasis on the fires of hell is not an antidote and need not be stressed, the matter of finding the magnetism of Christ, his teaching and the challenge of a renewal or re-born life must never be mitigated. Fear does not drive intelligent people to God, but His love attracts them. Divine forgiveness must be clarified continuously, for the old problem of guilt is ever present. Too many of the young people have more than dabbled with sin and would like to be re-instated with God and find a clearer conscience. But the problem is: How? Many mainline churches are not vivifying the answers, so the youth are attracted to fundamentalist churches despite their simplistic to naive ways of presenting the gospel. Most of the young people do not understand the theological differences, but when they find the redemptive message meaningfully relevant, especially justification by faith, they accept it and leave their more formal churches. A sincere, vehemently presented sermon does far more for them than an impressive liturgy. The same for the musical ministries. Many mainline churches have much sophisticated types of music which only specialists can appreciate. This misses the needs of many members. In general, the current need is for a stronger evangelical theology, a return to a critical neo-orthodoxy in which divine transcendence is given its due acclaim regardless of the place there may be for divine immanence. Such a theology can vivify biblical doctrine and yet communicate with a secular academia so as to be respected in our universities.

On the other hand, some people of evangelical backgrounds are looking toward more sacerdotal churches, which accentuate the sacraments with a stronger priestly blessing based on a more visible form of assurance. One such movement is to the Orthodox Church. Some former Roman Catholic priests have moved into its priesthood also. One aspect of their assurance is the idea that the Orthodox Church is institutionally and liturgically the oldest, springing from the church at Antioch, the first Christian community beyond Jerusalem.

Roman Catholics have problems of a little different nature mostly in America and countries like the Netherlands, where a few of their most reactionary theologians are found. The Pope has even been disturbed over some of their contentions. Also, women have been disturbed over not being admitted to the Catholic priesthood. However, the biggest Catholic problem has been the loss of so many priests. As a philosophy department chairman for several years, I have dealt with prospective and selected teachers in philosophy who were formerly prepared for the priesthood. Much of the problem goes back to Vatican II. For the first time, frank interchanges were made publicly on the variations in doctrinal interpretations. In time, however, many of the hopeful younger and prospective priests were discouraged by the hierarchy which insisted on ecclesiastical dogmatics with too little room for varied views or adjustments.

Today the Catholic laity are necessarily given more of a role in the leadership of practical churchly affairs and in the liturgy. Behind this trend is the nationwide loss of at least 6,000 priests. Some dioceses have far too few priests to serve the number of members. The Davenport, Iowa, diocese, for instance, has 86 priests for 116 churches, as reported by columnist William Simbro. He also reports that the National Conference of Catholic Bishops recently projected a loss of 43% of priests between 1966 and 2005. Since the later 1960's, 17% have dropped out, some to marry and some to transfer to the Orthodox Church or to none at all. Recruits are low in numbers today. One adjustment has been the training of laymen as assistants to the priest, a major help being pastoral or visitation ministers and liturgists. An indirect blessing, however, has been the greater serviceability and expression of the laity.

Quite recently the Muslims in the United States and Near Eastern countries conspicuously complained about a novel which to them was a discrediting of their prophet Mohammed. The reaction was so severe that they threatened to kill the author. I, for one, reminded my Islamic friends and acquaintances in print that this reaction, while perhaps legitimate to Khomeni, was not in keeping with their American citizenship, since our Constitution protects both freedom of religion and of expression. For the sake of contrast, I denoted that about that time many conservative Christians expressed disdain for the then current movie, "The Last Temptation of Christ," which fictitiously included Jesus' attraction in his last days to Mary Magdalene. Despite their negative responses, no Christians even thought of killing the movie producer, let alone the author. This reminds us that our religions, whatever their type, must avoid harsh forms of dogmatism, even when they think they are right ethically.

The latter thought is something Muslims in the United States must come to respect, lest they be dishonest as American citizens. There are some who are so fanatical that they are a serious threat to others of their faith, even their own kin, who, for instance, choose to marry persons of another faith. Surely, such thinking is a failure to respect the views of others in keeping with the spirit of American culture and its constitution. It violates religious liberty. Narrow-minded dogmatisms are not amenable to the freedoms accorded people by our constitution, the very principles they swore to uphold when they became American citizens. Upon coming to understand this and much more about our way of life in America, two students from the Near-East said to me, "We wish to become Christians." Whereupon I said, "Why?" Together they replied, with their many observations in mind, "You have so much more love in your religion."

One of the general weaknesses in most of our religions today is insufficient teaching of the religious interpretations of ethics. Despite the fact that some of our leaders hardly move beyond ethical issues, those who place emphasis upon doctrine, biblical studies and/or spiritual experience, whatever the denomination, are often atrociously weak in clarifying ethical and civic responsibilities. Why? For one thing the strong pietisms and doctrinaire positions of previous generations are taken for granted, as if inherited by the younger people who need to find a more vivid and relevant understanding of "the new birth" and the responsibilities it leads them to accept forthrightly.

Ethically speaking, three important areas which should be dealt with, especially among the youth, are drugs, sex and racial prejudice. If our people are to fully grasp their religious responsibilities, they must be taught the moral and civic implications of what they mean. In some of the other chapters, statements are made about drugs, especially alcoholism, and sexual irresponsibilities. Churches should have classes on these social problems. In addition, they must teach that racial prejudice is alien to genuine religious principles and commitments, especially if divine love is to be kept alive and brotherhood practiced in keeping with the teachings of Christ and the prophets. There are too many professing Christians, for example, who are prone to put down members of minority groups either personally or collectively. Many hardly even recognize the implications of observing, for example, what Dr. Martin Luther King stood for as both a religious and civic leader, who promoted non-violent protest against the injustices suffered by the minorities. How can these pseudo-religionists justify Christian Agápe or sacrificial love with such indifference? Little wonder, in many instances, that humanists and other unbelievers should distrust our church leaders. They see clearly our inconsistencies and hypocrisies. Ethical house-cleaning should never be obsolete in either the church or the world.

Just what is the underlying problem in religion today? It is akin to what was expressed above as the need for genuine faith commitments of a profoundly personal type. Next in importance is the need at all times for open-mindedness, a willingness to cooperate and learn from each other. But how? By placing the Spirit ahead of the letter and accentuating our commonalities before our differences, not only interdenominationally but inter-religiously, hence, ecumenically. In general, an insufficient clarification of the personal and social relevance of the biblical message is a part of our cultural cancer today.

Whatever the ethical improvements made in their religions, people must not forsake the most elemental features of prayer and penitence. Despite the weaknesses of dogmatic fundamentalisms, most of them may be credited with keeping these factors basic. Both John the Baptist and Jesus began their ministries with strong public appeals beginning with "Repent. . . ." Though fundamentalists commonly make such appeals in evangelism marked by emotion, often helpful to the less educated, the more middle-class evangelicals do so with more cultured, mild-mannered approaches based on fewer negative appeals related to the fear of hell and more positive appeals to the magnetic love of Christ, which Christians are called to reflect.

Roman Catholicism in the U.S. today has parallel concerns. According to the latest reports, fewer Catholics are going to confession and observing Lent today, both related to repentance. Their bishops claim that too few understand what sin is and see little or no need to repent, as reported in a Gannett News article. Yet much the same could be said for the near humanistic types of left-wing Protestants. Not long ago Karl Menninger of the noted Menninger Foundation wrote a book, *What Happened to Sin?*. Psychiatrists often see the problem when religious liberals do not. Whatever their branch of religion, people lack a religious vitality if they do not understand sin and the need of repentance linked with forms of "conversion," which lead to a new lifestyle.

Recently, news columnists have declared that the "baby-boom generation," which has now reached young adulthood, does not find the church doing anything for them. This writer's response is that such is to be expected, for many of the younger generation in particular do not want what the church can do for them. Most of these younger people do not prefer the moral responsibilities which are expected of people who are faith-committed to the Judaeo-Christian revelation of God. They want sexual permissiveness regardless of the consequences. For instance, in a semi-public meeting of nurses led by one of my former students, I heard some nurses literally scorn the expressed respect for the Ten Commandments.

The church can introduce these people to God and Christian ethics, but the sad fact is that many of our younger people do not want this relationship, because of the responsibilities that go with it. One of the major consequences of this trend is the implied invitation to the AIDS virus to do its worst among the people of our culture and increasingly among other cultures as well. Even though many high schools and colleges are today teaching our students about sex, many of those who are sexually active reject the use of condoms, for instance, even when supplied with them. This trend is a long way from two and more generations ago when most of our faith-committed young people were willing to remain virgins until they were married, or, if they failed to remain continent they at least repented of their sins and were willing to begin anew with the moral responsibilities accompanying their sincere faith-commitments.

Morally, today's younger generation remotely respects the church's endeavors, but they do not want to join its team fully, for they "want to have their cake and eat it, too," as the saying puts it. Most of them do not wish to dismiss God, but they do want to dismiss a responsible trust in God. They want free sex so badly that they are willing to reject genuine faith in God to have it, knowing that to try to have it both ways makes them hypocrites of the first order. They do not want to see our churches burn, but neither do they want to sincerely join the teams that keep them alive and vital to our culture and its values.

Another consequence of this debauchery is the splitting up of families and the increase in the number of single parent homes, most of which are fatherless domestically. In addition, it is apparent that the baby-boom generation has many unmarried couples living together under the pretext of economic security while really in the interest of free sex. It's time that we assert this without apology.

Americans and Westerners in general, it is time to overtly concede such moral debauchery and not casually look the other way. Our civilization cannot remain strong when we allow and even encourage the loss of our values, especially values basic to strong home-life. A German philosopher, Arnold Spengler, saw this trend on the horizon around 1900 and declared that Western civilization is on the way out, not just down but out. Though other noted interpreters of history in this century have not been so pessimistic, they recognized the problems of our "sensate culture," as Peterin Sorokin, the Harvard sociologist spoke of it, and conceded that without a visible recovery of moral and spiritual values we cannot save our civilization, which presently is at the bottom of a cycle. The "challenge" to our civilization, said Arnold Toynbee, is definitely moral and religious in nature, unlike the variety of challenges previous civilizations have had to confront.

Is it too much to say that our baby-boom generation has a very special responsibility to help prevent the collapse of our AIDS-ridden societies? What kind of future generations are they working for? Not much that is promising, for they are living primarily for self-gratification. Is our case hopeless? On a big scale, it almost appears so, but as philosophers like Whitehead, Schweitzer, Sorokin, and Toynbee all suggest, we must meet our basic cultural challenge and turn things around morally through spiritual re-commitments. Even Bertrand Russell eventually saw the errors in his positivistic philosophy, which for decades helped many academicians to renounce the morals of our Judaeo-Christian heritage. Russell even wrote a book in the mid-1920's attacking the institution of marriage. Many pseudo-sophisticates welcomed this. But Russell, when disappointed with his own family, who said they followed his positivistic philosophy, finally woke up and said, "We must return to the Christian ethic."

Realistically, is it too late for a big-scale turn-around? Time will tell — before long — but, unless our intelligentsia wake up responsibly, we may not only go down as a civilization, which we are doing, but *out!* Technology cannot save our civilization, for its methodologies must be meshed with our ethical values at their best, if they are to be truly serviceable. And this calls for a new generation of what Jimmy Carter referred to as "born again" Christians and other people willing to accept new beginnings under God. In short, the sex-crazed aspect of our cultural cancer cannot be healed without recovery of our best principles and values. Until our teachers and the leaders in our media recognize this and act to turn things around through the press, TV and radio, they will remain among the foremost perpetrators of our cultural cancer. Hollywood has an extra special responsibility in this regard. Without the leaders of our media becoming re-committed to our values, not the least of which is our sex ethics at its best, we cannot stop the cultural viruses from spreading. Only the recovery of morals based on religious principles can save us and heal the rot basic to our cultural cancer. Again, we must not only plead for our rights but be committed to our duties. Unless this is clarified in our schools and made commonplace in the workplace, our cultural cancer will continue to eat away at the fiber of our people's character and destroy us from within. There simply is no substitute for a vital personal theism to prevent this. Without it we cannot turn around our declining, sensate culture. Only if our leaders in education and industry will awaken in time can our cancerous cultural condition be contained.

Another symptom of our cancerous culture is what *Times* writer Charles Krauthammer calls our "mass hypocrisy." Relating this to what the American public sees to be the lowered sex ethics of political candidates, he asserts that people expect more from their leaders than of themselves. "Why should we care?" he states. "This is a country in which seduction trails only murder as the most popular form of TV entertainment, and in which condoms are handed out in the high schools. Yet, as voters, we profess shock that our candidates should behave as we do. Candidates overtly subscribe to family values at a time when our families are splitting apart. Over half the marriages in the U.S. end in divorce, twice the rate of 30 years ago." Krauthammer states that half of our children will live in single-parent homes before the age of 18, and today 25% of all births occur out of wedlock, five times as many as 30 years ago.

Not a working paradox, this to me is an out-right contradiction, a glaring reason for the mass hypocrisy. Though typical, it must not be condoned. Simply because many voters are hypocrites about moral values expected of political leaders gives no grounds for minimizing the seriousness of the matter. Our media and schools must vivify the importance of the virtues expected of our leaders and the responsibilities of citizens to extol and exemplify them. Krauthammer refers to a 1987 poll in which ". . . most Americans ages 18 to 44 thought that the rise of single parenthood and sexual permissiveness, and the decline of religious training of children, constituted a change for the worse." (*Time*, April 27, 1992). Thus citizens have little grounds for attacking faulty candidates related to these matters until they clean up their own act. It appears that similar problems exist among the British today. Without the moral housecleaning of all people in the West, however democratic, we cannot expect to eradicate our cultural cancer. Democracy cannot prove itself sound unless her people prove to be virtuous.

Today one of the basic moral issues and social tensions relates to abortion. I am against the practice, because a fetus is a human being even if in-the-making. Since it is a life, abortion is a form of homicide. Many women in favor of abortion argue that they can do with their bodies as they please. Just where do they get this so-called right? I've never heard anyone of this persuasion answer this question. An infant, after all, is not of the woman's body per se. She gives birth to a new life, a new person who is both a body and personality distinct from hers. Exceptional cases aside, the mother has no moral right to extinguish the life of the child. She has facilitated the appearance of that life but has not authored it. The child is a separate life from her own.

In addition, as John Silber has written, "If a woman can justify the termination of a pregnancy following voluntary coition, the same line of reasoning can be used by healthy and able-bodied men to justify abandoning wife and children and refusing to pay child support. In either case, personal convenience and comfort replace moral responsibility." Silber also shrewdly states, " Given the fact that a substantial proportion of the people in this country regard abortion as murder, it does seem improper to pay for abortion with tax money." Indeed, and all the more so when pro-choice people claim abortion is a private matter. This problem in general should remind us that we must respect human life, while we cannot do it justice without respecting the Divine Other apart from which we have no honor or purpose. As Albert Schweitzer put it, we must have reverence for life — all life. But, surely no form of life in this world deserves sincere reverence more than human life, which begins as a fetus with an innate drive to live and live some more. To squelch it is murder, and murder is sin, an insult to the Mind involved in its creation, design and organic fulfillment. Is it too much to expect our teachers to play fair with this perspective? To disregard it is an invitation to more moral debauchery, the core of our cultural cancer. To respect it is to respect principles intrinsic to an ethical theism linked with the person-producing order of creation.

A great betrayal leading to the loss of members in mainstream Protestantism is being fostered by several seminaries, which neglect the study of sound doctrine today and replace it with a humanistic confidence in social ethics as the answer to our society's problems. Their number 1 problem is the failure to see the distinctiveness of divine transcendence. Many of the teachers and graduates cannot even understand how a neo-orthodox theology, for instance, can be just as ethically minded while keeping redemption uppermost and basic to a remotivated people. Both Protestant and Catholic feminists, for instance, resist ideas of self-denial when they are stressing self-assertion. They and other "liberationists" seldom, if ever, see the need for a faith which begins with repentance and divine reconciliation. What is this but a new anemic version of the "social gospel," many of whose perpetrators seldom even mention Jesus Christ. How pathetic! Must the Church re-learn old lessons the hard way?

Until our religions undergo theological and spiritual renewals, our cultural cancer will not be cured, for our people will not be motivated. Biblically, God said, "A new heart will I put within thee." The left-wingers fail to understand this, let alone its need. The positive implications of what a vital faith entails will be treated in Part II relative to the religious implications of Logotherapy, the finding of meaning in life as important to the cure of our cultural cancer.

Chapter 7

The Phenomenon
of Alcoholism

Alcoholism is an increasing problem in our society. We must learn to face the facts of the matter and view it as frankly as possible. Dr. William C. Menninger, noted psychiatrist of the Menninger Foundation, puts it forthrightly when he says, "A national emergency would be declared if alcoholism were a communicable disease."

Alcohol is our nation's number 1 drug problem. Not communicable, alcoholism, nevertheless, constitutes the third or fourth leading health problem in our nation. That the disease is a social phenomenon of increasingly grave significance is borne out by the statistical facts. In 1940 there were about 40,000,000 users of alcohol in the United States, of whom 2,400,000 were "drinking to excess." About 600,000 of the latter drank "continuously" to the point of being chronic alcoholics. In just five years, by 1945, the number of American consumers of alcohol had increased 35%. By 1951, the number had risen to 65,000,000 of whom 4,000,000 were "excessive drinkers." In 1965 the latter figure became 9,000,000. Today it is closer to 12 million. One out of every four of these people or about 3,000,000 are "advanced cases of alcoholism." These figures have doubled since 1940. Think of it! Over five million people, one out every 48 citizens, literally enslaved to the liquid spirits. Just how many is that? It is an army of men and women marching ten abreast in military fashion past a given point for over 25 days and nights!

How are we to interpret "alcoholism" as such? All too popular is the idea that alcoholism is attributable solely to the physiological factors. This is too narrow a view, since it fails to see the total personality involved. Sometimes it is used as a disguise of one's own possible vulnerability to the disease, as though one were an "alcoholic" only if his body is heavily predispositioned with the problem, genetically or otherwise. Such a view must stand corrected from a psychosomatic perspective of the individual self as a whole being, not merely a body but a mind-body complex and the existentially conditioned total personality.

An alcoholic is one who cannot leave alcohol alone despite the problems it causes him and others. He simply must have his liquor, whatever the reasons – physical, emotional, mental, or social. Being under constraint, his indulgence is more than a moral choice or deliberation, though not unrelated to choices. While his problem has become physical, it is not limited to physical necessity, since deep-seated psychological factors are involved; therefore the view of "alcoholism" should not be restricted to the physiological perspective.

In support of this interpretation, may we consider the following factors:

1. Alcoholism is a progressive illness characterized by uncontrollable, compulsive drinking. "The alcoholic . . . cannot stop drinking even if he wants to, without help." (Council on Alcoholism, Abilene, Texas). An occasional drinker is not an alcoholic when in control of the situation. An alcoholic is one whose drinking complicates his life; he does not control it, for it controls him. When he sobers up, a single drink can send him under again. By no means limited to "skid-row," he is a habitual and compulsive drinker of any vocation or social station. Over 85% are employable, however. (AFL-CIO Publication on Alcoholism in cooperation with the National Council on Alcoholism).
2. Alcoholism is not a tendency that runs in families, studies have shown. Nor is the alcoholic particularly allergic or biologically necessitated toward becoming an abnormal drinker. The problem is developed gradually. Statistics show that comparatively few people become alcoholics prior to the age of thirty (E.M. Lembert, *Social Pathology*).
3. Alcohol is a drug. "Certain people cannot tolerate it or let it alone once the habit is attained." (Here physical factors may be related.) No one knows in advance whether or not he will be able to remain an occasional or moderate drinker. "A considerable degree of self-control is required to keep from passing the stage of light drinking

to moderate drinking and then to heavy drinking" (Harold Titus, *Ethics)*. Akin to this is what has been called a "moral disease" based on conflicts in the unconscious mind. This implies that the moral element is eventually qualified by factors "beyond the realm of responsible choice" (V. Ferm, *Encyclopedia of Morals)*.

4. Subtle "sociocultural situations" contribute to excessive drinking. Pressures and problems of social adjustment are reflected in the higher incidence of alcoholism among immigrants from northern Europe and Italy, especially the Irish. The Jews have a low incidence, largely due to religious conditionings of long-standing tradition. Among women alcoholics, there is a high incidence among divorcees (Lambert, *op cit)*.

5. There is a high incidence between chronic alcoholism and mental disorders. Psychologist L. F. Shaffer states: "In many instances the habitual use of alcohol . . . is the result rather than the cause of maladjustment. Many habitual drunkards continue their use of alcohol because of a persistent need for relief from adjustive difficulties. This psychological factor is probably as important. . . as is the more usually emphasized one of physiological habit." Shaffer stresses the need for mental adjustments to offset the psychological need for alcohol as an escape mechanism (Shaffer, *The Psychology of Adjustment)*.

Many people misuse alcohol because of hidden emotional pressures. "When a person uses alcohol to escape the problems and responsibilities of everyday life, or as an emotional crutch to feel superior and to build up his self-confidence, he is a problem drinker: chances are he has the disease of alcoholism" (AFL-CIO). Meaninglessness is a prime factor.

6. Though the alcoholic is "incurable," his illness can be arrested. Few chronic cases return to a normal life without help. This calls for their gaining insight into the problem, the understanding of the family, medical care, and adjustments relative to personal problems. For a pronounced improvement, as stressed by the National Council on Alcoholism, the first need is for the victim to face the facts, then concede the need of help and welcome it from his pastor, psychiatrist or A.A. Chapter. One out of six beyond age 65 is an alcoholic.

One of the more tragic features related to alcoholism, beside the terrible death toll it takes on our highways and its being the cause of half of our boating fatalities, is the growing number of alcoholics today among the homeless in our cities. Alcoholics and other addicts are filling the streets adding more and more to the return of "skid row." In addition families with children are "the fastest growing sector" of the homeless population while innumerable single people are joining them. Social authorities tell us that chronic alcoholics are the fastest growing group among the street dwellers.

Part of the problem is the relaxed regulation of public drunkenness and use of other drugs like cocaine. Soup kitchens do not meet all their needs, and the old flop houses are largely gone. Authorities tell us that "substance abuse" in 1990 virtually outstrips mental illness as a serious health problem. Since the 1970's homeless drunks seldom have found the jail cell a temporary abode, for most states have decriminalized public intoxication and forced the inebriates to take to the streets. One of the glaring economic consequences of this disease is the projected loss of 136 billion dollars in industrial productivity in 1990. Another consequence is the cost to the taxpayers. One Minnesota county has found that the annual cost of maintaining inebriates today comes to $23,000 per person. However, those randomly selected in their study often proved to have less control over their lives than the homeless, due to their chemical dependency on alcohol. Victims of alcoholism who are better off financially are socially tolerated today more than those who pass-by on the streets asking for handouts. It is questionable that this attitude is of any help. Perhaps it is time to remind everyone that playing with "fire-water" under any conditions is deleterious to our culture. The better educated people will need to take the lead in squelching the use of these drugs, alcohol being the most popular. But will they be able to do it without high moral incentives? It is doubtful, for as asserted above, too little of our education today is meshed with moral values. There is little hope apart from an enhanced religious understanding and commitment.

In conclusion, alcoholism must not be limited to a mere physiological perspective. It must be faced as a deep-seated malady of pronounced, social, emotional, and psychological conditioning. Related to the physical, it is of a psychosomatic nature, involving almost every aspect of the total self. In this respect it is not only a physical disease but an existential condition. Overcoming it is related to the strong personal resolve of the victim. Often this is possible only through a vital religious commitment. Either as a long-range tee-totaler or a day-by-day type with Alcoholics Anonymous, the commitment is essential as it affects the "total self." Called for usually is a new life-style that does not yield to peer pressure. Moral decision is basic here.

Is this really possible? Consider this recent report at the beginning of 1990:

> In this age of responsibility, more cities will celebrate this Sunday with alcohol-free family fests — and still have a bubbly good time. "Everyone's in a happy mood. Strangers wish 'Happy New Year' to each other," says Zeren Earls, director of Boston's First Night, the 13-year-old booze-less New Year's celebration that has spawned 33 other licensed followers. New this year: Denver; Elmira, N.Y.; and Waukegan, Ill.
>
> More than a half-million folk jammed Boston 1988 festivities at $5 a head. Kalamazoo, Mich., in the fourth year of its New Year's Fest, expects 10,000 people this Sunday ($6; kids under 5 free). Highlights: a tuba concert, jugglers, gospel music, Mexican folk dancers, fire-eaters and Renaissance musicians. And what about booze? Says Martha Ream, president of the Kalamazoo citizens group: "Nobody misses it."

Does this not allow for the moral involvement of the total self including the important role of the will? No chronic alcoholic willed to become such, but he did will to indulge and gamble with the consequences. Surely he must assert his will, though more strongly, to overcome the problem. Called for is all the help he can get while related to a reconditioned free will. How does one get it? Quite as the A.A. people have come to understand it, by experience. On a day-by-day basis, one must be committed or re-committed to the Divine Absolute as he sees it. This is the personal relevance of faith, which reorientates one's lifestyle, the social consequences of which are apparent to the individual, the family and community. Alcoholism is still our biggest drug problem, yet much that is stated here applies to drug addiction as well. It is dubious that our cultural cancer can be fully cured without the resolution of central problems of both — alcoholism and the other addictive drugs.

Part II

Prescriptions for Our Cultural Cure

Chapter 8

The University and Its Goals

During a discussion that followed an address by a university president, I asked him, "Sir, what do you mean by university?" He scratched his head, reflected with a wrinkled brow and said, "I really don't know." Perhaps his intellectual honesty should be shared by most of us in the university today.

While I do not presume to speak with finality, let me suggest that the term 'university' relates to an institution's concern for general or universal knowledge. It should deal with nearly all fields of learning and have several colleges through which to do so. At its best a university should view itself as a whole. As it realizes this, it will institutionalize the classical issue of the one and the many, principles which need each other. In order to fulfill this holistic perspective, a university should fulfill two basic functions of education: 1) specialization and 2) integration. If we may compare a university to a wheel, the spokes are the fields of specialization and the hub is the philosophical enterprise of correlating the basic findings of the specializations. The net result is integrated, systematic thought rather than piecemeal learning. In other words, a university should not only promote areas of specialization with depth but cross-fertilization with breadth. This is also the essential difference between training and education, the difference between the development of technique and the educement of insight. Without insight students fail to cultivate and transmit culture. It is not enough that we inform students bit by bit, but that we help them evoke understanding of both the universe in general and human existence in particular.

Though vocational training may be a subsidiary role of a university, it must not be allowed to usurp the centrality of integrated learning, for a university should do more than aid students in the economic devices of making a living; it should foster the art of living a life. The latter is cultivating an exciting habit of mind that weighs all issues of thought dialectically and regards knowledge as an end-in-itself and its own reward.

In short, a university based on these premises will promote the maximum maturity of the whole person. As it seeks to achieve this general goal, a university will have subsidiary goals that include the following:

1. It should train persons to think critically, scientifically, and constructively.
2. It should help them discriminate between cultural values of material, moral, aesthetic, and religious dimensions.
3. It should foster sound citizenship, enabling free men to use their freedom wisely.
4. It should supplement scientific and specialized learning with intellectual background a propos to any vocation through coordinated, not merely piecemeal, learning.
5. It should apprise persons of the great issues of our times, relative to questions of justice, freedom, nature, and human nature in the light of the principles of permanence and change.
6. It should inspire a philosophical perspective and evoke the student's enduring desire to gain in wisdom and find profounder meaning in life in moving into the future.

When these elements of education are fulfilled, a person educated in a university will be distinguished by no less than the following characteristics:

1. A thorough acquaintance with at least one discipline.
2. Ability to communicate well in one's own native language.
3. Ability to entertain new ideas in a changing age.
4. Ability to live cooperatively with other individuals and groups.
5. Ability to entertain oneself and develop a wide range of both cultural interests and inner controls.

6. Sensitivity to the larger spiritual order of which one is a part and one's awareness of one's measure of scientific understanding and control over the flux of nature.

The meaning of a university and its goals is a matter often neglected but one which must be reconsidered frequently, lest as a people we lose our way and fail to find and preserve goals for our civilization. As the university goes, so goes society.

As inferred above the university must combine the classic issues of the one and the many. Our cultural cancer in America can be overcome only as this is actualized through the coordination of the specialized fields of inquiry. At the heart of it must be liberal education, lest there be a failure to communicate across disciplinary lines. In general more educators are coming to see this, yet some of our schools fail to fulfill it. How can we have "university" if our programs cater to "diversity?" We need to lose sleep over this question.

For one thing a university diploma should not be valued simply in monetary terms. Yet too few college graduates today can discuss with acuity the intellectual issues of our day, though they can quote Sigmund Freud to help justify their sex life. The true university must foster not merely the quantitative interests but the qualitative, lest our society be cheated. High-class leadership cannot be given to subsequent generations unless academic achievements of this kind are realized here and now. In that event the superior students will be more than tolerated, for they will be respected as our prospective leaders of the future.

Unless our educational specialists are led into a more qualitative academic curricula, we cannot expect much to improve. They must come to be more like scholars and not drags on scholarship. Will this come about? I trust it will, because our administrators are beginning to see where lies our basic problems and answers. Legislators are beginning to show concern, yet not with total trust in monetary answers alone. Our house-cleaning must begin within the walls of academia.

One of the big problems at this time is the need to change "the myth of the student-athlete." The college drive for winning sports contests, while not all bad, is such that the athletic programs have become business enterprises. Amateur athletes are getting little moral guidance and too frequently little of the education they matriculated for. Far too many college athletes do not even approach graduation. The system they join is an educational fraud. Fewer than 30 percent of the football and basketball players graduate today, a rate obviously much lower than that of the more typical students. There are a few exceptions among some reputable universities, but most schools are closer to one which graduated six out of 58 basketball players between 1973 and 1983. What a farce! Some schools are beginning to improve the picture, but little will happen for the better until our athletes are taught they must earn their privileges by *maintaining* no less than a 'C' average or what is commonly called a 2 point average within a range of 1 to 4, the latter being a straight A average. Falsifying entrance exams also must be eliminated as well as wooing recruits by money and other favors. Such unethical practices must be exposed and stopped. A university must make this one of its goals in this decade, lest our educational betrayal be pushed to the hilt.

A recent poll by the sports agent Ralph Cindrich reveals that many athletes have received bad academic guidance. No less than 25% of the top pro prospects in football were polled near the end of 1991. Of them 99% expect to have a professional career in sports, while 98% believe they will be sufficiently prepared to enter another field if necessary. Many are simply misinformed and prone to wishful thinking. Many prove incapable of monetary management. The survey also disclosed that 57% felt prepared adequately for professional coaching positions. Besides these tendencies, 10% do not regret taking steroids despite the health hazards. One of the consequences of poor guidance among athletes is the tendency of all too many to crimes like stealing and rape. This writer has known of such cases and finds them related to financial troubles and loss of moral principle. The latter has much to do with their receiving no introduction in college to ethical studies through philosophy or religion. One case in point, a university administrator removed an athlete from a course in ethics, lest his grade therein be against his athletic future.

One of the major adjustments called for throughout all higher education is the blending of the sciences with the humanities. Some months ago Rex J. Beaver, M.D. of the University of California LA Medical School strongly asserted that the modern mind has sold out almost completely to the idea that science has all the answers. "One by one," he said, "all the evils of the world fall prey to the most powerful of scientific weapons — explanation." Man against nature has been displaced by science against nature. Such concepts as human will, badness and laziness have been displaced by conditioning and bad genes. Moral weakness has been reduced only to disease, alcoholism being a case in point.

All sorts of objective explanations of our lives are given, which imply that we have no free will as knowing subjects. Stress is one of the common explanations, though unheard of generations ago. Beaver states frankly that the craving for scientific sounding explanations has gotten out of hand. The big need of the hour is the recovery of our free will. We must assume more responsibility for our actions and stop the experts from exploiting our frailties. There is a need today to relate our behavior to our desires, inner directives and decisions rather than to our deterministic "pop psychology." This would help restore human dignity. Pain would remain a part of life to be dealt with scientifically, but the individual as a person, not merely an organism, would still fight the problems subjectively, not just "some army of self-declared experts," as Beaver puts it.

In reaction to this a behavioristic psychologist said, "Beaver has rejected the scientific study of behavior" by not accentuating the causes of behavior. In responding to the latter, I maintained that Beaver was not rejecting science but re-orientating it, culturally. A behavioristic psychology de-mans man of his manhood. Even after causal explanations are given him, a patient must return, after all, to a human existence that demands either/or decisions, either to accept or reject what he has learned. Only a moral agent could profit from any explanation. The alcoholic may understand his plight causally but unless he freely asserts himself (a self-caused cause) to seek help he will not surmount it. This is why A.A. has proven to be one of the best therapeutic agencies for alcoholics. It deals with persons as willful selves, not merely as organisms. We need more than explanatory causes; we must see ourselves as part of both the causes and the answers.

Beaver is right in asserting that we must rehabilitate the will of persons. Behaviorists reduce us only to animals, if not to mechanisms. Not all wrong, they are not all right, for their naive strait-laced logic ignores the dialectical problems of the self — in this case deterministic causes versus freedom (self-caused causes). B. F. Skinner even denies that we have moral freedom or even consciousness. He reduces us to laboratory rats. Such a psychology does not blend with the new physics, which allows for unpredictabilities.

Furthermore, to insist on a totally deterministic view of psychology and not embrace Beaver's view makes the scientist an enemy of the humanities, the logic of which is that the humanities should be removed from our schools. Total determinism is antithetical to human dignity and responsibility. Existentially, the behaviorist I have referred to cannot consistently allow for his own religion, which has a strong but not excessive place for free will. His position, however, could be qualified legitimately if he modified his closed logic in favor of a both/and paradox which interrelates determinism and freedom. The psychobiology of R.W. Sperry gives support to this possibility, for though it sees consciousness to be a product of physical processes, it can in turn affect them even within the brain traffic. This is not unrelated to a recovery of the conscious will of man related to all his academic undertakings.

So, in general, the university must warrant every student the possibility of not only a specialized area of study but a holistic view of man and society. This demands the recovery of philosophy as the central discipline of thought so that specialization will not obscure integration in education and that diversity will not deviate us from university. Without such a recovery, what we referred to in Part I as the educational betrayal will win the battle and diversity will abrogate university.

Chapter 9

The Recovery of Our Constitutional Principles

We need to see that religious expressions in our schools are not unconstitutional, for our constitution is not against religion simply because it separates church and state. Church implies institutionalized religion. Separation thereof from the state does not mean the separation of the state from religious principles without which we would not even have our constitution. How so? Our constitution relates to the dignity of man, which is not a humanistic self-concoction. No one has honor, save as granted it by an Other.

If all forms of religious expression in public places are off base, then the founding fathers who drew up our constitution were off base. Though not institutionally or theologically alike, they looked to God as the source of human dignity. When problems were confronted in drawing up the constitution, they themselves went to their knees in prayer during the Constitutional Convention itself. Benjamin Franklin had made the suggestion, which was respected. A precedent had been set by Thomas Jefferson, who advocated a whole day set aside for prayer when the Constitution of the Virginia Commonwealth was in the making. The conference members agreed to meet in a local church without being sectarian.

To dismiss religion from our public affairs is to undercut our strongest social bond. Even Gorbachev of Russia has come to see this and to see that an effective social ethic can be recovered in his land only as religion is kept alive. Our founding fathers represented this view in principle, and to dismiss all school prayer, for example, while not to be required absolutely, is one way to abrogate the morals most loyal Americans wish to keep relevant to their lives and social objectives. Currently there are complaints by some humanistic persons against high school students holding extracurricular meetings for Bible study, prayer and religious self-examination. Omaha's Westside High School is one such site where teenagers began such a group a few years ago. The U.S. Supreme Court is considering whether protesting officials have violated club members' right of free speech by denying them permission to meet after school hours. Reactions have pleaded for freedom to think philosophically or religiously and for the right to meet during off-hours the same as several other extracurricular groups. How pathetic the situation at a time when our youth are under so many negative pressures including drugs and pregnancies. Permission to meet in special study groups need not imply a direct endorsement of what is being studied, only a democratic right to do so.

The basic problem is a philosophical one based on the failure to see the difference between "religion" and "religious institutions." To avoid fostering the latter is not to dismiss the former. Without religious recoveries our society will continue to deteriorate and our constitution be forsaken. The cliché "the separation of church and state" hardly does justice to the First Amendment to our Constitution, which said Congress shall pass no law establishing religion or forbidding it. An honest appraisal of the founding fathers and their work by no means allows this to imply that government and religion should have no relationship. They favored a government based on religious principles and to the glory of God and His Kingdom. We of today cannot be true to our founders if we disregard this view and blindly assent to a secular state that dismisses or disregards our moral foundations.

It is often said that religion should have nothing to do with politics. Not so. Without religious principle we would not have our American Constitution. The Declaration of Independence initiated our nation on religious principles, resting its principles four times on God. Upon signing the Declaration, John Adams stated the day (July 4, 1776) should be observed not only with brilliant festivities but "solemn acts of devotion to Almighty God," as writer George W. Cornell has observed. (And what of the Pledge of Allegiance?)

Basically the challenge given to the divine right of kings had religious implications. The "unalienable Rights" of men were seen to be "endowed by their Creator." Not merely obvious or innate, they were regarded as derived from the "Laws of Nature and Nature's God." The founding fathers looked to "the Supreme Judge of the World" for the moral rectitude behind the independence of the 13 colonies. In addition they expressed reliance on "divine Providence" in all undertakings.

All of the 56 founders were religious men, some deists, who accepted a divine creation of the world combined with virtue and the afterlife. Student of the Bible, Jefferson overtly said he was a disciple of Jesus. Influenced by philosopher John Locke, he appealed to the "natural rights" as "evidence" of Deity, the Designer of nature's design.

The sessions of the Continental Congress were opened with prayer, a practice retained by our congress until today in the summer of 1787, when drafting the constitution, the delegates became embroiled in a critical conflict. It was then that Franklin suggested they pray for "illumination" upon appealing to Jesus' words: "Except the Lord build the house, they labor in vain who build it." Intercessory prayers were conducted daily after July 4th up to September 17, 1787 when the Constitution was adopted.

George Washington said that religion and morality were essential to "political prosperity." Jefferson saw religion as basic to moral law. Here is Washington's prayer for the United States:

> Almighty God: We make our earnest prayer that thou wilt keep the United State in thy holy protection; that thou wilt incline the hearts of the citizens to cultivate a spirit of subordination and obedience to government; and entertain a brotherly affection and love for one another and for their fellow citizens of the United States at large. And finally, that thou wilt most graciously be pleased to dispose us all to do justice, to love mercy and to demean ourselves with that charity, humility and pacific temper of mind which were the characteristics of the Divine Author of our blessed religion, and without humble imitation of whose example in these things we can never hope to be a happy nation. Grant our supplication, we beseech thee, through Jesus Christ our Lord. Amen.

D. James Kennedy reminds us today that the constitutions of all 50 of our states appeal to God. Also, most of the prominent monuments and buildings in Washington, DC have provocative religious statements inscribed on them. The first settlements and colonies were all led by religious leaders and their charters based upon religious convictions. All of these tentative and later confirmed commonwealths looked to God as the one who "governs in the affairs of men," as Franklin had said. All the presidents from Washington down appealed to Almighty

God in their inaugural addresses. Though our society of today may betray these principles in favor of forms of pagan practices, we cannot be true Americans, nor our cancerous culture be cured, if we do not clarify afresh for all citizens, especially our children, what our constitutional principles are and look to for authenticity.

Speaking of what our constitutional principles look to, one of the needs of all our people, including the members of the Supreme Court, is to realize that our laws and judges are not the highest reference points for either sound citizenship or morality. Those judges are wrong, who, for instance, regard with indignation if not contempt the vocal anti-abortion exponents who look to an authority higher than those who adjudicate our laws. Our founding fathers, who provided for the judicial branch of our society, among others, saw that without reference to God as the seat of all morality and justice our legal and political principles would be vacuous. Furthermore, human dignity would be fictitious were it not for the Great I Am who grants us such honor. Without it there would be no ultimate basis for respecting one another, a matter positively essential to implications of the justice basic to our constitution.

Benjamin Franklin stated clearly that the Constitutional Convention in May of 1787 needed to begin daily with prayer. Stressing divine Providence such as superintended the American cause during the war years, he said forthrightly that without God's guidance ". . . we shall be divided by our little, partial local interests, our projects will be compounded, and we ourselves shall become a reproach and a by-word down to future ages." This applies to our generation as much as to his. (Cf. Harold V. Milligan's editing of *The Best Loved Hymns and Prayers of the American People*, Garden City Pub. Co., 1982).

Unless our leaders in law and jurisprudence recover respect from such matters our society will be completely undermined by the relativisms of our intellectual life, including law itself. Among our professional people today, none need a recovery of ethical insight more than those in the legal profession. Prelaw students should be expected to study philosophical and religious ethics, lest their profession continue to suffer from deleterious indifference to the principles basic to our laws and men in their profession be concerned merely about monetary gain. Supreme Court Justice Anthony Kennedy recently stated that lawyers are not measuring up. He even said, "We see shoddy practice in every court in the country including the Supreme Court of the United States. . . ." (*Time*, Nov. 12, 1990). Yet he sees some hope for improvement as experienced attorneys pass on skills to the neophytes, especially through the American Inns of Court, an 8,000 member association including judges. We hope that ethical principles will be related to these skills. Our judges should set the example here and be expected to be specialized in the various schools of ethical thought, both philosophical and religious. Otherwise they, too, foster the moral and social relativism weakening our culture.

As we approach the 21st century, we must ask ourselves; Can America continue to lead the world in the right direction, or even lead at all? Though there is much in our society which spells debauchery, we need not succumb to failure if we keep our constitutional principles before us clearly and with relevance to all aspects of our nation. Industrially and technologically, the U.S.A. has proven to be remarkably successful, as we all know, and has helped defeat Nazism and Communism. But will this lead us into a new type of isolationism, not only politically but economically? We must seek to keep democracy alive through a more international economic order, but it must be done clearly in relation to an international moral order not unrelated to the U.N. Charter. Stressing what the respective cultures have in common ethically, we must lead and yet solicit help in feeding the hungry and destitute, especially in the Third World. As Henry Grunwall has stated recently about America, "We have learned much more about the connection between the abundant life and freedom." Communism, he suggests, is too much like an unbending feudalism to produce abundance.

Today, Europe is trying to become a community-at-large based on international economic cooperation, but will it rely on a free market economy as military interests are curtailed? Will the U.S. combination of ideals and freedoms prevail? Or, will economic warfare pick up momentum so as to hinder progress? We wonder. Will ethnic nationalisms mount up or not? It appears so in the Balkian states.

Grunwald is correct, we believe, in asserting that, "Ideally, the world needs a new view of sovereignty and new structures that would give peoples a sense of autonomy and identity, but within larger regional and rational economic groupings. The U.S., which gave a huge push to the formation of the European Community, can help develop such structures." But how? It seems to me we must return to what President Eisenhower stressed before we were ready for it: A United States of Europe. Why should we care? So that needed reforms may be brought about much in keeping with the freedoms of our constitution and so democracy may prevail everywhere. Surely, we are not so poor as a nation that we cannot assert international leadership toward such ends in the coming century. Many Americans today think we are being surpassed economically by the Japanese. Should this be viewed with acquiescence or as challenge? It need not be either an optimistic or pessimistic view, as Grunwald suggests.

Our main problems are not from without but from within. We have long emphasized the search for rights and privileges over duties, as observed above. Our founding fathers saw freedom based on fulfilling our obligations, and our nation was to be a major example as a democratic republic. Today our people need to recover their sense of duties and responsibilities, which our founding fathers interrelated. We can reverse the negative trends seen above in education especially. Improvements supported by the computer age can enhance our cultural as well as business interests if we relate them to our social and political problems while mindful of our role in the world at large. To keep our distinctive role alive and well we must consistently observe the great principles of our Constitution.

The Supreme Court must retain our constitutional principles and be the vanguard for keeping them relevant to every aspect of our society. But the Supreme Court is really betraying true Americanism today when it castigates prayer at public school graduation exercises. Recently the cited prayers of Rabbi Leslie Gutterman were non-institutional and non-sectarian in nature. They were in no way related to the "separation of church and state." For the justices to attack their place at Bishop Middle School of Providence, RI was for them to represent no absolute reference for political ethics itself. To be consistent they should repudiate the founding fathers for appealing to God in the Declaration of Independence and should denounce Benjamin Franklin for appealing to fellow designers of the Constitution to pray when they confronted a knot in their dialectics. In addition, if the Supreme Court justices think they are right they should denounce overtly all our presidents for referring to God in their inaugural addresses.

The action of the justices shows how they are on the side of the moral and intellectual relativism that is sucking us under as a culture and civilization. The logic of their prayer ban spells an atheism which provides no respect for moral or spiritual ideals or absolutes beyond the relativistic claims popular in our schools today. Educational relativism is tributary to our sensate society and the moral decline of our culture. It fails to meet or challenge the debauchery that is "putting us on the skids."

To denounce institutionalized religion planted within our schools is one thing, but to renounce religious principles is another. To ban all prayer in academic circles is such a renunciation. The action invites the collapse of Western civilization, as several specialists have or will endorse, as the failure to meet our civilization's "challenge." Unlike the various challenges to 21 civilizations, which have collapsed before us, ours is moral and spiritual in nature. Fundamental to this is the need to see that even our laws require a higher reference point to be authentic. No law and no temporal judge, even on the Supreme Court, is the highest reference point. Only the eternal God with His implicit righteousness, as biblically revealed, can play such a role. Our founding fathers saw this, and our generation needs to recover their type of faith as reflected in the great Charter they drew up for our nation, the United States Constitution. The alternative is to betray its intrinsic values and continue to feed our cultural cancer through moral indifference, anti-religious sentiments and relativistic judgments.

The Pledge of Allegiance must not only be recited in our schools and civic clubs but understood, especially the words, "one nation, under God, indivisible. . . ." School children must be taught the meaning thereof, and college students must come to understand how it pinpoints the unity in plurality so basic to our republic and crystallized in *E Pluribus Unum* as inscribed on our coins. Fundamental to this is the philosophical first principle of all creative thought, the one and the many, so basic to true democracy and our republic, which looks to these principles.

While preparing for this book I have begun to wonder whether some of our leaders are beginning to think in this vein. Recently, the columnist Cal Thomas conceded that "the moral light" is going out today. "For many," he says, "the physical, moral, psychological and spiritual consequences of unrestrained living are now being worked out on psychiatrists' couches." Even children are in need of such help, often due to "freelance sexual recreation," as Thomas puts it.

Thomas supports our claim that the Constitution pre-supposes a moral order, which must be enforced by law if not accepted freely. To disregard the implications of this is what to our founders was "sin." Between the lines of the freedoms it protects is the freedom to sin, but this does not mean that all choices are good. We must see that freedom is not an end in itself; it must be linked with our moral and spiritual ends, which are righteous and/or loving in nature. Thomas quotes Jack Kemp, Housing Secretary, who forthrightly states, "Democracy without morality is impossible."

Thomas agrees that popular moral relativisms, together with the elimination of all prayer and Bible reading in public schools, have led to our legal system replacing God by the government and, I would add, an implied egocentric humanism. Thomas rightly criticizes various TV talk shows for presenting persons of chastity and fidelity as freaks. When I wrote to "Donahue," I asserted that too often the show exposes inferior brands of religion without giving opportunity to persons specialized in ethics and religion to give corrective response; hence millions of Americans are propagandized to think that much that is phony or outlandish is perfectly OK. Thomas agrees that our culture cannot prevail without respect for the eternal principles recognized by our founding fathers and made implicit in the Declaration of Independence and the Constitution. He is right, for our society cannot remain or become healthy in a moral sense if people do not adhere to the principles overtly and latently expressed in the Constitution. The torch of moral truth must be reignited in our time.

A few years ago when William J. Bennett was Secretary of Education, he was criticized for statements favorable to religion. He saw that it was wrong for educators to regard religion as off limits or out of bounds. Textbooks, he observed, deliberately avoided religious matters, even to give credit where credit was due. He saw how students were being cheated of much cultural understanding when kept ignorant of the roles religion plays in today's world and in our own American history, which has been influenced much by our Judaeo-Christian ideals and lifestyles. Bennett was labeled an "ayatollah" when he supported prayer and the posting of the Ten Commandments in our schools. It is this type of phenomena which made sense of a Chinese Communist's words to a returning missionary awhile ago, "Just remember, we will defeat you from within."

Many pseudo-intellectuals refuse to concede that many of the big issues of our day are religious in nature. William Bennett would agree that without respect for the Divine Absolute we will be sucked under by the quicksands of relativism, which give us no moral undergirdings. Bennett sees what many cynics and atheists fail to see, that religion at its best is "a wellspring of civic virtues, which promote hard work and responsibility along with concern for community and country." He says, "It is a call to kindness, decency and forgiveness." To have disdain for such things is to have it for ourselves. It is a loss of values essential to a meaningful life. This relates to what Viktor Frankl calls "the new neurosis" of our time, the sense of one's meaningless existence. To violate or ignore the values indigenous to our constitutional principles is to invite the moral sterility, which undermines a democracy. Americans and all Westerners need to be re-awakened to the first principles of our society, lest our cultural cancer continue to debilitate our civilization and cause it to collapse. Supported by a variety of thinkers who interpret historical trends and troubles, Arnold Toynbee reminds us that our sensate culture needs to be motivationally re-directed through a return to the best in moral and religious values, lest the eleventh hour of our civilization slip into the twelfth. We can turn things around only if we re-consider the principles of our American Constitution and their religious implications.

But right here is where the Supreme Court recently betrayed the spirit of true Americanism by disavowing a place for prayer in our schools, even at Commencement exercises. This spurns respect for the Absolute beyond the relativistic opinions and judgments popularized in our schools today. For the judges to insist on such a position is to support or espouse a pro-atheistic philosophy, which provides no ultimate reference point for political ethics and law. If they think they are right they should overtly castigate the founding Fathers for appealing to God in the Declaration of Independence and the Creator in the Constitution. The all too popular cliché, "the separation of Church and State" may imply separation of government from religious institutions but not from religious principles. Likewise, the judges should denounce the constitutional delegates for resorting to prayer and all our past presidents for referring to God in their inaugural addresses. The recent action by the Supreme Court is blatantly in support of the cultural nemesis which is defeating our society from within. And what is this but what serves the Communist ambition, cited above, to defeat us from within.

All moral and political judgments which sooner or later reject or overlook the divine Absolute logically support the very relativistic notions which are undermining our civilization. They encourage moral indifference and anti-religious attitudes, which lead us astray and violate the meaning of what the Pledge of Allegiance refers to as "one nation under God indivisible. . . ." The latter spells unity amidst plurality and multiplicity, so basic to our republic as such. *E pluribus unum* is possible only as the majority of our citizens and leaders look to the Absolute One amidst all our many opinions and sentiments, which in themselves remain amorphous and sterile. Without belief in God we have no absolute reference point for morality, justice and law. The judges are not the highest level of appeal, nor are the laws per se, for both must look to the

Supreme Moral Judge. To fail to acknowledge such is only to exacerbate the cultural cancer of our society. To overcome such internal weakness demands the recovery of faith as the "absolute relation to the Absolute" without which there is little or no cure for our cultural cancer, whose most serious virus is the relativism fostered by our educational system and its social expressions.

Chapter 10

The Subjectivity of
Scientific Objectivity

Presupposing what is meant by the sciences based upon the scientific method, we must raise the basic philosophical problem of epistemology as the springboard for what follows in the philosophy of science. It is a matter of perspective. How do we know the sciences? And what is involved in knowing them? are the basic questions. Upon entertaining these questions, we are already considering what belongs to our thesis: the subjectivity of scientific objectivity.

Germane to this endeavor is the better grasping of the epistemological tension or dialectical issues within scientific understanding itself. Characteristic thereof is the age-old problem of thought identifiable as continuity versus discontinuity. Coming up for basic consideration in this context is the more immediate issue of subjectivity versus objectivity. Our purpose is to pose some of the keynote issues or unresolved tensions, which arise in science, centering about the scientist's own involvement in his scientific knowledge, i.e. the relationship between what he knows and how he knows it.

The locus of the basic tensions that appear in scientific understanding is already suggested. Essential to scientific understanding is the interrelation of the scientist's own subjectivity as a knowing subject with nature's objectivity as observable phenomena. It is intensified by the primacy of the presumably objective method deployed in the sciences. Succinctly, the underlying issue, then, is the subject versus the object or the knower versus the known.

What is the core of this basic issue? In question form, it is this: Are these two epistemological factors perfectly symmetrical, or are they disjunctive? Is there total apposition between the subject and the object, or is there about as much discontinuity between them as there may be continuity? Admittedly, the scientist can ignore this question as he goes about his work, but the philosopher in general and the philosopher of science in particular should never overlook this question and its primacy. The reason for this is that where a thinker stands in his epistemology will affect his total perspective and interpretation of all subsequent issues entertained.

Underlying the thesis of these pages is the claim that the epistemological issue can neither be bypassed in the philosophy of science nor be resolved either rationally or empirically. Neither an idealistic, realistic or scientific solution does justice to the problem and its answer. Subordinate to this contention are the following three elements:

1. The scientist-in-action cannot be completely objective, for his own subjective consciousness is very much involved in his endeavors, i.e., his own intellectual constructs and psychological capabilities affect his work.
2. The philosophical implication of this is that much in scientific understanding is intrinsically paradoxical, i.e., we cannot evade the conceptual tensions and dialectical problems of opposites which arise when essential, but necessarily opposite, ideas meet and clash — often beyond, or short of, a neat rational resolution or synthesis.
3. As a consequence, one to which we cannot do justice in the present undertaking, a homogeneous philosophy of either materialism or idealism is highly questionable and a realistic picture just as tenuous, for neither scheme can obviate the existential creativity of the scientist as a knower in combined continuity and discontinuity with what he observes. This may mean that it will be necessary to settle for a kind of Kantian phenomenalism or critical realism which concedes that we can know things only as they appear to us, in which case our knowledge is relative or limited, pragmatic or operational. This, in turn, implies that though the sciences become legitimate, instrumental schemes, they are not completely authoritative.

Having considered our purpose, keynote issues and thesis, we would do well to delineate some of the more specific epistemological tensions confronted in science today. Basic among them are the necessary presuppositions of the scientist-in-action. Fundamental is the presupposition of his own consciousness, its capabilities and mental constructs and involvements. Sir Arthur Eddington (1882-1944), noted British astronomer of this century, was exceptional in his sensitivity to this point. Justifiably qualifying the empiricism of John Locke (1632-1704), he said, "I think that those who wish to take cognizance of nothing but the measures of the scientific world made by our sense organs are shirking one of the most immediate facts of experience, namely that consciousness is not wholly, nor even primarily a device for receiving sense impressions." This, in turn, means that the scientist's mind not only receives perceptual data in an experience or observation but brings special insight to it. Consciousness supplies a creative element that transcends, and even affects, the perceptions. No one needs this reminder more than the Behaviorist in psychology, who detests the acknowledgment of a significant consciousness in the animal and human subjects he observes, yet all the while is presupposing, but ignoring, its role in his own observations.

The consciousness of the scientist is both akin to nature's processes and transcendent of them. This implies continuity and discontinuity. If not, there would be no science, for there would be neither the wonder nor curiosity nor ingenuity of the scientist, on the one hand, nor his awareness of the objectivity of things, on the other. Scientific understanding presupposes this subjective factor, whereby the knower transcends what is known while also having affinity with it at the same time. The scientist's affinity with nature is seen in his mental reflection, logical deductions, classifications and correlation of perceived data. As Alfred North Whitehead once stated, "Thought about nature is different from the sense-perception of nature." Indeed, the one is communicable, the other not.

Having some affinity with the objects of phenomena of nature, the scientist reports on things presumed to be independent of himself, but, paradoxically, he cannot extricate himself from his position as a subject-observer, correlator and interpreter of what he reports. His perceptions are very much his perceptions, and his logic and mathematical correlations perhaps even more so. As a reporter, then, he is an interpreter. What he reports is to some degree refracted by how he perceives what he perceives or how his own consciousness is involved in both his perceptions and his reasoning as well as their creative interrelationship. This is phenomenological.

Akin to the presupposition of his consciousness is the scientist's creative insight, logic and ingenuity as intrinsic to his subjectivity and essential to his knowledge. Mathematics is a basic form and product of his creativity. As A. N. Whitehead, himself a great mathematician and philosopher, has said, "Modern mathematics may be the most original creation of the human spirit." Whitehead was epistemologically sensitive to the role of subjectivity, even though he was a metaphysical realist, who also saw mathematics to be an objective set of principles Platonically writ large in the nature of the universe. Whitehead saw how mathematics was brought to experience as an antecedent guide of sense perception, apart from which sense experience in general was apt to be a cacophonous hodgepodge. Mathematics is a type of reasoning which both transcends and relates itself to observable phenomena. But what is this creative relationship within a man's conscious experience but an existential paradox of continuity and discontinuity?

Whatever the scientist gleans as working data is subjectively correlated by his mathematics. His logic and related symbolism provide him with a unique language and calculus. This relationship of two kinds of logic, the inductive and deductive, frequently characterizes the scientist's work, for often the inductive and deductive types of logic are blended imaginatively into a single insight, operation or task. Such creativity has never been fully accounted for and remains an epistemological paradox of opposites which meet, not as a rational synthesis, but as a practical working team. The two kinds of reasoning remain distinct, never homogeneous yet creatively operational. Functionally, the logical methods of induction and deduction become a harmonious duet in the scientist's mind, but each plays a different chord. Being different modes of thought, they are no more resolvable into a perfect homogeneity than a marriage union makes for a neutral sex. In fact it is just at this point that classical and modern realisms break down as they attempt to make a rational fusion out of an existential both/and paradox.

Strange, indeed, too, that abstract constructs like time should help the scientist to measure and control his concrete observations and treatment of natural events. Time consciousness is a subjective awareness not measurable by either sense experience or objective methods, save in artificial manner. Kant saw time to be an a priori category of the mind, not based upon experience, but brought to it and creatively combined with it in a practical reason or "synthetic judgment." Modern physics with its stress on vibration could not have arisen without abstract ideas of time applied to specific instances. Whitehead once said, "The paradox is now fully established that the utmost abstractions are the true weapons with which to control our thought of concrete fact."

Scientific learning usually begins with a problem around which facts are gathered toward its resolution. But without his intervening hypotheses, the scientist gets almost nowhere. As conjectures deemed apropos at the moment, his hypotheses serve as testable targets of further inquiry. Yet it is here that his creativity, imagination and insight come to bear, often with great impact, even though there is no scientific rule by which any hypothesis may be derived from a problem. Rather, a helpful hypothesis is derived creatively from the scientist's combined observations and logical deducements, even intuitions and hunches at times. Henri Bergson (1859-1941) saw intuition as fundamental to knowledge and as "the immediate data of consciousness." Is not consciousness a trans-objective phenomenon that accounts for and guides, if it does not control, the objective methods of inquiry? How can we evade the issue of the subject versus the object? The primacy must be given to a subjectivity that understands, and is in charge of, objectivity — the objectivity of both content and method.

Then, too, as physicist Erwin Schrödinger (1887-1961) points out, the last 50 to 75 years have seen a great change in the conception of matter; it is much less materialistic than a century ago. The basic concept is one of form, not substance. As such, matter in the form of energy lends itself more to our minds than our senses. Also, physicists Niels Bohr (born 1885) and Werner Heisenberg (born 1901) have seen that the object has no known existence apart from the observing subject; thus the Cartesian dichotomy between object and subject is not so pronounced today. We can never observe the object without our own activity being involved, even to the extent of modifying it upon observing it, as Heisenberg has shown. Schrödinger even says the relation between subject and object does not lend itself to a quantitative meaning based upon physical and chemical measurements, lest there be an incongruity between the problem and its answer. In seeing this epistemological issue, Bohr, Heisenberg and Schrödinger are exceptions among scientists. Their view actually has much in common with the phenomenological view of Edmund Husserl (1859-1938) and most existentialists of today. Consciousness is a primary datum, not merely a secondary consequence.

It is the focal point of the subjectivity that transcends objectivity while linked with it.

The new quantum physics sees a mutual causal relation between the subject and object; not only does the object impress the subject, but the subject the object. This view is more adequate, since physical action, as Schrödinger points out, is always interaction or something mutual. Thus we see how objectivity and subjectivity are by no means disrelated physically and, likewise, epistemologically. This position anticipates Roger W. Sperry's claim that within the brain there is a mutual cause and effect relationship between physical and conscious activity, without the latter being reducible to the former. The mental actually affects the physical, as Sperry asserts psychosomatically in his psychobiological theory of an "emergent consciousness."

The epistemological problem of the scientist's involvement in what he knows, combined with the empirical and trans-empirical nature of his involved consciousness, was once expressed by the philosopher Johann Gottlieb Fichte (1762-1814) when he said: "All consciousness of objects outside of myself is determined by the clearness and exactitude of my consciousness of my own states, and in this consciousness there is always a conclusion drawn from the effect in myself to a cause out of myself." Not only is clearness of consciousness important together with insight into causation, but also the extension thereof: in the form of instruments, which vivify both factors and better coordinate the subject and the object, as in the case of a measurement. Even so, an instrument is limited to doing only what it is designed to do by the scientist himself. This makes the instrument both a help and a hindrance. It is seen to be a most pronounced limitation in the light of Heisenberg's "principle of indeterminacy." The physicist, for instance, is both helped and hindered by the use of his micrometer. He is hindered, because particles of light are refracted by the micrometer as he uses it, thus conditioning and limiting what he observes. Here is another paradoxical tension reminding us of the combined continuity and discontinuity between the scientist as a knowing subject and the objects which he knows.

P.W. Bridgman, Harvard physicist (1882-1961), once asserted, "The fact of the limitations of the human mind must be accepted and emphasized." Today many leaders in physics and astronomy help vivify this, having moved away from the 19th century deterministic view of the universe to a 20th century awareness of the unpredictabilities confronting the scientist today. The newer view is wholesomely humble; instead of regarding scientific theories as if metaphysically final, it treats them as operational or pragmatic. Heisenberg's indeterminacy principle contributes to this newer view, which comes closer to acknowledging the subjectivity of scientific objectivity.

There are other limiting factors which affect the scientific approach to knowledge. In recognizing them, however, we do not detract from the legitimacy of that approach; we merely indicate further epistemological problems intrinsic to it. First, scientific research is restricted to what both its method and instruments are capable of finding. For example, the telescope clarifies certain data of nature, but is in no way an interpreter thereof; that is to say, it is in no way involved in either a teleological, causal or other explanation. Second, scientific classification gives information, but does not necessarily include everything in the subject being classified. Frequently, the scientist may justifiably neglect the human element and data that do not fit in with his immediate concerns. Third, there are qualities or characteristics of wholes that are not recognized in the parts of some phenomena. The more complex levels of reality may not always yield to the simpler units being dealt with. To think that the simpler units are more basic reality than the more complex relationships may be a fallacy of reductionism. To explain the sunset as so many electromagnetic vibrations is still not to account fully for the sunset as typically experienced, though it helps explain the light and colors involved. The same may apply to the chief difference between the Gestalt and Behavioristic schools of psychology, as well as the difference between living organs and organisms. Fourth, the uncritical attempt to explain things by one principle or type of interpretation is a frequent misuse of the scientific approach. To explain some historical or sociological developments solely in terms of climate or natural resources or biological factors or cosmic cataclysms, or to explain human conduct by glandular secretions and social pressures, may be oversimplifications. To draw big conclusions from meager evidence may be the danger. A person's emotional experience is seen one way by a laboratory psychologist, another way by a physiologist, another by a chemical biologist, and another by a physicist, and still another by a bystander, while seen distinctively by the person himself. Thus, the whole of things is not seen from any one perspective. Fifth, the later stages of some things may be as real and as important as the earlier, and might be seen to be even more determinative of the nature of things. To genetically trace everything back to limited beginnings is apt to be too exclusive. The Aristotelian principle of nature's process as one of potentiality moving into actuality helps sharpen the matter. Alfred North Whitehead's modern view of the cosmos together with his principle of "prehension" might also vivify it. Not just the origin and survival of man are important, but the "arrival" of man may support it, too. On a more elemental level the unifying factor in organisms, both as they evolve and grow, suggests the same principle. Sixth, another factor is that the scientist himself is dependent upon his own sense organs and mentality. Though instruments extend the range thereof, limitations are still prevalent, and after data is collected and organized, inferences must be logically deduced and mathematical correlations applied. Fundamental here are the assumptions and postulates of that mind-at-work. Seventh, closely related to this subjective factor are the theories erected even during experimentation, as a creative imagination must take over where uncertainties are manifest. Thus, the creative and conditioned standpoints of the scientist himself as an observer cannot be overlooked. To take these points seriously is to respect the subjectivity of scientific objectivity.

The underlying epistemological problem is sharpened further in a phenomenalistic way, when we remember that the sciences themselves have unfolded some of the limitations of human knowledge, especially pertaining to our limited sense perceptions. Our eyes, for instance, failed to see the breathtaking beauty of many of the stones we may have walked on today, because our eyes are receptive to barely an inch of the mile-wide spectrum of cosmic light rays between them and the sun. But truly breath-taking beauty is released for us when the apparently drab-looking stones are placed under an ultraviolet ray lamp. Thus the relativity and limitations of our sense percepts constitute another aspect of the epistemological tensions within scientific understanding. We are reminded of Kant's legitimate skepticism, when he said we cannot know *das Ding an sich*, the supposedly objectively real thing-in-itself, because all we have are impressions of it. These are but appearances based upon combinations of sense perceptions and a priori mental categories.

The Viennese psychologist Rudolf Allers (born 1883) was right when he stated that "science both begins and ends with the mystery of the scientist himself." This further implies that scientific learning rests upon what is prescientific or trans-scientific, and what is existentially a part of the knower himself in his situation. Even Aristotle conceded the matter, though he did not stay with it consistently, when he said that the demonstrable rests upon the undemonstrable. The undemonstrable is what is anchored to the scientific knower himself, who transcends what he knows by impression and demonstration, even as he conditions what he knows by the way he knows it.

It takes a conscious and even self-conscious subject to make any kind of inquiry. If this unique phenomenon, in this case the scientist himself, were reducible to the chemical and physical levels completely, it is dubious that there would be a scientific inquirer with his scientific pursuits. The higher functions of life and conscious activity may not be completely explained by the lower functions. The need here is for a holistic point of view, whereby not only do we see the higher levels of activity in terms of the lower, but wherein the lower levels are not explainable without the higher. Such a holistic view implies that the whole is needed to explain the parts, and the whole is a distinctive organism that is greater than the mere sum of its parts. When we apply this holistic principle to the consciousness of the scientist and the epistemological role of his consciousness, we begin to see more clearly the issues with which we are already engaged.

The scientific reductionism of the scientist-in-action by some interpreters is a deleterious bit of philosophizing. Though the extreme Behaviorist in psychology, who deals only in things physically measurable, has every intellectual right and reason to operate from within his limited frame of reference, when he threatens to reduce us not only to the animal level, but to physico-chemical processes and to a deterministic set of stimulus-response nerve mechanisms and patterns, he is limiting the view of man, especially when he neglects the epistemological factors already considered and philosophizes accordingly, as does B. F. Skinner (born 1904). Can the scientific psychologist justifiably do this to you and me? In a sense, he can. But can he do it to himself? It is as dubious as a snake swallowing his own tail. As Carl Gustav Jung (1875-1961) has said, "I cannot experience myself as a scientific problem."

It is here that the epistemological tension of subjectivity versus objectivity is perhaps most pronounced. "If I could eliminate myself," one scientist was known to have said, "then I might give a truly objective report." But his big word "if" expresses the crucial issue, because the scientist is existentially involved in his own pursuit, which is to say his subjectivity is primary, and whatever objectivity is achieved in his work is subsumed under his subjective deliberations.

We have touched upon the basic epistemological tension relative to how we know our sciences, but some of the broader philosophical implications might well be considered before closing the discussion.

Moral freedom is an aspect of subjectivity and consciousness, which has some bearing upon the problem before us. Yet most of the sciences, even those centering in man, are developed on the premise, if not presupposition, that all things are determined. Perhaps the matter is not an either/or but a both/and paradox. Though the physician and psychiatrist deal with their patients in a deterministic context, they must assume that their patients can either accept or reject the diagnosis and counsel received; and what is this but the acknowledgment of moral freedom?

Sometimes it takes a deterministic argument to temper a deterministic argument. When the glandular theory of psychology was being stressed for a specialized course in an eastern university to the point that every personality was explainable by the ratio of glandular secretions in the body, a student put a postscript on her final examination. It read like this: "I have tried to answer the questions with reasonable objectivity; however, I could not agree with the professor's glandular theory because of its exclusiveness; however, he will have to excuse me for not agreeing with him. My glands wouldn't let me."

Even the scientist-in-action makes crucial decisions and judgments, does he not? He also trusts his colleagues in the laboratory. Even his personal philosophy as a man can affect what he does as a scientist. Albert Einstein is one scientist who overtly conceded this, saying a man's motives and ambitions very much affect his work. For one thing, Einstein spoke of "a faith which looks ahead." Similarly, the noted physicist Max Planck (1858-1947) said, "The disjointed data of experience can never furnish a veritable science without the intelligent interference of a spirit actuated by faith." Thus the scientist's outlook and attitude has much to do with the outcome of his endeavors. From the negative standpoint sometimes the problem of misconstrued, misinterpreted or ignored data comes to bear on a scientist's work. One form of this is a possible over-enthusiasm for a certain theory; this hinders his consideration of other theories and may delay scientific progress. The writer knows of a Ph.D. candidate in biology who could make no headway on his dissertation, because two of his advisors had opposite theories to which they were attached dogmatically with emotional passion. What does this suggest, again, but the existential subjectivity involved in scientific objectivity? Its locus is the consciousness of the individual knower, a matter respected by phenomenology.

Sir Arthur Eddington, Max Planck and Albert Einstein are some of the most noted twentieth-century scientists who have shown how questions of morals and values also influence the scientist. Most of the scientists involved in the Manhattan project during World War II, the project which led to nuclear fission, became well aware of this. Surely the involvement of the scientist in such ethical considerations is not a dead issue in our day.

In general, it can be concluded that the scientist himself is much involved in his knowing experience. Epistemologically, he is a conscious, creative component of his scientific work. To see this is to acknowledge existentially the subjectivity of scientific objectivity. It is to concede that we cannot do justice to any of the subsequent facets of the philosophy of science until we have reckoned with the basic epistemological concerns. Most germane is the keynote phenomenological issue of the subject and the object with the primacy given to a conscious subjectivity in charge of scientific objectivity. Hans Reichenbach (1891-1953) conceded this, when he saw how objective phenomena are matters of relation between the observer and the observed. He said, "The only path to knowledge leads through conscious awareness of the role that subjectivity plays in our methods of research." Hence, we must not overlook the subjectivity of scientific objectivity. To do so is to violate the primacy of the knower, who not only is aware of facts but also values, even the values of the scientific data per se.

warrant academic quality through discursive thought basic to intellectual maturity.

But our cultural condition is not hopeless. Our cultural cancer can be cured if we re-awaken to the needs and sources of our virtues and reckon seriously with the intellectual issues posed mainly in Part II. Both teachers and our public leaders as well as parents and serious-minded students must wrestle with them, so that hopes may be renewed and constructive redirection fulfilled through fresh reappraisals of what made our nation great in the first place and what will preserve and improve it.

If educators show a willingness to qualitatively improve all academia and if students show evidence of greater concern for our values at their best, there is hope. But this hope is conditional. It must be more than a matter of sentiment; it must grow with intellectual, moral and spiritual maturity, and this through hard work, higher standards and intense study of the qualitative philosophical matters essential thereto. Quality must redirect quantity; our ethical ends must control our empirical means.

As stated above, education must be designed for more than making a living in favor of what makes for living a life. Studies in the humanities must no longer be side-lined but interwoven with the scientific and technological studies and advancements, which will be future assets to our civilization only as guided by our ethical and spiritual principles at their best. When this relationship is kept uppermost in education and not peripheral or subsidiary, we can overcome our cultural cancer — from within. We can do so, yet to do so calls for remotivations akin to what Toynbee meant when he said, "We must pray for a reprieve." An inner illness demands an inner cure. I want to believe we can realize it if we wake up soon. Only then, to adapt the words in Isaiah 49:17, will "your builders outstrip your destroyers."

Chapter 11

The Paradox of
Determinism and Freedom

Though it is an old problem in classical thought, the issue of freedom versus determinism is still a vital matter in modern psychology and philosophy. B. F. Skinner, the chief spokesman for behaviorism, said in his book, *Science and Human Behavior*, "That man is not free is essential to the application of scientific method to the study of human behavior."

Though seldom recognized or conceded, this statement and the perspective beneath it represent one of the modern dogmatisms par excellence. It capitalizes on a basic bit of illogical cerebration concerning which many psychologists look the other way, if they recognize it at all. Skinner is guilty of what in logic is called *petito principii* or the fallacy of "begging the question." This is the tendency to presuppose the answer in attempting to prove it. Skinner's *modus operandi* presupposes that there is no such thing as moral freedom, and then he proceeds to demonstrate the matter. In other words, he fails to look for freedom, since he has already ruled it out. But, even for him to rule it out from the start is for him to choose to do so, which is an epistemological presupposition of the very freedom being negated. This is a flagrant violation of logic.

For Skinner to deny both moral freedom and consciousness, as he does, is to deny the reality of choice, decision, deliberation, self-control, subjectivity, personhood, and responsibility. It is to espouse total determinism even to the extent that each of the students in the study of psychology itself had no conscious choice in the matter of selecting it as a specialization. The logic of that is that they merely floated into the field or they were completely necessitated by circumstances beyond their control. Such total determinism is anti-existential in the sense that it implies that a human being is not a person or subject-self. It means that we are all little more than hockey pucks shoved about completely by the forces of nature and/or society.

Though we may not be perfectly free, since partly determined by physical, biological, economic, and social factors working upon us, human beings are at least partially free, just as you are free this moment to continue to consider this discourse or to turn it off. Also, certain pressures were upon you to get out of bed this morning, yet you could have rolled over and defied the alarm clock, as you undoubtedly have done on occasion. Freedom implies that you can even defy social mores and precedents under which you are commonly constrained. This reminds the writer of a student who defied social pressures to run naked through the business section of his town.

To respect the role of moral freedom in life is to allow that a person is more than an organismic object, since he is a personal subject as well. Such a subject can to some extent effectuate his human existence as well as destiny by his decisions. A subject is what knows the object and gives it significance, for subjectivity is at the center of knowledge and experience. The object does not know or experience the subject, let alone anything else. A subject not only transcends an object but, to some extent, even transcends himself by introspecting and freely asking questions about himself. It is doubtful whether any student would become interested in psychology itself were this not the case. The ability to ask questions about oneself calls for a subjective consciousness that can do such a thing.

The recent Nobel Prize winner in physiology, Roger W. Sperry, is a noted psychobiologist, who has shown from a laboratory perspective that consciousness emerges from the bodily process and can, in turn effect the bodily processes. One feature of consciousness, in this two-in-one relationship, is freedom, Sperry maintains, even as thought is related to the brain. Sperry overtly states, "Conscious mental forces do govern and direct the nerve impulse traffic and other biochemical and biophysical events in the brain and, hence, do have to be included as important features in the objective chain of control." Consciousness, Sherry explains, is an integral aspect of brain activity as supported by the emergent brain patterns and consequent mentalism. While interacting with the physical processes, from which it has emerged, consciousness psychosomatically effects them as well. Sperry speaks of this relationship as "emergent interactionism," which explains why psychic events are not only consequential but also causal in nature. Thus, while physical factors play a basic role, the emergent consciousness is a type of freedom or self-caused cause that accounts for volition and deliberation.

As conceded above, deterministic forces influence us in our concrete human existence, yet a conscious freedom of the will is also real, as Sperry's approach to a functioning consciousness suggests. This makes for measures of self-control. In recent months, this writer managed to lose forty pounds. It called for a self-determination or freely espoused self-control and deliberation. Few, if any, forms of conditioning demanded that it be done, but it took a conscious desire and decision to change the waistline and scale indicator. At such a point, freedom or volition is seen to be fundamental to a self-control, though not out of relation to a plan. But, even a plan reflects a matter of deliberation based on freedom.

Speaking of self-control, it is easy to assume that animals have no such capacity, but such an assumption can be questioned. Take my pet dog Duchess, for instance. Ostensibly, she displays a type of self-control. On days that the garbage collectors disturb the tins and bins outside the house, she barks vociferously out of discontent of the noise and her territorial consciousness. But in the middle of the night when dogs-on-the-loose make similar noises around the tins and bins, Duchess merely offers a soft, subdued bark. Why? She knows she should not disturb the family asleep. She has a pronounced measure of self-control. No one has conditioned the dog in this respect.

In this connection, we note that D.O. Hebb, distinguished psychologist of McGill University, says, ". . . thought is the integrative activity of the brain," and it "overrides reflex responses and free behavior from sense dominance." In this context Hebb says that free will is a cortical component that makes for the "control of behavior by the thought process." Surpassing the mechanistic behaviorism of Skinner, and anticipating the work of Sperry, Hebb states that free will, while having a physiological basis, belongs to the "relative autonomy of the activity of the cerebrum." In light of what Sperry and Hebb have to say, it is important to reject Skinner's presupposition that there is neither freedom nor consciousness in man. Surely upon denying us our consciousness Skinner had to have a consciousness with which to do it. Skinner's presupposition of a totally deterministic psychology rules out freedom and is a serious form of reductionism; it reduces man to an automaton of nature and a pawn of society. Violating human subjectivity, it fails to see how conscious subjectivity emerges from physical objectivity in a two-in-one relationship. Such reductionism de-mans man of his manhood.

Even higher animals are to some extent subjects and not merely objects. This is because they, too, have a consciousness that affects their experience and the bodily processes involved. In this respect Ivan Pavlov set a false precedent in psychology by overlooking the role of consciousness in the dogs with which he experimented. Only as a dog had a consciousness could it associate food with the bell through the conditioning process involved. While the association of food with the ringing of the bell led the dogs' salivary glands to flow, it took more than a stimulus and response sequence of events for it to happen. It was only by the dogs' consciousness of food when the bell rang that their salivary glands began to flow. Salivary glands per se were oblivious to the bell associated with the food save for the mediating input of a consciousness which could coordinate the two factors involved and account for the basic association. The underlying oversight contributed to an erroneous, delimiting formula, long known as the S-R. The stimulus-response formula stressed by behaviorism is faulty in that it omits the mediating factor of consciousness. The formula should read S-C-R with consciousness being the mediating factor that relates response to stimulus. Such an adjustment blends with the psychobiology of Sperry and Hebb.

In Pavlov's train, Skinner's position is too mechanistic as it ignores the cognitive dimensions of a mediating consciousness. While today there is a movement in psychology called "cognitive behaviorism," the designation is really an unacceptable contradiction, because behaviorism per se rules out the cognitive element; to rule it out and in at the same time is hardly a working paradox. To continue to respect an objective scientific approach to psychology may very well be in order, but to rule out the creative cognitive consciousness of the scientist behind the method is out of the question. Furthermore, to fail to keep physical processes and consciousness an interrelated team within the subjects being studied will be a gross violation of personality and another invitation to a mechanistic reductionism. While Skinner's position rules out this writer's position, this writer's position rules him in without selling out to him.

B. F. Skinner dwells frequently upon the conditioning factors that have contributed to a person's background, but often he makes it sound as a strictly mechanical process of the S-R pattern. He tells, for instance, of how patients in a mental hospital were reconditioned, to some extent, when he offered them rewards in the form of candy bars whenever they managed to avoid urinating in their clothes. But overlooked by him is the fact that the patients had to have a conscious desire of the reward. Without the conscious desire for the candy, there would have been no re-conditioning. The same is true of young children. In order to stop wetting their clothes, they must come to the point of wanting to do so. And what is that willful desire based upon but the personal appreciation of aesthetic, social and sanitary conditions. Without the freely chosen preferences of their consciousness, progressive habits would not develop.

Back in the 1920s psychologists like William McDougall and Hugo Munsterberg were well-versed in the pro-behavioristic methods of modern, mechanistic psychology but held to a more balanced or temperate viewpoint. Actually, their methodology was one of a scientific determinism, but they saw that the danger in carrying it too far lay in denying man as a conscious being, who could freely adapt himself to situations and have self-chosen ends and means. Anticipating developments in the behaviorism of Watson and Skinner, they saw that a psychology totally restricted to a mechanistic biology implied a dangerous determinism that neglects the teleological and purposive aspects of mentality. As Alfred North Whitehead once stated, "Scientists animated by the purpose of proving that they are purposeless constitute an interesting subject for study."

Even the scientist-in-action demonstrates the moral freedom of his consciousness as he makes crucial decisions and value judgments. Common in this respect is his purposive choice of selective data to work with within certain areas of concentration and specialization. Albert Einstein was sensitive to this and said that even the scientist's motives and ambitions affect his work. This reflects the primacy of subjectivity in that it is in charge of objectivity. Without a creative, subjective consciousness it is dubious that there would even be such a thing as scientific objectivity. Scientific objectivity is not merely a product of stimulus-response relationships of experience; it is also a product of conscious deliberation. As for the value judgments involved, they can be either helpful or harmful. Pharmaceutical scientists working on the release of thalidomide some years ago made a judgment as to when to stop experimenting with it. Had they adjudicated that it called for a dozen or more relationships for experimentation they may have prevented the tragic births of many defective babies whose mothers had been led to use the drug. The tragedy was related to the free decisions of the scientists involved, decisions which proved, in this case, to be deleterious.

What was the underlying problem? It was that a pure objectivity was lacking. Quite as one noted scientist is known to have said, "If I could eliminate myself, then I might give a truly objective report." On the other hand, without the conscious level of creative thought as centered in the scientist's subjectivity as a man, there would be no scientific objectivity, for scientific objectivity is a product of the thinker's creative ability to coordinate induction and deduction or sense data with mathematical analysis. This belongs to a functioning consciousness, not merely to a physical process per se.

As Sperry and Hebb have pointed out psychobiologically an emergent consciousness includes moral freedom and self-control. Sperry, as mentioned above, shows that conscious psychic factors can affect the nerve impulse traffic of the brain and nervous system. This may be illustrated by the person who chooses to concentrate on sex, for instance. As he does so, his genitals are literally affected. Or, take the sickly person with presence of mind enough to think of pleasant thoughts or the meaningful values of life; his health can be improved. Norman Cousins tells of how his very serious physical disability was to a great extent improved through good humor. Also, many an ill person has testified as to how religious thoughts and commitment have led to his physical improvement. Such things are germane to psychosomatic medicine today, as accentuated by personnel of such institutions as the Houston Medical Center and the Menninger Foundation.

If a totally deterministic psychology had all the answers, a child, for instance, would only have to read his arithmetic book and follow the logic involved in order to learn elementary mathematics. But the fact remains that he must choose freely and deliberately to learn more or less by rote his multiplication table and some of the clues to long division. The same for spelling. Often there is no substitute for conscious memorization. The writer has known students raised in a Deweyite "progressive school" where such conscious deliberation was depreciated. They were very poor spellers, because a mechanistic association akin to a Skinnerian conditioning was not enough. Much needed was a conscious deliberation that implied self-discipline. Such indispensable self-discipline implies a subjective consciousness that affects the lower elements of psychology quite in keeping with Sperry's observation that consciousness can affect the nerve-impulse traffic of the brain.

Even though physicians, psychologists and psychiatrists must to some extent deal with their patients or counsellees deterministically, they cannot do so exclusively. They must assume that when patients return to everyday life they can either accept or reject the diagnoses, prescriptions and advice given them. What does this imply but an existential acknowledgment that moral freedom is intrinsic to concrete human existence. Sensitive to what this means, Leslie Paul writes, "The reintegration of the human personality sought by psychoanalysis (for instance) is nothing more nor less than the restoration of the power of free judgment." So, when psychology moves into the clinical domain it must treat a person as more than an object and respect him as a conscious and free subject. Often this is actually being done in practice while preempted in theory.

Even after causal explanations of behavior are given, a clinical patient must return to a human existence that demands that he either freely accepts or rejects what he has learned about himself. He can have all the causal explanation of his behavior that is possible, yet if he ignores his capacities as a moral human agent he will not profit from the explanation. Consider the alcoholic who causally understands his plight. Unless he freely asserts himself, which is to imply a self-caused cause, and admits his problem and need of help he will not surmount it. This is why A.A. has proven to be one of the best therapeutic agencies for alcoholics. It is not enough that we learn the causes of behavior; we must see ourselves as willful agents who belong to both the cause of the problem and its answer.

One of the keynote marks of free will is our awareness of it as in the case of deliberately concentrating on what is being contended or argued in this moment. When we freely concentrate on something we can transcend the disturbances around us and choose to let our minds focus attention on the topic, idea or activity at hand. Consider the basketball player at the free throw line, for instance. Truly remarkable is his ability to concentrate amidst the roar of the crowd. To be sure, he is habitually conditioned in some measure to do so, but his success is in large measure a product of self-chosen, conscious deliberation and concentration. Yet even as we dwell on the subject at hand, for instance, we can elect to let our minds turn away from it and dwell on other subjects. Though sometimes our attention wanders inadvertently due to distractions, there are other times when it is deliberate as when we are bored with a topic being discussed. A truly creative feat of human consciousness is the ability not only to associate one thing with another, such as these peculiar markings on paper with words and their meanings, but the profounder ability to concentrate on the topic. Without similar ability a strain of music would hardly be a delight. In the present moment of concentration, there is a recall of previously struck notes and an anticipation of those to come. Such an experience is more than a physical process, for it is also a matter of an interrelated creative consciousness at work.

The contentions being made in this discourse are in no way meant to imply that Skinnerian behaviorism is all wrong; it is simply not all right. Bending over backward to prove they are scientists, the behaviorists use a straight-laced logic of cause and effect, which, while having its place, ignores the more dialectical problems of the existing self. That kind of psychology cannot be "lived out," because it is too exclusive in claiming to be "the whole cheese." Skinner goes wrong when he philosophizes as if men were merely complex laboratory rats. He denies human dignity in his book *Beyond Freedom and Dignity*, but as Alfred E. Koenig wrote in reply, "Freedom and dignity are beyond Skinner!"

There is no doubt that we need causal explanations on a physical level, whenever apropos, but what about the self-caused phenomena, centered in consciousness, without which a man is not a man. If consciousness and moral freedom are to be ruled out entirely, psychology must be the blatant enemy of all humanistic studies and activities including ethics. To reiterate what Rex Julian Beaver of UCLA Medical School has said, "The lust for scientific-sounding explanations is completely out of control. It is time to rehabilitate the concept of the will .... Ultimately, we must assume responsibility for our actions...." The total determinism of behaviorism is a dogmatic view that cannot be lived on the everyday level of life. It is objectively on the balcony of the spectator rather than in the arena of the participant.

A totally deterministic psychology not only disallows human responsibility but implies that everything belongs to a closed system that disallows novelty in human existence and an open-ended future. Spontaneity and creativity are barred from serious consideration, even as moral conscience is depreciated if not violated. William James as a psychologist preferred a certain amount of "loose play" in a pluralistic world, lest a type of fatalism rule out all freedom. James saw that without freedom there would be no place for regret, even as what ought to be the case is impossible. He was right, for such things as praise, blame, honor, reward, and approval would make no sense apart from freedom. Even punishment as something of which a person is at times deserving would make no sense morally. Merely to apply it as a form of social conditioning would keep it mechanistic without any ethical implications such as justice and injustice. James also saw that man is not only a product of his environment but a creator thereof. He can criticize it and help ameliorate evils in society. This implies moral freedom. Such activity is different from the billiard ball that is moved when another strikes it; it is self-caused activity.

In a world like ours loyalty to a cause or person makes no sense unless we are to some extent free moral agents. Similarly there would be no sense to the virtue of honesty, if we are determined robots of necessity. Freedom and deliberation imply the ability to select an action before we do it. Despite deterministic and conditioning factors that work upon us, a free self can choose between alternatives, and ethically, often does so in the light of permanent standards. To explain a delinquent's conduct solely in terms of heredity and/or environment is to rule out his moral capacity. Such thinking is simply a more sophisticated version of comedian Flip Wilson's flippant excuse, "The devil made me do it!"

There is no doubt that human beings are to a great extent conditioned beings, but not exclusively. Parents wittingly and unwittingly do much to condition their children in such things as good habits, but we must ask the underlying question: Why? Such conditioning is not merely a mechanistic cause and effect relationship, for it is tied in with moral and social as well as aesthetic values. To condition a child to hang up his or her clothes, for instance, is linked with aesthetic values related to neatness and becoming demeanor. Often, then, values supersede and guide our behavior. This makes our behavior more than a mechanistic set of S-R relationships, for the intermediating factor of consciousness effectuates certain kinds of response over others, while all the while alternatives are before us. Scientific thinking does not provide for social, moral and aesthetic values, for they are more than mechanistic. Nicholas Berdyaev points out, for instance, that the creativity of the artist is based upon a free act that supersedes sheer necessity.

In addition, freedom is basic to the social values intrinsic to democracy. Such values are appreciated not by a mechanistic, physical process per se but a free-thinking consciousness. Values must be espoused by such a consciousness through moral commitment, not mere happenstance. Slavery, for instance, was both instigated and renounced through the moral freedom of people, who once thought it to be good practically but later thought it to be bad ethically. Surely this was not solely a matter of conditioning but a matter of moral decision. In addition, how could the practice of slavery be renounced at all after centuries of social conditioning that condoned it? It called for progressive minds and thinking that stood head and shoulders above popular consensus. Not conditioned thinking, this was new and creative thinking, a product of a consciousness that was also a moral conscience. Such thinking shows that man is more than a cog in the necessitative network of direct causes and effects comparable to a mindless machine. His response to moral principles and aesthetic and spiritual values give clue to his fuller nature.

While determinism has long been a working scientific postulate, it is often overlooked today that present trends in the sciences rule against total determinism. The new physics, the basic physical science, is much less deterministic than 75 to 100 years ago. It does not banish freedom but actually rules it in. As the noted physicist Arthur H. Compton has said, "There is nothing known to physics that is inconsistent with a person exercising freedom." Physicists have come to recognize many unpredictabilities in nature that offset the old determinism. To accentuate this, Comptom says, "The ability of a man to raise his arm freely was attested long before the well-tested laws of Newton." This is something that thinkers like B. F. Skinner seem to overlook or have failed to catch up with. As Compton forthrightly states, it is ". . . no longer justifiable to use physical law as evidence against human freedom."

Some behaviorists in repudiating moral freedom say it bespeaks randomness. This reflects a prejudice in favor of a total monistic view of nature and society and fails to recognize that even among deterministic forces many of them work at cross-purposes, as it were. Often an individual must lean toward or away from a deterministic force as he adjudicates circumstances. He does this freely. Freedom, then, is not randomness but deliberation, a product of conscious subjectivity related to, yet more than, the physical processes.

Among human beings conscious reactions to deterministic factors can make a great difference in their thought and behavior. More than mere mechanistic response to stimuli, some reactions are interpretive responses in which their consciousness effectuates a more creative type of experience. Willful defiance of what comes naturally may be common forms of such interpretive reactions. For instance, many a cigarette-smoker has exceeded his mechanistic conditioning by renouncing the habit and deliberately re-orientating his nervous system. Also, many a person has defied hunger pangs for the sake of civic or religious principles, and many have held in check their sexual impulses for moral reasons. Sometimes there are even intellectual implications related to a person's reaction to something. Are not these types of self-control expressions of the moral freedom of the person who, therefore, is not totally determined? And are not these qualifications of a popular scientific determinism tributary to overcoming our cultural cancer today? Morals imply responsible behavior, but how can this be actualized socially unless people are regarded as free moral agents, who are not completely determined robots of either nature or society. This concession is essential to the overcoming of our cultural cancer today.

Chapter 12

The Anthropic
Principle of Science

It was mentioned in passing that Sperry referred to the cosmic implications of the electro-neural aspects of consciousness, since they constitute a causal force, not merely a consequent. Mental factors are distinguishable while linked with the physical processes; they are even interreactionary. In a sense, this in principle is related to what some astronomers are contending today from another angle.

Some British astronomers these days are giving special attention to what they call "the anthropic principle" relative to cosmology. This implies that among the basic constants of nature there are "coincidences among the numerical values" thereof. The appearance of man as an observer of the cosmos is related to these "coincidences," especially in view of the fact that we are "carbon-based organisms." This view challenges the notion that we human beings are mere accidental phenomena of the universe. The "coincidences" of nature's laws are not accidents, hence man as the conscious observer is not an accident either, for he has been provided for or occasioned by the laws of the universe.

Astrophysicists John D. Barrow and Frank J. Tipler in their recognized book, *The Anthropic Cosmological Principle*, maintain that in recent years cosmologists increasingly relate mind and observership to the physical phenomena. This implies renewed respect for man's distinctive place in the universe. They declare this: "Although we do not regard our position in the Universe to be central or special in every way, this does not mean that it cannot be special in *any* way." This suggests that the laws of the universe at least provided us the privilege of being observers, which, in turn, means that they gave occasion to the evolution of intelligence. Without this no one would even be asking questions and pursuing answers.

The "anthropic principle" deepens the link between the inorganic and the organic realms, and it vivifies the connections between the laws of nature and "the chain of properties required to permit life." The existence of life may be just as remarkable as the existence of the universe itself, say these astronomers. One Britisher known as B. Carter even emphasizes the stronger Anthropic Principle that "the Universe must be such as to allow for life together with the creation of observers within it." Yet there has been an interest in the possibility that our universe is one of many, with different sets of "constants." At any rate, the Anthropic principle has led to some new developments in the physical sciences. Some scientists retain a purposive element in nature by relating evolution to a universal teleology. Though teleology has been renounced by some scientists, Barrow and Tipler show to the contrary that "teleology has on occasion led to significant scientific advances." The "coincidences" mentioned above are really the consequences of the numerical values of the basic constants as reflected in the electromagnetics of physics. In addition the new quantum mechanics involves observers most noticeably, for they even affect what is observed.

Sir Bernard Lovell asserts in response to Barrow and Tipler that few, if any, astronomers deny the evolution and expansion of the universe while accepting the Big Bang theory of a beginning and "the coincidences relative to our existence." But they differ over whether the expansion will continue forever or will eventually cease. Yet they agree that biological evolution could not have occurred on earth if the rate of expansion had been markedly different. Conditions being what they are have made man inevitable.

Sir Lovell agrees with the Anthropic Principle declaring that "man is, of necessity, inextricably involved with the fundamental nature of the early state of the universe." He states that this leads to the conclusion that "the Universe is made for the sake of Man," words quoted from Peter Lombard of a few centuries ago. This includes the prophenomenological view that objects of investigation cannot be interpreted without the interaction with conscious beings. Sir Lovell says, "If the cosmology of today with the strange coincidences leading to the anthropic principle survives similarly, then both scientists and theologians may at last speak with the same confidence about man's relation to the universe."

Physicist John Polkinghorne of Cambridge states that the anthropic principle raises questions that go beyond the power of science to answer and that may call for "a new natural theology." Akin to Hebrew thought and contemporary existentialism he sees man as a psychosomatic unity. Carbon-based life is essential to this, yet we know little of its origin. The anthropic principle implies, however, that we must move from physics to metaphysics, thus "a deeper explanation of this principle is called for." Two insights need to be re-evaluated today: First, the revised concern for the teleology of the world implying a design in nature or a "Cosmic Architect." The latter implies the sustenance of all physical processes, making the world capable of producing living beings. Second, there is the re-evaluation of man's self-understanding in relation to the universe. For man to appear the universe had to be as vast as it is, giving us time to appear. Yet, the Cosmic Architect as scientifically deduced is not one to give man a hope; it's too impersonal. Hence, Polkinghorne states, "The only God who can offer individual hope is the One who is encountered in personal religious experience. . . ." While these astronomers favor a teleological view providing for man and basic to a new "natural theology," it leans toward an impersonal deism but must be supplemented by the ethical theism discussed above.

The anthropic principle implies a person-producing universe. Only personal subjects are knowers who can pursue the sciences. Two contemporary philosophies respectful of this are personalism and existentialism. Both allow for phenomenology, the study of consciousness as basic to the subject-knower. Epistemologically, they blend basically with the anthropic principle, which enhances the personal dimension of reality deemed by these philosophies to be the greatest. Here astronomy and the humanities may be allowed to meet. The anthropic principle also gives cosmic support to psychosomatics in medicine as well as the new mentalism related to the psychobiology of R. W. Sperry's "emergent consciousness theory" dealt with in the next chapter. In addition, it gives support to the burgeoning interest in consciousness reflected in contemporary anthropology — due to the recognition of man as knowing subject, not merely a social unit. Thus, the anthropic principle enhances respect for man as distinctive, for he is the conscious observer of all phenomena.

An astronomer at a famous observatory was loquaciously stressing the vastness of the universe and how infinitesimal man was, thus so insignificant. Finally, a lay listener commented, "But remember, sir, you are the astronomer." We must turn to what is implied in being a conscious observer. But before doing so in the next chapter it must be asserted that the observer is a cognitive and subjective conscious being not unrelated to what we commonly mean by the person and what religion means by man as a spirit. This makes relevant the question whether science and religion are at odds. The "anthropic principle" referred to helps us relate the matter to the issue of creation versus evolution. Must they be dichotomized? Not so.

Though the two Genesis accounts do not teach evolution directly, they are not alien to it. Most critically minded theologians, who do not settle for dogmatisms, find the issue to be no major problem, for they see evolution as a divine method of creation. How so? The laws of nature are deemed the laws of God, the immanent intelligence within or behind them all. Where there is design there has to be a designer. Witness the evolution of the human brain — and frame. Just since the Middle Ages alone men have grown remarkably in size, however we account for it, which we can.

Related to this correlation of nature and intelligence is the fact that we cannot avoid the mystery of what Aristotle was the earliest in the West to respect strongly as the First Cause of life and planets. Yet it does not matter how we originated or arrived here, even if through a terrestrial "soup." The marvel is that we should be here at all. The British astronomers of today who recognize "the anthropic principle," recognize the remarkable fact that the conditions of the universe were just right for the appearance of the subjective, conscious intelligence that observes and appreciates nature's phenomena. These scientists are amenable to a purposive cosmic process, hence a pro-religious teleology. Another noted astronomer, Fred Hoyle, states explicitly, "The creation issue cannot be dodged." He does not necessarily endorse a kind of magical, literalized six days of creation (there being no reporters on deck) but the marvel of the beginnings of our galaxy and others related to the Big Bang theory. There had to be a first cause.

The total separation of evolution from creation is unnecessary if not ignorant. Fundamentalism, whose first premise is biblical literalism, is at fault, for it fails to integrate systematically religion with science and philosophy. On the other hand, atheists fail to see that we can be religious, even evangelical, while critically minded at the same time. No literature has been so scrupulously studied scientifically as the Bible in the past two centuries. Unfortunately, fundamentalists who have not made studies such as Pentateuchal criticism, often drive the enlightened student away from religion because of their disrelation of religion from science. Dogmatism is common among both fundamentalists and atheists. As for the latter, in a discussion on the philosophy of science a woman vehemently shouted with the foulest language that she was an atheist. Later I asked her this: "When you dismiss God, what are you dismissing?" She replied, "I don't know."

What is the underlying problem here? Both fundamentalists and atheists lack either the ample faith or the intellectual ambition to go through the woods of critical inquiry about the Bible and theology to gain mature understandings of the numerous things involved. Sad to say, many on the one side are self-proclaimed preachers, who do not dare, if capable, to attend accredited schools of theology, where critical issues of any kind are not feared. On the other side, there are many lopsided teachers who know their specialties but not how to integrate them philosophically with other disciplines. When we trust completely either type it's like accepting as a physician a person with a first-aid course.

How pathetic are the many Americans who identify emotionalism with the best religion. Dogmatic fundamentalism is the main cause, while ignorance is often linked with it. The short-cut to authority is biblical literalism. But, if fully accepted, it should return us to slavery, for instance, which is endorsed in Ephesians, Chapter 6 (to mention again but one of many problems). What really matters is the biblical message of man's redemption, whether or not human language, thought forms and contexts are fully equated with it. Human reason cannot be identified with absolute truths, because it is a finite instrument, not a perfect tribunal. The humanly finite and the divinely infinite are as qualitatively different as milk and water, though related on a faith-subsumed basis.

We need to see with our Founding Fathers that without belief in the Divine Absolute we lack substantial ethics in society. Without it today our superficial relativisms will continue to suck us under as a culture and civilization. Educators have special responsibilities in this respect, for our failures in these matters are leading to the downfall of American education, basic to our cultural cancer today. As asserted above, the number one weakness here lies at the doors of our colleges of education, who are betraying us due to their weak curricular requirements and failure to turn out philosophically minded teachers who can think dialectically, not just with simple logic. Furthermore, all conscientious students need to wrestle with the basic philosophical question: How do you know what you know? This applies to all specialists including mathematicians and scientists as well as theologians. Without such tussling we remain intellectually immature. When we face the related scientific and religious issues honestly, they need not be at odds. Nobel Prize winner in physiology and authority in psychobiology Roger W. Sperry has stated that he agrees with me about this. Science and religion can be a working team.

What is recognized today as "the anthropic principle" is a scientific view which enhances respect for the distinctiveness of man, without whose cognition based on a creative consciousness there could be neither science nor religion. This is not to say that the two disciplines are perfectly symmetrical, but it adds to the assurance that science and religion need not be at odds. Both are pertinent to human existence and spring from the epistemological fact that a creative consciousness is basic to their human relevance. Not due to an accident but a product of the laws of the universe basic to a cosmic consciousness, they belong to "the anthropic principle" making man of special consequence as the observer of these laws and interpreter of their significance. We must now examine more explicitly what it means to be an observer.

Chapter 13

The Emergent Consciousness Theory

It is apparent that some behaviorists in psychology have gotten around to modify their claims under B. F. Skinner. The modifications finally have come to allow for types of cognitive behaviorism.

But for this new trend to be respectable, it must pull away from Skinner's denial of consciousness and free will, which reduces human beings to mere mechanisms or animals, at best, completely conditioned by stimulus-response nerve systems. For there to be cognition, there must be the phenomenon of a conscious subject, not merely the processes of a physical mechanism. A subject can know an object but an object cannot know a subject, let alone anything else.

The best antidote to a mechanistic psychology that reduces itself to a study of behavior alone is the work of Roger W. Sperry of California Tech, a Nobel Prize winner in physiology and brain specialist, who has developed a theory in psychobiology known as "emergent consciousness." This allows for what he calls "the new mentalism."

Sensitive to the fact that value judgments and the dignity of man have been undermined in today's culture, Sperry seeks, in part, to clarify their place in the light of recent scientific findings. Seeing how human acts follow patterns, not merely events, of brain excitation, Sperry takes issue with the reductionistic views of such experimentalists as Pavlov, Watson and Skinner. Their stress upon the conditioned reflex theories of behavior overlooks, Sperry contends, the role of consciousness within the causal sequence of cerebral events. Many brain researchers have simply neglected consciousness and given it little or no place in psychology. The causal sequence of electro-physico-chemical events in the brain have not been acknowledged to be influenced by conscious phenomena such as thoughts. Taking issue with this view, Sperry overtly states, "Conscious mental forces do govern and direct the nerve impulse traffic and other biochemical and biophysical events in the brain and, hence, do have to be included as important features in the objective chain of control." The basic consequence of this is that conscious subjectivity cannot be ignored as a mere epiphenomenon or byproduct of the objective physical processes. Consciousness is seen to be an integral aspect of brain activity.

Accentuating the role of emergent brain patterns, Sperry is on the side of mentalism, mental events being important to functions of the brain. Despite the less measurable nature of sensations, percepts and concepts as well as images and feelings, consciousness is observed to interact with the physical processes in a psychosomatic manner. Sperry accepts an emergent theory of the mind in which both continuity and qualitative discontinuity between the physical and conscious levels are maintained. Dependent upon cerebral mechanisms, consciousness functions from within them while also influencing them; it affects both the physico-chemical processes and the Gestalt-like patterns of the nerve impulses. This interactionary and emergent theory makes Sperry's psychobiology more holistic than various laboratory psychologies and is, therefore, pro-existential, since it sees the "wholeness" of the knowing self.

In asserting that the conscious mind influences the physical factors involved, Sperry maintains that the emergent brain patterns of consciousness have a causal control power over the cellular, molecular and subnuclear particles of the brain. These patterns are mental forces which govern the flow and "patterns of impulse traffic" or cerebral excitation. The holistic factor is that just as the lower functions contribute to the higher, the higher functions also influence the lower. The conscious properties of the brain process both encompass and transcend "the nerve impulse traffic" in the brain. This makes consciousness transcendent of the bodily processes while at the same time linked with them. Just as the organism as a whole has causal effects on the constituent cells and molecules, so, too, the conscious properties of cerebral activity affect the subsidiary events in the patterns of neural excitation. This places the conscious mind in a position that transcends matter, Sperry acknowledges, without its being disembodied from the biophysical laws behind the nerve impulses.

Sperry points out that the work of the electro-physiologist is not changed by the influence of consciousness, provided he sticks to neurophysiology; however, he needs to take special care when he traces a sensory input to conscious levels to explain how either a percept or volitional response is produced. The latter is linked with the fact that individual nerve impulses operate within larger circuits, which have their own characteristic properties and dynamics. "It is the emergent dynamic properties of certain of these specialized higher cerebral activity patterns," says Sperry, "that we interpret to be the substance of consciousness." Furthermore, it is these mental phenomena which, due to their emergent properties, influence, even determine, the flow of nerve impulses. "The neurophysiology controls the mental effects, and the mental properties control the neurophysiology," says Sperry. Consciousness is said to be "a dynamic emergent property of cerebral excitation" that supersedes the physicochemical forces, yet is interdependent with them. Thus Sperry's hypothesis is one of "emergent interactionism" with a hierarchy of cerebral activities involved, ranging from the electronic and material, on the bottom, so to speak, to the consciously ideational at the top. The functions are distinguishable while interrelated. Philosophically, this means that any dichotomy of the mental and physical is to be questioned.

Sperry sees all levels in the hierarchy of brain activity, ranging from the subnuclear to the psychic, to be real and important, while the distinctive matter is that the higher can control the lower. By his interrelating the respective levels, Sperry salvages consciousness from its scientific neglect. Psychic ideas are not only consequential but causal, he points out. Instead of merely being "parallelistic" and "noninterventionistic," they are an integral part of the brain processes and essential to action. Holistically, they are subjective experiences, whereby consciousness is allowed to be conceived as "an emergent dynamic property of cerebral excitation, inseparable from the material brain process, but different from, and more than, the collected sum of the physicochemical components." Consciousness, then, like life itself is more than its constituents and more than the sum of its parts. It both includes and transcends the nerve impulses quite the way organic properties include, yet transcend, the cellular, the cellular the molecular, and the molecular the atomic.

Not merely things which intervene in neuronal activity, conscious or mental forces, rather, *supervene*. This implies that the brain responds to the Gestalt-like patterns, qualities and forces of excitation, and not merely to individual elements of excitation. Mental factors are as causal as atomic relations. The biochemical and electro-physiological factors alone are not enough, then, to account for conscious cerebral activity. The resultant patterns of conscious activity must be included — even though as yet there is no strong hypothesis for the way in which cerebral tissue generates conscious or mental experiences. The nature of the unifying forces that cause patterns of excitatory events to yield conscious cerebral entities has yet to be determined. A photographic technology likely will be needed for recording the cerebral activities which to date can only be deduced from indirect and inadequate samplings.

Psychobiology's breakthrough to consciousness or the human mind is such that the philosophical dichotomy of mechanism and mentalism is largely resolved. The psychobiological perspective is seen now to rest on a bipolar, interactionary system which embraces different types of brain activity ranging, as was suggested above, from the sheer electronic to the consciously ideational. Included in this hierarchy of events is the mental force of one idea helping to evolve another; also the mental force of self-determined acts. Though deterministic elements play their role, a conscious free will or self-determination is also real. The latter point should help meet the objection of Edward H. Madden, for instance, who says he is not in full agreement with Gestalt psychology, since he seeks to combine determined behavior with responsible, self-caused behavior. Sperry pulls the two strands together when he says, "I subscribe to the view that each mental choice is causally determined, but on condition that the phenomena of consciousness are not excluded from the causal sequence." This implies what we might interpret to be two kinds of causation, the external and the internal. By the latter, we mean the self-caused causation of consciousness per se or that which makes it a force, not merely a consequence of other forces.

Sperry's position is very much in agreement with the new physics articulated by such men as Bohr, Heisenberg and Schrodinger, who concede that the observing subject and the object need each other, and their relationship does not lend itself to a physicochemical reductionism. The new quantum physics sees a mutual causal interrelationship or interaction between the knower and the known. This lends itself to psychosomatics as well as to existential epistemology. Sperry's position also supports Brand Blanshard's philosophical judgment that consciousness is not dismissable. Science cannot dissolve the mental process and has "no pigeonhole for consciousness;" therefore, it must be prepared for revisions centering around the difference between events as phenomena and events as cognition.

In addition, Sperry's breakthrough to the mind goes so far as to embrace unconscious psychic desires and even instincts. For at least three decades the word "instinct" has been taboo around many psychology and biology labs, but Sperry sees the need of its recovered respect. For a long time no conceivable means could be found by which an inherited behavior pattern could be directly integrated with brain functions. Only experience, environment and conditioned reflexes were traceable to fetal development. Sperry states that experiments have since contradicted earlier claims, showing even that "nerve fibers do indeed grow and connect with the utmost precision within the brain center," and that "an entire evolutionary tree can be built in terms of inherited behavior traits. . . ." Environmentalists in psychology and education will need to give a new ear to those who respect heredity.

The recovery of mental forces as forms of inner causality can have important implications for the future of both psychology and philosophy. If it proves true that mental phenomena are real entities and efficacious factors in controlling cerebral activities, undoubtedly consciousness or the human mind as such will be given renewed scientific status. In addition, it would do much to heal the theoretical tensions between the different schools of psychology and bridge the gap between the objective and subjective types. Laboratory psychologies and psychoanalysis will become more of a working team.

Philosophically, such prospects will, in turn, strengthen the holistic views of the human subject and help resolve the tension between freedom and determinism as well as increase respect for the existentially concrete self, who is either a whole self or no self. This, in turn, will help enhance human dignity and the role of consciousness in the development of human values, something which has been neglected in much modern thought.

Sperry realizes that even a partial solution to the remaining problems will have increasing philosophical implications, enabling men to decide with greater assurance whether consciousness is cosmic or individual in scope and whether free will and determinism are reconcilable. Thus, the scientific verification of the distinctiveness of consciousness or mind is most provocative. As Sperry himself states, "In any search for meaning, identity, ultimate goals and values or for new ideologies, the nature of mind and its relation to physical reality becomes central and basic." Among other things, the simpler philosophies of sheer materialism, bolstered today by behaviorism and dialectical materialism, will be offset by fresh regard for the distinctive capacities of the conscious human subject, including the scientist himself.

Sperry's emergent theory and holistic view sees consciousness to belong to the brain processes, but at the same time, is more than the neural events comprising them. Phenomena like colors, sounds, sights, tastes, smell, and pain belong to the inner experience and are such in their own right. Though interrelated with neural events, they are emergent from them and belong not merely to the parts that are tributary but to the holistic level of consciousness that is unique. Since he upholds the distinctiveness of conscious, subjective experience, it is easy to see why Sperry is opposed to epiphenomenalism and behaviorism. But he is also opposed to panpsychism, the view that all reality is mental. He is too much of a realist to condone such a notion. Yet it is apparent that Sperry gives mental properties per se no precise locus within the neural system. Perhaps that is expecting too much; nevertheless, Sperry holds to a type of two-in-one "interactionism" of mind and body that ascribes to conscious phenomena a causal power — a reason for saying mental phenomena are real in their own right. This kind of interactionism, we must declare, is perfectly feasible in a way that Descartes' interactionism was not due to his rigid dualism of mind and matter. In one of his articles, Sperry, therefore, could say teleologically, "Consciousness . . . has a reason for being, and for having been evolved." It is more than a passive phenomenon, for it is active and causal.

Sperry is convinced that the unity of mind and brain provides a bridge between science and values. This is due to the enhancement of the scientific status of subjective experience together with the negation of the exclusiveness of the mechanistic, deterministic, and reductionistic aspects of behavioristic psychology. Subjective value judgments are not only caused but are causal; they are causal determinants with objective consequences. Sperry speaks of "the strategic control power of human values functioning as universal cerebral determinants in all social decision making," and he pleads for "a more active involvement therein on the part of science." In making such claims Sperry believes that the traditional pattern of separating science and values must be put in question.

Sperry also allows for moral freedom. While deterministic factors are involved, the matter of free will and choice are not abrogated thereby. Freedom of choice belongs to the conscious mind and is a part of the causal sequence of decision making that affects the course of events, including ethical matters. Value judgments are to be treated as causal agents in this context, and values are subject to scientific analysis. Sperry states, "For neuroscience it suggests a design principle for understanding brain organization and cerebral processing as a goal-directed, value-guided decision system, replacing older 'stimulus-response' and 'central switchboard' concepts that arose out of spinal cord physiology."

Philosophically, Sperry even dares to challenge the claim that we cannot derive an ethical "ought" from an empirical "is," or that science cannot be prescriptive, since it is descriptive. He does so on the basis that human values are inherently properties of brain activity, and it is only confusing to treat values as though independent of the functioning brain. Values are based on facts, which interact under the influence of "innate and acquired needs, aims and motivational and other goal-directed factors" based on biological heritage, experience and the acceptance of ethical principles based on social relationships.

Scientifically, Sperry's "emergent consciousness theory" has done much to counteract the exclusiveness of materialistic views of man. Basic to the respect for values and the choices thereof, consciousness becomes central to the qualitative levels of life, which make for a vital culture. It is indeed essential to the cure of our contemporary cultural cancer, for among human beings conscious reactions to deterministic factors can make a great difference in their thought and behavior. More than mere mechanistic response to stimuli, some reactions are interpretive responses in which consciousness effectuates a more creative type of experience. Willful defiance of what comes naturally may be common forms of such interpretive reactions. Many a person has defied hunger pangs for the sake of civic or religious principles, and many have held in check their sexual impulses for moral or religious reasons. Sometimes there are even intellectual implications related to a person's reaction to something. Are not these types of self-control expressions of moral freedom of the conscious person who, therefore, is not totally determined. And are not these qualifications of a popular scientific determinism tributary to overcoming our cultural cancer today? Morals imply responsible behavior, but how can this be actualized socially unless people are regarded as free moral agents, who are not completely determined robots of either nature or society?

Would that our educators take Sperry's theory of consciousness seriously today, lest consciousness be spurned as distinctive of creative thinking persons and education continue to adapt itself solely to the mechanistic, materialistic views of men as animals. Our cultural cancer today strongly relates to this one-sided position.

Chapter 14

The Key to a Stronger Morality

The same thinker who has done so much to revitalize the place and role of consciousness scientifically today is also interested in ethics. R. W. Sperry as a philosophically sensitive scientist believes that there can be a scientifically grounded ethics. He does so inasmuch as he has overtly denounced a completely materialistic view of science. We have seen above where he as a brain specialist has come to see also the causal reality of mental or conscious forces, which are cognitive. The brain's cognitive functions shape both personal and social behavior and thereby relate science as processes to the values and beliefs held by the consciousness which emerges therefrom. Sperry even asserts that the higher such values are religious and philosophic ones.

On what grounds can ethics be grounded scientifically, then? By the interrelatedness of physical processes and conscious ideas. Both belong to the conscious self. Hence, science and religion need no longer be kept disparate. In the mid-1960's, Sperry came to the point of seeing that conscious experience had "an integral, causal control role" in the processes of the brain. On such a basis, Sperry could regard mental and/ or spiritual forces as the highest of the emergent properties of the brain and as basic to what is meant by a person. They also had downward effects on the lower properties of the brain traffic, thus allowing for psychosomatics. A cognitive subjectivity was given scientific respect after decades of neglect if not obfuscation by consistent appeals to physical objectivity.

In short, mental vitality received a new respect and was recognized to have a type of force of both cosmic and personal qualities. Chemical phenomena of the brain are even "programmed" by the more dynamic mental factors, yet do not interfere with the physical phenomena as such. This is a two-in-one relationship. Sperry states, "The subjective dynamics of mind and consciousness transcend and control brain physiology at the same time that they are determined by it." The freewill and determinism paradox discussed above is allowed for and does not exclude moral responsibility. The forces involving ethics, education, politics, and religion are purposeful yet just as real as the electronic bases of what is physical. Science, ethics and religion can now be teammates in our endeavors to improve world civilization through values derived from each.

In this newer outlook, Sperry no longer sees the need of separating the sacred and secular perspectives. Dualism is not condoned, which is to say that an otherworldly or supernatural frame of reference for morality is not needed. Yet Sperry claims that transcendent values are seen to belong to "scientific reality" linked with this life and world. He does not assert it, but Sperry describes a type of monism or pantheism, which embraces an evolving nature, meaningful and value-producing in itself without looking to another realm. On this basis it is immoral to demean or eradicate any species and deplete resources without good cause. In fact, Sperry sees morality now based on whatever preserves the quality of life in this world. To him this looks to what is transcendent while having global relevance. Sperry appears to mean by "transcendent" any of the phenomena which belong to consciousness. This is akin to what he means by the mentalist paradigm which offsets the old behavioristic psychology. Allowed for is the causal control power of the higher conscious forces over the lower physical phenomena — but now seen on all levels of nature. Physical reductionism does not have the last word. Moral and religious and social forces within cognitive consciousness are also of scientific significance. The question of their objective validity is not the central issue but their "causal control power" or their efficacy as beliefs within human behavior. Free will as a form of self-determinism is seen to be acceptable. Science becomes more prescriptive of values, meaning that we can move from fact to *ought*, contrary to Moore. This writer's disposition is to favor the latter, were it possible, but Sperry does not demonstrate it reliably except to say that some ideas in the brain are beliefs, and beliefs yield values. Perhaps this is adequate for a mentalist psychology.

Sperry believes that his position is ample for attaining "a unifying ultimate frame of reference," which can provide a code of ethics for all mankind. His ultimate reference is not the various belief systems throughout the world, though they might someday converge in favor of a global view if allowed to blend with the scientific perspective by updating doctrinal aspects. The good and right will have to be seen as whatever harmonizes with or "enhances the orderly design" of the evolving nature. Evil would be the opposite. Implied is the reverence for nature as the "infinite wisdom," which proves the ultimate reference for ethics.

Theoretically, it seems feasible to relate, but not identify, Sperry's pro-scientific ethics to what for several decades has been called "the new morality." Sperry's position could give a boost to what it represents at its best. The new morality is the sequel to the relativistic brands of thought, which have nearly typified twentieth-century education, viz, empiricism, pragmatism, humanism, positivism, and existentialism — but with positive efforts to adapt *Agápe* or the Christian ethics of self-giving love to concrete life-situations.

With pronounced respect for individuals and their circumstances, the "new morality" is precisely articulated by Joseph Fletcher as "situation ethics," a moral outlook which tries to avoid the extremes of codified conduct, on the one hand, and normless relativism, on the other. Its presumed strength centers in the "secularization" of the sacred; its probable weakness lies in concessions to the profane, including compassion toward the "sexploitation" of personality and the condoning of the socially conditioned criminal.

The new morality wisely relates the Golden Rule to everyday social relations, transferring its expression from institutional forms to mundane affairs. Codes and catalogs of conduct are secondary to personal decisions as it seeks a faith-conditioned liberty without license, not unlike Augustine's dictum: "Love God and do what you like." But when Agápe is "secularized" will it not degenerate in quality unless men also like the righteous principles that God likes?

Is the new morality likely to be a bane or blessing in our society? Does it foster genuine moral responsibility or obscure it? Does the secularizing of the sacred lead to an easygoing tolerance of most anything in the name of freedom, or does it muster the moral stamina of the individual to withstand conformity? Does the secularization of Agápe-love reduce it to a humanistic sentimentalism severed from either idealistic or divine ideals, or are there no real grounds for them today? Is it an accomplice to the "God-is-dead" humanism paced by Nietzsche?

When plagiarized pragmatically, with the support of psychologist Eric Fromm, is Agápe-love reduced to an egocentric means rather than a divine end? A practical solution rather than a sincere inner motivation? These are some of the issues at stake.

Joseph Fletcher's view tends to make Agápe as secular as T.V. and apple pie. But in seeking to make the divine Absolute of Love relevant to the humanly relative, does he not threaten to make the relative absolute? Unless consistently God-centered in every sense, what prevents self-giving Agápe from being perverted by Eros, the self-gratifying loves that range from sex to success, symbolized today by the vanishing virgin, the debauched businessman and the punk politician, who suspend virtue for vanity or mammon, who give only to get.

The keynote issue is this: How can we avoid either a faithless moralism or a normless relativism? Akin to this socially is the question: How can we resurrect our "sensate culture" through an ideational" one (Sorokin) in today's "eleventh hour of Western civilization," unless we meet its basic "challenge," which is moral and religious in nature (Toynbee). Cultural hope lies chiefly in the recovery of our religiously grounded moral stamina, say Schweitzer, Whitehead, Tillich, Berdyaev, and others. In view of this, is it not possible that much in our twentieth century education literally has betrayed us for placing premiums on socioeconomic adjustments without teaching us how to think philosophically, ethically and religiously? In this hectic period of cultural and personal insecurity, what is the answer? Will the new morality suffice? Does it want the fruits of sacrificial love perhaps, without adequate faith-fed roots? Does it want a quantitative horizontal relevance without a qualitative vertical reference?

If we are to develop a new morality which will re-direct our culture constructively, we must be pro-scientific with Sperry while re-conditioned ethically and religiously by the spirit of Agápe, the highest form of love. Not self-gratification or only neighborliness, it is sacrifice, a self-giving to others, which seeks no reward for itself. One of the basic areas of life to which this must apply is matrimony. At a time when half of the marriages in America end in divorce and one out of three are involved in physical abuse, I hereby submit in behalf of the highest type of love a list of proposals entitled "Ten Commandments of A Happy Marriage." (Submitted to *Reader's Digest* about four years ago, it was rejected, but within a couple of months they published an article entitled, "Ten Commandments of a Good Marriage." Whence their idea? You be the judge.) The following are "the ten commandments" originally proposed as basic to a new and renewing morality:

1. Never hesitate to express your affections with reasonable modesty. Kiss one another goodbye and hello daily.
2. Don't the two of you get angry at the same time. There is no need to develop the habit of arguing. Listen to your partner with respect and express your views tactfully with regard for your mate's opinions. Give ear to the opinions of your parents and in-laws, but at the same time live your own life without their domination.
3. "The family that prays together stays together." Couples are no stronger morally and emotionally than that to which they are committed. Grace at mealtime goes a long way toward cementing relationships in the home.
4. Form good habits personally and domestically. Aristotle said, "Two-thirds of life is habit." Good habits should cover everything from keeping clothes orderly to a joint bank account to budgeting and going to church.
5. Do things together. Avoid anything like a "golf widow" or a competitive career, especially when there are children. Homemaking should be honored as a great art and privilege.
6. Give each other time for himself/herself. Allow time for personal interests such as hobbies, tinkering, music, sewing, and a little socializing.
7. Do not feel that you must have a complete home all at once. Enjoy the thrill of procuring furniture and furnishings a piece at a time. Look forward to improvements rather than back at major achievements in the home.
8. Do not think of sex as nasty but as a gift of God to express mutual love through a kind of symbol or sacrament of mutuality.
9. As for conjugal relations each should think in terms of making the other happy. Husbands should avoid rushing into the act without wooing the wife through foreplay.
10. Eros love (sexually prompted love) is self-gratifying but needs to be qualified by Agápe (sacrificial, out-going love). In all aspects of marriage the partners should seek to give to the other and not just get. When this is a paramount concern and practice a marriage will weather many a storm. Extended to all social relationships this quality of love can provide the new morality needed by our whole society today.

Yet the stronger morality of expendable love to which we refer is not only individualistic at its base but social in its outreach. In this respect there are several civic responsibilities involved, a few major ones worthy of our consideration in this context. Education, religion and legislation must work together to fulfill these responsibilities. This can be done if the new morality espoused keeps sacrificial love relevant at all times both personally and socially, while pro-scientific adjustments called for by Sperry are always pertinent.

It goes almost without saying that the moral decline in America is not only related to the high incidence of drug consumption and distribution but the lowering of sex ethics. Premarital sex is almost taken for granted. Half the marriages in the United States end in divorce and commonly not long after the marital commitments at that. An authority states that during the past year in the U.S. as many lives died in mothers' wombs as in all our wars put together. Surely, this is a loss of respect for life itself and the dignity it represents.

Besides the rise in child abuse is the rapid increase in organized pornography., An imprisoned murderer of young boys has admitted the following in a letter: "Pornography is a widespread social problem, so prevalent that many people accept it as normal. . . . Pornography was a determining factor in my downfall . . . (including) photographic, or art books. . . . Sexually arousing materials became an obsession. . . . I lost all sense of decency and respect for humanity and life. . . ."

Today, pornography is linked with a crime syndicate not unlike the Mafia. The infamous spread of foul literature related to sexual abuse actually has become a big business. Even certain families are tied in with it, as the Attorney General's Commission on Pornography has disclosed. Much of their profits have been deposited by the millions in foreign banks. In one case, 200 lesser corporations designed to hide the money have backed hundreds of hardcore pornography bookstores throughout the United State and Europe besides various video producers of obscene movies. The moral aspects of this social problem is intensified by the fact that lawyers behind the corrupt business argue that laws against it are an illegal restraint of the freedom of expression. This underlines my assertion that many, if not most, people in law and legislation fail to study ethics or take it seriously. It is time for conscientious people to stand together in plugging this social sewer. Freedom of expression does not mean that "anything goes." True freedom is a responsible freedom. A closer look at the American Constitution, taken elsewhere in this book, confirms this. Still there is a frivolous attitude reflected in much so-called art today, simply because our society has held to a robust tradition of the freedom of expression. As editor David Gergen has viewed it, some artists "want it both ways," i.e. through their obscene works they want to destroy our values while expecting the government to pay their bills and apply no restrictions on funding the National Endowment for the Arts. As Gergen puts it, "No society, even one as tolerant as this one has usually been, is willingly going to pay for its own demise." Indeed, for tax-payers to pay for the smut expressive of moral decay perverts the very idea of freedom. "If artists insist on a wholesale denial of any standards, they will wind up wrecking the very institution they claim to need." Congressional leaders must see that such practices reflect the cultural cancer we need to cure.

As for another civic problem, all good citizens should be sensitive to how we are treating the earth upon which we are so dependent. Sperry's view of ethics would support this. Besides the threats to the ozone layer around the globe due to the fumes and gases we are releasing from industry and automobiles, we should be aware of how we are destroying vegetation even in the forms of huge forests and jungles in North and South America.

Environmentalists are specialists in this subject, who, together with their activistic followers, are trying to be better stewards of these natural resources. Many have paid a big price for their convictions. Among them over a thousand lives have been taken by landowners and ranchers who in recent years have resisted their efforts to save the Amazon Basin both for humanity's sake and that of animals. Specialists inform us that today the equivalent of a football field of all these woodlands and jungles are being slaughtered per second, per second, mind you! A big percentage of these areas are being deliberately burned. In the United States, the loss of woodlands has resulted in the heavy erosion of the land often linked with treacherous floods, since our rains are forced to run off the soil. Another consequence is the lowering of the water tables throughout the continent, a problem intensified by the industrial pollution of what water we do have.

Is not this problem of our environment a moral and religious issue, which should be of great concern to our legislators and politicians? Should it not be of concern to anyone who wishes to save our resources for the benefit of our grandchildren and theirs? Legislators should be sensitive to these phenomena and our responsibilities relative thereto. They are both global and local in scope. Some concerned citizens are persuaded that many industrial leaders are looking the other way, desiring that we forget about such matters. But the big oil spills in rivers and at sea must not be forgotten.

The recycling of waste materials is also an environmental problem. In the U.S. 160 million tons of solid waste are discarded annually. Experts say that the United States recycles only 10% of its solid wastes. Some big newspapers, fortunately, are using recycled paper. Yet we are wasting enough aluminum cans to equal many large airplanes per year, our entire commercial air fleet, in fact. A university journal stated recently that 88% of the unrecycled paper amounts to 33,000 trees — wasted! Great amounts of glass are not recycled and 2½ million plastic bottles are thrown away every hour and 2 billion razors disposed of each year. Compare all this waste to the fact that thousands of school children in India, for instance, do not even have reasonable amounts of paper and pencils to write with. What a travesty of civic responsibility! Surely the new and stronger morality cannot condone but must inspire us to act both religiously and scientifically with a social concern at all times at home and abroad. This, too, is essential to the cure of our cultural cancer.

One of the needs of our time is for an increased concern for the mentally ill. Mental and emotional distress are having a devastating effect on the young. Teen-age suicides are more prevalent than ever. Frequently they struggle with alcohol, crack and sexual promiscuity. A sense of meaninglessness encompasses them. Even younger children sense it. A report from the Institute of Medicine in 1989 estimated 7.5 million children suffer from psychological illnesses, 12% being below the age of 18. A sharp increase of about 50% hospitalized cases was observed between 1980 and 1986. Suicides tripled between 1960 and 1967 among those ages 15 to 19. One of the basic causes of these trends is unhealthy emotional homelife. Often children do not feel loved; often they hate themselves, especially when they have a strong sense of guilt.

One basic need of youth, like others, is for a philosophical sense of "who I am." Unstable families related to broken marriages and economic instability accentuate this problem. Very often children and youth are severed from the emotional stabilities and moral values once proferred them through church and school. Wealth is not the answer either. They need a sense of belonging, worth and identity, which clothes and cars do not satisfy. Pressure from parents to get good grades for high school and college often accentuate the problems. Only one in five children who need therapy ever receives it. One elementary need is for the entire family to have one meal together daily; togetherness of this kind builds emotional support and encourages respect for curfews and other youth regulations.

In addition, a shameful indifference to the plight of the mentally ill who are homeless has left thousands in our cities stranded on our city streets and in our jails. Many among them are schizophrenics and manic depressives; many live in squalid, make-shift shacks and transient hotels without ample food and medical care. Many have dementia related to AIDS. What is behind all this? One big factor is the release of patients from state mental hospitals when a change in attitudes favored the idea that they could fare better on their own. New drugs were thought to be ample, and government forces thought confinement competed with the civil rights of people. Between 1955 and 1990 the exodus caused a drop from 552,000 to 119,000, according to a report by Anastasia Toufexis in October, 1990. Budget-cutting was also a factor. The consequence is that only immediate, temporary cases are being treated in hospitals. In Vermont, there is a better out-patient system aided by support groups and services, which relieve patients of a sense of being "locked in" and give them more freedom to decide things for themselves, even rendering services to others in need. This kind of programming also proves therapeutic to the participants, and it confirms that the basic answer to the mentally disturbed is for the rest of society to be more attentive to their needs. Indifference, incidentally, is the most serious of what classical theologians spoke of as "the seven deadly sins." It is still the most prevalent in the 1990's. It is ignoring our problems in society, one symptom being the low voter turn-outs at election time. This problem, too, must be adressed if a stronger morality is to help cure our cultural cancer.

Basically, to make for a stronger morality which addresses contemporary problems we must learn to relate theories of right and wrong to concrete situations. This demands more educators studying ethics both philosophically and religiously so that principles may come alive with relevance to people's everyday life. It is a major failure in education to back away from this philosophical responsibility. To continue to do so is to contribute to the insidious forces making for our cultural cancer from within by sucking the life blood of responsible living from our citizenry. How can our many irreligious families be of help here when teaching ethics is ignored in the school system? Sperry's pro-scientific view of ethics may help some, though it is doubtful that it can do much unless linked with conscientious religious convictions. We may possess opinions galore, but convictions must possess us. It is not enough to be mandated by external law. As a people we need to be mandated inwardly by a sensitive conscience. The medieval theologians were close to the truth when they asserted that the worst of the seven deadly sins was indifference. Is not this form of non-commitment basic to our cultural cancer? Is not its eradication essential to a higher and stronger morality?

Does religion really make a difference relative to crime? The crime rate in Scandinavia and Finland is remarkably low today, because religion is taught in their schools. Today the state of North Carolina does not release prisoners unless they have been spiritually rehabilitated. Chuck Colson, the one-time supporter of the Watergate scandal, was converted to Christ in prison, and his life and life-style turned around conspicuously. He became an ordained minister and founded the very effective Prison Ministries, a devotional and study movement which has done so much to similarly change the lives of hundreds of inmates. My son, a minister linked with the program in prisons in North Carolina, has observed first-hand the effects of this Christian witness and cannot say enough in its favor.

The writer does not wish to leave an impression of denominational bias, but the following is a factual report to hundreds at a church conference in western Michigan. At the Methodist conference after World War II, a clergyman of another denomination, who was the chief chaplain at the Great Lakes Naval Station in Chicago, reported that during the war years the station had extensive records of their servicemen, including their religion. He asserted, "Among the hundreds of men who committed crimes and caused disturbances of one kind or another practically every denomination was represented." "But," he said firmly, "there was not a single Methodist among them." Was this merely a coincidence? Not at all. They were taught in their homes and churches that Christian salvation was not only a faith-commitment which justifies the faith-committed person or saves the soul but an activated responsibility indigenous to the pursuit of a holiness which overtly expresses love of neighbor and applied social righteousness. Their spiritual progenitor was John Wesley, whose main concern was "to spread scriptural holiness throughout the land." Admittedly, some Methodist leaders have since "fallen from Grace," and some leaders have neglected divine transcendence, a theological blunder, but the pursuit is still alive among most of such designation.

In short, sincere religious faith does make a big difference. Where it prevails, crime rates are reduced and much of the immorality of our cultural cancer is curtailed. When the biblical clarification of the meaning of life is vivified for people and an activated devotion is made widespread the social debauchery of society is visibly reduced. The healing of our cultural cancer becomes not only a hope but an experience.

But our school texts and the American press do far too little to remind the public of how much we owe to religion to prevent errant behavior from adding more and more to our social ills. Sincere religion does much to prevent crime, drug dependency, teen-age pregnancies, alcoholism and AIDS. Currently a few columnists and social scientists are beginning to acknowledge that religious inspiration behind clean living spells hope for the future. Sad to say, however, secularists among our writers and teachers are quick to criticize religious leaders while looking the other way when it comes to the sensuous perpetrators of a debauched type of entertainment.

Evangelical and conservative interpreters of religion have high standards of life and do the most of all segments of Western and American societies to prevent anti-social behavior. One columnist recently declared, ". . . how much safer and serene . . . our lives would be if everyone practiced what the religious right preaches." This is much like Benjamin Franklin's assertion, "Where would we be without religion?" Modifying his earlier deism under the influence of the New England preacher, George Whitfield, a close colleague of John Wesley at Oxford, the two became friends and together founded the academy which became the University of Pennsylvania. Typically any delinquent persons associated with evangelicalism repent and have their lives converted or have their lives turned around. Without genuine faith commitments, people remain sluggish about moral and social responsibilities. Others often are persons who have been at least indirectly influenced by the religious convictions of those around them.

The writer Irving Kristol in the Wall Street Journal in February 1993 stated that there are three main influences upon "modern conservatism:" religion, nationalism and economics. "Religion," he asserted, is "the most important, because it is the only power that, in the long term, can shape people's characters and regulate their motivation." He strongly asserted, "It's the traditional spiritual values that we as individuals need. . . ." The family values stressed by President Clinton and former President Bush have no stronger supporters than the sincere faith-committed people who often prove to be the role models of their communities. But in saying this we by no means imply that spiritual devotion must relinquish the use of critical intelligence in any form of studies including those of the Bible. Democratic freedom is never true to itself without the moral and intellectual responsibilities coming from the hearts and minds of dedicated people. Just as this is the key to a decreasing crime rate, so, too, it is the main moral clue to curtailing our cultural cancer in general.

It is well-known that the present generation of up-and-coming parents belong to the "baby boomers." Early in 1993 *Time* magazine referred to them as "the generation that forgot God." But it may have been more accurate to have said they "neglected" or even "rejected" God. Most of this rejection is linked with either a naive understanding of God, such as the comic strip concept of God on cloud nine or a lack of exposure to mature views which are more apt to blend or at least relate religion to theologically tenable principles and critical insights. The failure of these parents to have attended good Church School classes or youth and young adult studies in religion has had much to do with their lack of interest and often paucity of religious understanding.

This phenomenon is intensified by the fact that the children of many such parents are being raised with an even more serious lack of religious understanding. Many public school teachers and college professors display a similar paucity of spiritual insight and prove to be religious defectors. As expressed elsewhere in this book, much of this is due to a lack of introduction to critical studies in religion and a weakness in dialectical philosophy.

Yet today many newer churches are popping up under modern methods of salesmanship. Arousing the curiosity of this "lost" or "directionless generation," to adapt the N.T. words of Jesus and Peter, many baby boomers are beginning to return to the church, though often bouncing around in search of what they want on their terms. Often by over-accommodating them, standard brand churches minimize their historic heritage. As Richard N. Ostling put it, "The returnees are usually less tied to tradition and less dependable as church members than the loyalists." Even so, the drop-outs are much greater in number than the returnees. Bringing up children causes some of the baby-boomers to concede the need to re-think things about God. But as Wade C. Roof, a sociologist, points out there is a growing number of what he calls "believers but not belongers." It appears that these people often have strange notions about God and religion. Also, many hesitate to make sincere spiritual commitments for fear of having to assume the high moral expectations that go with them. But some churches are adapting their programs to reach the unreached, the deviated and less enlightened.

Still, nearly half of the children born in mainline Protestant churches, we are told, leave them for good, and millions of members are dropping out. Why? My observations tell me these churches have become more liturgical without fostering clearly an evangelistic punch-line and appeal. Preserving the bureaucracy and systems of the churches is more important to many leaders than putting people on the spot and winning them right where they are. Too many clergymen become power-seekers. Methodism, while quite virile, is a case-in-point. Baptists, Presbyterians, Episcopalians, and Disciples of Christ, likewise. Social ethics often supersedes redemptive doctrines. The churches which are really flourishing are those which address the needs of the people as they see them. Informal methods are replacing the formal. Spiritual renewal is what the real returnees are seeking, not mere tradition and conformism. Their prosperity and broken relationships have not brought them peace of mind. Yet, many also want to be challenged, not just mollycoddled — redeemed, not just reformed.

But over-accommodating the returnees may prove to be a big mistake, if it does not lead people to a fresh regard for what the returnees are most ignorant of, viz. the heritage and sound biblical doctrines of the church. It may be important methodologically to adapt to cultural changes, but in itself that is insufficient. People need to find eternal truths relevant to them in the midst of their temporal activities and strivings. Support groups and single-point ministries can be helpful, but they are not ends-in-themselves. Grasping the redemptive message of the Bible must be kept central. Only then will the baby boomers find the saving Grace, which can regenerate and remotivate them while pointing them to the higher happiness and stronger morality. This, too, is germane to the contemporary cure of our cultural cancer.

The people of America and the West need to be reminded that no nation has survived, as Will Durant claimed, without a moral code supported and inspired by religious convictions. Science and technology alone cannot save us, for they belong to our expeditious means, not our moral ends. Reducing education to mere training we are losing our moral directions. Stressing the primacy of our best methods and techniques, we are losing our best values and virtues. The overall result is that our cultural vitality is being radically weakened if not depleted. Back in the 1950's Supreme Court Justice William Douglas saw these deleterious trends and indicated that the problem is not merely a neutrality toward religion but an obvious hostility toward it. As Jesus once said, "He that is not for me is against me." In principle, it couldn't be said more plainly.

Unless we become overtly committed to our spiritual principles at their best, we cannot develop a stronger morality, for the cancerous bacteria of secularism will sap our moral strength from within. Our sensate culture must be turned around by a recovery of our qualitative values and principles, those which our founding fathers and mothers saw focused in God. To remain indifferent to the need and terms of this recovery is to invite the death of our civilization. It's a matter of the decisions and commitments of our people, for a cultural cancer is not merely physical; it is moral and spiritual in nature.

Chapter 15

The Dialogue of
Science and Religion

Some time back, the positivist A. J. Ayer had a debate with F. C. Copleston, an Anglican philosopher of religion, broadcast on the B.B.C. After coming to a close stalemate relative to metaphysical arguments, they turned to a more empirical perspective, though Copleston was more inclined to recognize scientific limits in explaining man, especially as a moral being.

Ayer insisted that the only things meaningful were the empirically verifiable, while Copleston acknowledged metaphysical issues that could be pushed beyond our empirical observations. For example: Why something rather than nothing? Not empirical, the "why" is still meaningful, for the world is not self-explanatory. It points to a necessary causal metaphysical seat of meaning. Since Ayer could not accept this, the discussion moved to what is contingent while removed from analytical or logical necessity. Copleston stood for a rational both/and synthesis epistemologically, whereas Ayer did not, sticking to an understanding based on perceptions not integrated with formal logic and in no sense metaphysical. To Ayer sense perception and analytical thought like logic were both used by the scientist but not as a synthesis used in separate moments.

Also excluded by Ayer were ethical principles. They were held only to be emotive and non-cognitive since not verifiable as he saw them. Copleston refused to accept this limited view of all meanings. He maintained that there are some propositions which are not verifiable, even in principle, but which can be accepted as true or false. For example: "Atomic warfare will wipe out the human race." Though not empirically verifiable, the statement yields meaning or is intelligible.

Copleston asserted that God points to a metaphysical reality which transcends sense experience. Yet he could say, "it does not follow that one could not have another type of experience of it." The latter implies that we need not rule out the metaphysical nature of God. But Ayer found anything "metaphysical" difficult to grasp on his terms. Copleston's reply was that God is hypothetically unique and not describable in ordinary empirical terms, lest God not be God. It does not follow that there can be no knowledge of God, though admittedly the philosophical knowledge of God is only analogical. Copleston stated that if God is personal, He is capable of having relations with human beings. "And it's possible," added Copleston, "to find human beings who claim to have a personal intercourse with God." Ayer conceded this point, for it implies an empirical meaning and that such experiences were eligible for psychological study. He also conceded that the proposition "God exists" could be "a perfectly good empirical proposition" quite like "a conscious mind exists." Yet Ayer did not want to concede a metaphysical reality behind the experience in the way Copleston did; only God as an experience was allowed for.

Copleston closed the discussion by saying the "principle of verification cannot itself be verified." To attempt to make it so leads to an infinite regress. I agree with this. Yet, I should like to add that the same applies to reason's analytical statements basic to metaphysical theories and those like logic combined with sense perception in the sciences. This is to say that neither can reason verify or prove itself. Its first principles are intuited, and any proof as in simple geometry, for instance, must presuppose them. This is no proof.

What then are we led to but the practical Kantian synthesis based on the creative thinking of the conscious existing self. Existentially this settles for neither positivistic security nor metaphysical objectivity, for it is an epistemological both/and kind of thought that is paradoxically relevant to the knower but neither rationally nor empirically objective. It is creatively subjective. Without this epistemic creativity, there could be no type of theory in either science or metaphysics.

Even so, the empirical concession to religious experience made by Ayer and supported by Copleston is another matter. While not a product of pure reason nor pure empiricism, I maintain it belongs to the holistic conscious self to whom the religious experience is relevant, though more as an empirical consequence of what the religious existentialists mean by encounter with the Absolute. As a psychological aspect of existential relevance, religious experience is meaningful while not in itself religiously authoritative. The Transcendent is the source of authority; the conscious human existence the seat of its relevance. So while both Ayer and Copleston make provocative points worthy of our consideration, their respective emphases must not be alienated, for they both belong to the creative knowing subject, the holistic conscious self. While a rationalistic metaphysics is insecure, so is an exclusive empiricism. While God is a trans-rationalistic transcendent Being-of-all-beings encounterable faithwise, the encounter has no less than psychological relevance to the existing self. In this respect a psychology of religion has its place, for the psychological factor of religious experience is an aspect of what is meant by the existential relevance of God. Yet the empirical phenomenon or relevance should not be confused with what is relevant — in this case what to Kierkegaard is the Transcendent Absolute beyond all that is relative.

The book *Issues in Science and Religion* by physicist Ian G. Barbour is a brilliant delineation of just what the title suggests. It is a lucid, penetrating and systematic discussion between science, philosophy and theology on the cardinal issues they confront together in historic and contemporary thought. As a tripartite study, it summons the view of the leading exponents of the respective fields of inquiry who have contributed to the issues. The basic zone of communication is that of philosophy of science in dialogue with the philosophy of religion.

In taking a historical approach leading up to contemporary intellectual frontiers, Barbour presents valuable cross-sections of various schools of thought in medieval and modern interpretations of the world in science and theology before doing the same with contemporary philosophy of science and theology. This provides background for the author's creative synthesis of the respective disciplines by making current process philosophy the bridge between current scientific findings and theological concerns. Through this creative cross-fertilization a coherent schematism is constructed, even as the weaknesses of logical positivism are overcome and the limitations of both science and theology duly acknowledged.

Barbour's strong point is one of keeping alive the dialogue between science and theology as "complementary languages" while showing that neither discipline is all-inclusive. Epistemologically, the author soundly recognizes the involvement of the knower in what he knows in either field and that there is no complete dichotomy between objectivity and subjectivity, since the knower creatively makes contributions to what he knows. Though neither science nor religion should be overly identified with a metaphysical system sometimes superimposed upon it, both disciplines use metaphysical categories whether or not they intend to.

The basic objective of Barbour is to set forth a so-called "theology of nature," which interrelates the contributions of science and religion. In so doing Barbour clarifies the role of God in nature, something minimized today by neo-orthodox and existentialist theologies. By theology of nature Barbour does not simply mean a revival of "natural theology" based on arguments for God from either rational speculation or empirical evidences in nature but rather an attempt to view the natural order of the sciences in the light of historical revelation and religious experience. By this an integrated Weltanschauung is made possible in which intellectual compartmentalization is overcome by philosophical coherence.

As suggested above, process philosophy becomes the bridge. This is because it can embrace the fundamental findings of both modern science and religious experience. Implied here is a new view of nature centered about the relation of God to nature or creation. Both scientifically and theologically, this calls for new perspectives. In place of the old static and mechanical Newtonian view of the world as held formerly by scientists, a dynamic concept of a continuing creation is espoused. Seeing creation as a dynamic process the new view allows not only for biological evolution but the new physics with its less deterministic outlook and unpredictabilities. Barbour contends that the new view is as biblical as it is scientific. In this respect the process philosophies of Whitehead, Hartshorne, and Teilhard de Chardin are summoned to integrate the different methodologies, so that divine creativity is seen indigenous to the processes and laws of nature.

This philosophical synthesis or theology of nature overcomes the old mind-body dualism and separation of living and non-living phenomena. A reductionist view of man as in Behaviorism is surmounted in favor of personal unity. Mind and brain are not viewed as separate entities but as different perspectives, one from within and the other from without; the same for free acts and deterministic explanation. "In general," says Barbour, "either/or dichotomies turn out to be not mutually exclusive competitors but alternative types of analysis useful in differing contexts."

Thus Barbour holds to a holistic and "unitary view of man which admits many-leveled complexities." The higher levels are not reducible to the lower. Like the current organismic theory of biology, the whole is seen to be greater than the sum of its parts. The classical dualism of body and soul is seen to depreciate the unity of a person, while both science and the Bible defend such unity, thinks Barbour. Stronger both biologically and theologically is the contemporary psychosomatic view of man, which embraces several levels of activity. Such an integral view of man sees him very much within nature while transcending it. (B.F. Skinner could not do his work as a laboratory psychologist if he did not transcend the chemical and physical levels to which he would reduce us.)

In looking to process philosophy as a frame of reference for his theology of nature, Barbour differs from classical theologies by viewing God's activity in nature as a dynamic, organic and creative process. Not a necessitative process marked by determinism and complete sovereignty, divine activity rather bespeaks novelty, indeterminacy and emergence. Viewed as immanent and even in process of self-fulfillment God is very much involved in the processes of creation and its teleological thrust. Determinism is disavowed in favor of divine persuasion and sympathetic participation. Freedom and creativity are combined with divine causality.

Yet, much like Whitehead, the author also sees something of divine transcendence, since the world depends more on God than God depends on the world. Distinct from the world while working within it, God is not identified with a pantheistic view. Nor is the orthodox doctrine of creation ex nihilo to be accepted, thinks Barbour, for it is neither biblical nor a propos to a continuous creation in tune with today's physics and astronomy. Much like Whitehead and Hartshorne, the author sees God changing in experience while eternal in character and purpose. Also with Hartshorne, he sees God lovingly sympathetic through his participation in the creative process and struggle against evil.

Barbour's theology of nature, which is akin to contemporary "process theology," does not sell-out to either naturalism or natural theology. With neo-orthodoxy he sees Christ as the basic revelation of God; with existential theology he sees personal commitment essential to religious understanding; with linguistic analysis he sees the distinctiveness of religious language in worship. While faith in God as a redeemer related to historical revelation supersedes faith in God as creator, Barbour contends that the latter must not be minimized; hence, his theology of nature links God and nature, lest nature be left devoid of meaning and the activity of God outside historical revelation likewise. Though laws of nature are human constructs they reflect patterns in nature which bespeak divine activity, intelligence and order.

It can be said that Ian G. Barbour fulfills a superb task of correlating scientific findings and theological observations. Seeing the need for a theology of nature, he moves beyond the weaknesses seen in those theologies which have neglected the idea of a continuing creation and turns to process philosophy as a bridge that makes not only for wholesome dialogue but provocative integration of thought. Scientific findings and theological insights are correlated in such a way as to provide a dynamic view of creation that is as scientific as it is religious and as religious as it is scientific.

It is important that we recognize that religion requires methods of various types. Even so, those who settle for an equation here are remiss. Unless God is in some manner implicit within or in relation to our religion, it is not religion. That being the case religion may include a methodology or technology but is not restricted or equal to it. This distinction is basic to a theological perspective in contrast to a sociological one.

As Paul Tillich states, "Looking at God, we see that we do not have Him as an object of our knowledge but that He has *us as the subject of our existence*." Here is the cardinal issue: While we cannot know God perfectly in His aseity neither can we get away from God, nor can our religion be totally alien to Him. Why? Because God is the very "ground of our existence." God is "Being as such," as Tillich puts it. This is in accord with the philosopher Martin Heidegger's view of the Sein of Dasein or the Being of our existence. It also blends with the Biblical claim that in God, "we live, move and have our being." (Acts 17:28)

While transcendent of all beings including ourselves, God is still "the ground of our being," the immanent "is" of our existence, and our existence includes our religion. As such God is existentially relevant to us in our concrete existence, though our religious expression and methodologies of worship and doctrine are inadequate, since finite. Finite as we are, Tillich recognizes that we have "an ultimate concern" for God, which while not synonymous with God is in *apposition*, to God. In this respect God is "the depth dimension of ourselves." This means that God is *essential* to our human existence per se, an existence that *includes* religious yearnings, methodologies and expressions. Since man is held to be created *imago dei*, man has a nostalgia for the God who is the ground of his being. It is this which gives rise to religious belief, expression and methods of worship.

Tillich is influenced by Soren Kierkegaard, who sees God as the Unconditioned or Absolute beyond all that is conditioned and relativistic

— yet God as such is relevant to human existence psychologically and faithwise. Tillich sees this relevance anticipated in man's "ultimate concern," i.e. concern for the Ultimate or Absolute, a concern that is in response to God as the very "ground of our existence." God, then, is not totally removed from man but addresses man, who has such a yearning or concern, though often man misinterprets the Absolute and settles erroneously for his "tin gods." Nevertheless God is concerned about man's ultimate concern, for He is the immanent "ground" of man's very existence or being. Man does not simply concoct his ultimate concern, for God has an investment in man's religiosity and is not altogether alien to it.

Since God is Being as such and is the "is" of our existence, He is not oblivious to our religion — especially when He is understood to be the God of Love. Rather, God is the very basis of our religion, as deficient and finite as its concepts and methods may be. God is working from within our yearnings and "ultimate concern," since God is not only transcendent but immanent, even working through our methods of religious experience and expressions. God is "Being as such," which includes the idea that we cannot shake Him off. He is confronted in the Being of our human being, a human being which includes the religious dimensions of our existence or particularity of being. Though God is more than our beliefs in God, for His aseity supersedes all our finite concepts, God addresses us through our nostalgic yearnings for the Ultimate — which He is. God, then, does not snub man's yearnings and expressed religiosity, for they have a finite affinity with God. In this respect God can be known faithwise. Indeed, faith in the Absolute God is essential to a vital religion and essential to all theology, theology being a part of that religion. "Faith," said Kierkegaard, "is an absolute relation to the Absolute." While this implies a personal "leap of faith" it is from within an existence that is religiously real, though limited not only due to finite thought forms but man's fall or "estrangement" from "the ground of his being," as Tillich puts it. Religion includes belief in God, but God is not dualistically removed from or oblivious to that belief — lest He be irrelevant to man. God is even the ground of that imperfect belief; hence, he has an investment in man's belief and religious methodology, which is to say that religion is something more than its "technology," for God is involved in it. Just as God is the "ground of our existence," with all its finitude, so, too, He is the "ground" of our religion with all its finitude. There is no religion without God both within and beyond it. Why? Because God, while transcendent, is also immanent, and He "has us as the subject of our existence," as Tillich puts it. God, then, is the Being basic to our human being, and as such is also the ground of our religious existence, i.e. our yearnings, concerns, religious methods, symbols, and expressions. Were this not so, worship would be totally enveloped in our own ideas and there would be no encounter with "the Living God." Encounter with God is on the condition of faith or "total self-commitment," while, to Tillich, this is no less than a reverence for the Being of our existence, an existence, I remind you, that is at least partially religious and to which God is not oblivious.

In view of the above, religious methodology (deemed by social thinkers as a technology) without God in some sense implicit within its finitude would be only a meaningless methodology, perhaps a struggling for God but not a finding. On the contrary, since "Being as such" (God) is the ground of our existence, God is fundamental, too, to our religion, though far from identical to it. The net result of this is that while religion *includes* a technology, it is far more than that, for God is immanently involved within it. This is the difference between a sociological view of religion that reduces it to a technology and a theological view that sees religion to include technology without being totally identified with it. The one view is *about* religion from the outside; the other is an interpretation *of* religion from the inside. The latter is not hesitant to include religious doctrine and revealed content as important aspects of religion. A religion reduced to technology alone does not do them justice, let alone introduce men to God. Called for is a higher view of religion that is more than method (techne), since it confronts God from within concrete human existence. This is possible when God is seen to be the Being-subject of our existence not unrelated to the "I AM" (Being-subject) who confronted Moses and the "I Am" repeatedly referred to by Christ in the Gospel of John.

If we can keep alive a vital dialogue between science and religion, we can do much toward curing the cultural cancer of our time.

Chapter 16

The Answer to Materialistic Biases

Not long ago the editors of a student paper quoted Karl Marx as though his well-known remark was an irrefutable observation: "Religion is the opiate of the people."

The philosophical truth is that his statement is both true and untrue. The word "religion" stretches like rubber. It all depends on what kind of religion is referred to. What Marx especially had in mind was the authoritarian structure of the Russian Orthodox Church when it was confirming the nineteenth century Czaristic rule and making the people much too obeisant and leaders uncritical of that partnership. In this respect Marx was right.

However, too many of our professors and students are negative toward religion in America because of ignorance. Often their backgrounds are either religiously nil or are of the uncritical, dogmatic and/or fundamentalist brands of religion that eventually turn them off. They know too little, if anything, about the more mature, intellectually honest types of religion led by theologians and religious philosophers who are familiar with the critical biblical and scientific issues and are not afraid to wrestle with them.

One of the leading such thinkers in twentieth century Russia was Nicholas Berdyaev, a Bolshevik without religious background, who became a Christian through philosophy. When he taught philosophy at the University of Kiev (later Moscow) in the 1920's he was twice sent to Siberia for criticizing the Communist regime. The third time he escaped in 1927 to Berlin and moved to Paris in 1928. Cambridge University honored him in 1948. Berdyaev's many books have done much to help the intelligentsia of Europe and America, especially the "white Russians," to see the philosophical deficiencies of Marxism while being constructively critical of both the East and the West. He also had contributed much to bringing Christian theology to a more mature stance relative to spiritual metaphysics, eschatology and ethics.

While, on the one hand, fundamentalisms create religious problems for critically-minded people because of their dogmatisms, on the other hand, many so-called educated people lack understanding of the more mature brands of religion, which do not duck any of the critical questions. These more liberal types in the past two centuries have applied more pro-scientific study including "higher criticism" to the Bible than has been applied to any other literature. Furthermore, most of our social legislation since the 1890's has been initiated by religious social critics and lobbyists. Many of them were labeled "the social gospel" people in the 1920's and 1930's because of their social activism. One of the leaders in this field of socially-applied religion was the late Dr. Jack McMichael, Philosophy Professor at Concord College in West Virginia, whom Senator Joseph McCarthy before a congressional committee tried to "black ball" as a Communist. Dr. and Mrs. McMichael paid many a price for their ethical convictions.

The fact remains that Marx was both right and wrong in contemporary terms due to the ignorance on both sides of the fence — belief and unbelief. Few agnostics and few fundamentalists alike have gone through the woods of critical inquiry about religion. The result is that ignorance prevails among both brands of thought. Both need to realize that it is more commendable to ask honest questions than to merely accept dogmatic, pat or biased answers. Whatever is accepted should be based on sound intellectual inquiry and integrity. Seldom do the mentioned extremists of either type demonstrate this. They are fearful of an open-minded approach to religion with critical intelligence. The fundamentalists are afraid they will lose the "paper Pope" as the authoritative base for religion, and the agnostics are afraid they will learn how religion can be vitally relevant to our lives and give us an ethical motivation for living and cleaning up the world.

Many of our college teachers are behind the times intellectually in keeping science and religion alien to each other. Though not identical, to be sure, they can be viewed today as complementary approaches to life. When Bertrand Russell, the outstanding British mathematician and philosopher wrote his book, *Why I Am Not A Christian*, the noted Scottish theologian John Baillie stated, "Were that my understanding I wouldn't be a Christian either." After years of expostulating an anti-religious philosophy that included the rejection of the institution of marriage, Bertrand Russell changed his attitude noticeably. This writer is one of the very few people who know that he deeply regretted the conduct of his family, all the more so when his son said, "But, dad, we are simply applying the logic of your positivistic philosophy." Eventually, Russell said to students at Columbia University, "We must return to the Christian ethic." In his book, *The Impact of Science on Society*, (p. 59) he stated overtly: "The root of the matter is a very simple and old-fashioned thing, a thing so simple that I am almost ashamed to mention it, for fear of the derisive smile with which wise cynics will greet my words. The thing I mean . . . is love, Christian love or compassion." Lord Russell then added, "If you feel this, you have a motive for your existence, a guide in action, a reason for courage."

So-called process philosophy is at present doing much to demonstrate that science and religion are complementary. The same for the psychobiology of the Nobel Prize winning physiologist R. W. Sperry. For a good discussion on the latter, see his August 1988 essay in the *American Psychologist* entitled "Psychology's Mentalist Paradigm and the Religion/ Science Tension." In that article he even says he agrees with me that the dichotomy of science and religion is passé. Physical processes and human consciousness are interrelated, the latter emerging from the former, he shows, hence allowing for values and morals and a religious perspective as much as a scientific methodology. Thus Marx was right to some extent in his day but not in ours.

It was inferred above that it is erroneous to assume that science has all the answers. Those who claim such a view either wittingly or unwittingly subscribe to a view akin to logical positivism. This implies that nothing is intelligible which is not based on scientific verification. The exclusive criteria are the two which are fundamental to the sciences, sense perception and logic, yet not as synthesized but as kept separate kinds and separate moments of thought. This position disregards the ability of the scientist himself to creatively coordinate the two kinds of thinking in a given moment. The result is a philosophy or type of thinking that cannot interrelate the kinds of phenomena dealt with in the sciences so as to be relevant to the concrete existence of the individual. Atomistic in nature, it makes no contribution to the holistic character of the self and his existence nor to his cultural values.

Being given to an imbalanced empirical thought the positivist is an extremist who looks upon moral thought as merely emotive or sentimental, lacking in scientific grounds. An atomic bomb can be said to be able to kill 25,000 people, a verifiable fact, but there are no grounds for declaring it morally right or wrong. Science simply affords no basis for ethics. Moral issues in human existence are merely emotive, yet R. W. Sperry is presently seeking to provide for a scientifically based ethics. Will he supersede Dewey's position?

Much in our universities today is so scientifically biased that humanistic studies are almost scorned in some institutions. Usually they are schools which neglect philosophy and do not require it of their students, especially within imbalanced programs in the physical sciences. Called for is more respect for the phenomenological studies, which accentuate the primacy and creativity of consciousness. Studies in existentialism stress the primacy of the individual conscious self, who is even basic to the sciences. Would the sciences be possible without the creative thinking self? In another chapter the matter was clarified under "The Subjectivity of Scientific Objectivity," the basic issue being how we know what we know.

Due to its restrictions, positivism is an educational threat to our culture, for it negates the basis and the importance of ethical values. A leading spokesman for positivism, A. J. Ayer, actually speaks of moral issues as "nonsensical" rhetoric. The basic reason for this imbalanced position is the failure to keep alive within the sciences the holistic, existential self, who is central to a phenomenological involvement of knower within the known. The result is the sterility of the areas of life which yield values and moral principles. Consequently, it leads to a loss of ethical strength and cultural depth. This is deleterious to our educational endeavors, contributing much to our cultural cancer today. Let's consider some of the specific implications.

In the 1980's science seemed to reach its zenith. It appeared to be man's salvation through its release of so much technology — but it was also a damnation due to the limits of human nature. Even war was thought to be made obsolete. Had the search for scientific solutions gone too far? Computers took over the world, not as monsters of science fiction but as workhorses on our desks in almost all fields of endeavor. Environmentally, we came to the point where our earth and its resources as well as animals were threatened with extinctions. More than that, as William F. Altman has put it:

> Two specters that haunted the decade, AIDS and environmental apocalypse, dramatically showed that science is no cure-all. AIDS was a deadly reminder that some human behaviors may always be

risky. Rising levels of atmospheric CO_2, and the depletion of the ozone revealed that the risks often exceed expectations. No longer are such issues the province, solely, of the scientist's skill. Increasingly, the search for scientific solutions requires complex choices from a society that, paradoxically, seems overwhelmed by the pace of change.

To refer again to just one of these overwhelming changes, it has been shown that the earth's woodlands and jungles have been depleted already at the rate of a football field per second! Is a positivistic view of science and technology all we need to stop its threats? Hardly. They must be integrated with the moral sources of our values, lest the threats become an actualized downfall. Though such choices may be complex, they must be made.

It hardly needs mentioning that our culture is greatly influenced by our economy, which accentuates material values. Though they may be our lesser values qualitatively, they are important. Our American democracy is based on various forms of freedom of a moral quality, but it also allows for freedom of a materialistic type, which relates to our capitalistic system marked by freedom of enterprise. But as significant as we believe this is, it still leaves us with the disturbing social phenomenon of unemployment.

Like their predecessors Presidents Bush and Clinton in early addresses to Americans, said that we must supply work for all who need it. But it is doubtful that our government can or will be able to warrant this cherished dream without investing more taxes to help fulfill it. For years this writer has maintained that we must resurrect systems comparable to the New Deal policies of the C.C.C. (Civilian Conservation Corps) and the W.P.A. (Works Progress Administration), which proved very helpful to hundreds of thousands of American citizens, who were unemployed in the 1930's.

Why is it that so many people today rely on government relief funds when they could be given jobs linked with environmentalism and the improvement of our national and state parks, libraries, schools, museums, hospitals, and even highways? Other types of jobs might relate to the fine arts, their activities, and facilities. From these types of opportunities much good could be realized, including more dignity given to many of our oppressed people, including the homeless. In addition such types of employment might well help mitigate the use of drugs and the number of addicts and alcoholics through the medical surveillance of these people and improved social relationships among them. It is not enough to acknowledge the problem. We must be embarrassed by it and take action, and if we fail to do so, critics from other countries will continue to have much to say against our economy in favor of socialism which claims not to have the problem of unemployment. Perhaps it is time for the people to again "march on Washington" in this interest or for our people in Congress to lobby for it. Unemployment, too, is tributary to our cultural cancer. Do we really care?

Are the social sciences catching up with philosophy today? This is a legitimate question and can be answered affirmatively. Basic to the answer is the contemporary scientific and philosophical discovery of the phenomenon and role of consciousness. A philosophy that is akin to existentialism today is phenomenology. Their common rootage lies in the primacy of consciousness and the subjectivity thereof basic to all knowledge. Here we must reiterate that the Nobel Prize winner in physiology, Roger W. Sperry of California Institute of Technology, has propounded a psychobiological basis for his "emergent consciousness theory" fundamental to the newer cognitive trends in psychology. Since I have written considerably on this, especially in my book, *The Creativity of Consciousness:* an empirico-phenomenological psychology, I will only assert here that it overcomes the lop-sided, physical psychology known as behaviorism. Such an adjustment is much-needed in our time.

However, another pro-phenomenological development, even more current, is the "burgeoning interest among anthropologists in the application of existentialism and phenomenology to ethnographic material." This is to quote Dr. Steven Klein of the University of North Carolina. As a Ph.D. in both anthropology and philosophy, he wrote the following to me as an editor of a book he was soon to finish: "Over the past few years several of us have presented sessions in existential anthropology to the national anthropological convention, somewhat surprisingly to overflow crowds." Dr. Klein specifies applications to various world cultures, including East Africa and Japan. At the University of North Carolina, he says, graduate seminars are now linking leading existentialists like Merleau-Ponty and Heidegger to anthropological studies. Dr. Klein adds, "The anthropology department here has already begun to attract graduate students, several with undergraduate degrees in philosophy, because of this emphasis."

About five years ago, a student in sociology and anthropology at Marshall University expressed to me that he believed that a phenomenological approach to anthropology was very much in order. I encouraged him to pursue such a study, but he received no encouragement from his department. I hope that has changed.

What must we deduce from these new trends? It is the fact that the social sciences are beginning to recognize that even scientific objectivity could not exist without the existential-phenomenological subjectivity of consciousness. Only a conscious subject can know anything, though, as Sperry points out, consciousness emerges from the physiological processes of the brain and nervous system, while it, in turn, affects and often controls such processes. Indeed, it took a conscious man like B. F. Skinner to deny that we have consciousness! It even takes consciousness to make theoretical errors.

In general, another provocative consequence is that science and values are seldom deemed to be as alien to one another as in the past. As seen above, Sperry actually contends that ethics can be scientifically prescriptive and not just descriptive. Philosophically, this implies that the sciences and their methods presuppose phenomenology. They belong to the consciousness of a concrete existing man. To be sure, the social sciences are catching up with philosophy. Klein's work is truly exemplary.

Some of the more discerning psychologists and psychiatrists of today have come to recognize that psychology and religion have some related problems and related answers. One such psychiatrist is also a writer, M. Scott Peck, M.D., who while reluctant at first to face up to such possibilities, after studying them with care arrived at the point of seeing the human psyche from a combined perspective. Without stressing it in so many words, Peck came to a holistic, pro-existentialist view of the self to which the gaining of meaning is pertinent and religion often an open-door to such a possibility.

In his book *The Road Less Traveled*, Peck integrated the strongest insights of psychiatry with those of religion. In his book, *People of the Lie*, Peck uses this perspective to probe the basic problem of human evil in a somewhat new way. Evil people, he denotes, fail to face up to their own problems while pushing others down. In this regard he is highly illustrative and analytical. The study is a strong analysis of the psychology of evil and human encounters with evil in everyday life. Evil, says Peck, is a type of disease not yet scientifically diagnostic. Evil in most any form including illness and phobia is to Peck, "any defect in the structure of our bodies or our personalities that prevents us from fulfilling our potential as human beings." (p. 125)

The latter refers to what Abraham Maslow speaks of as "self actualized" persons. Eventually, Peck assures his readers that this attainment is more than a matter of resolve. It is commitment to the values that matter most in life, the highest of such being intrinsically religious. Existentially speaking, Peck not only saw this in relation to his objective studies but subjectively as well. He writes not with finality but as one who must say, "I am learning" (p. 10), and an important aspect of it is the illuminating influence of his own Christian commitment after years of examining Buddhist and Islamic mysticisms. Without apology, he states, "My commitment to Christianity is the most important thing in my life and is, I hope, pervasive and total." (p. 11).

This daring and creative study leads Peck not only to an objective psychology of evil but to a hope for healing human evil. Basic to this is the willingness of people to face up to what is inwardly "displeasing to themselves." This is akin to "the high voltage" of exorcism and power-seeking as well as to Satan worship and various forms of "group evil" linked with crimes and the atrocities of war as well as many industrial policies today. Peck speaks of "people of the lie" because he sees lying as both "a cause and manifestation of evil." It is related to narcissism, a common form of it being among people of power from parents to kings. Socially it has such proportions that it effectuates national pride. (Evil is "live" spelled backward.) Peck even states that we must respect what many theologians have said: Evil is the concomitant of free will as a price we pay for our power of choice. (Kant in his philosophy of religion saw this as the perversion of the free will he stressed as native to human nature.) The eradication of narcissism is essential to the elimination of group evil . The group mind depends on the individual mind. Until the latter is changed the former cannot be. As religion has recognized, the change of history's course may depend upon a change of heart in a single person. The battle between good and evil must be settled in the sacred soul of the individual, says Peck. He sees narcissism and laziness at the root of all human evil. He states frankly what has long been needed to be said by our social scientists, ". . . personal purification is required not only for the salvation of their individual souls but also for the salvation of their world." (p. 253). In other words, unless our society is changed for the better at the grass roots it will not be changed at all.

Dr. Peck has taken a scientific approach to evil but is shrewd enough to see that it cannot be removed from the moral perspective, if decent lives are to be lived. Moral judgments of others, however, are not fair until we have purified our own motives before making them. Evil people avoid self-criticism and such self-inventory. The more we examine many contemporary forms of evil the less reason for pride is discovered. We need to make judgments, but they must be wise and in accord with the best spiritual leadership, as Peck concedes (p. 11).

As much as science can help clarify issues for us, it is "a major pitfall" to give science too much moral authority. For one thing, the sciences are constantly changing and amount to the best judgment of most scientists at a given time, while often they are "as lost as the rest of us," says Peck. Science, too, has its tentative fads; the last word is never in. Debates must continue relative to science and morals. The burgeoning psychiatrical interest in the sources of our prejudices, fears, mental ruts and the like may be the opening of an important door to fresh insight. Yet specialists must be careful in not becoming too negative . . . even toward themselves as therapists. It is questionable, therefore, that science can continue to be value free. This is because the major threats to our survival do not come from nature out there but from human nature in here. Evil must be curtailed from within the human soul, Peck declares, yet not apart from scientific scrutiny. Evil can be overcome and healed only by the love of individuals for others, and this implies love as sacrifice. Such love is not mere sentiment but activated self-giving, expendable love, what the New Testament stresses as Agápe. Out-going, it seeks nothing for itself. It is the antidote to materialistic biases including narcissism and much mental illness. And until it becomes more common to men's ethical motivations, we cannot eradicate our cultural cancer based on selfish and materialistic ambitions and biases.

Dr. Peck is correct when he asserts that we need salvation for both our souls and our society. Men need to be remotivated from within spiritually. As stated above, our major threats to survival are from within. That we may better correlate and apply spiritual remotivation to our social problems we do well now to relate this issue to the problem of crime, which is a major challenge to the Church and every facet of civic responsibility today.

It was asserted above that we need more prisons to help combat crime. But will this prove to be the way to stop crime? It will not. The punitive approach has its place but should not be regarded as a cure. It is very much linked with our materialistic biases and fails to emphasize our cultural values and what they can do for criminals themselves. The noted authority on this subject Charles Colson is promoting a movement today which has mobilized over 20,000 volunteers supporting a prison ministry of spiritual and moral reform, the results of which are phenomenal. It actualizes what Peck has expressed in principle.

Colson asserts that the United States has stricter dealings with crime than any other democratic country with budgets amounting to billions to handle over 550,000 prisoners. Has our crime rate lowered? It has not. Many citizens feel far from secure on our streets and in their homes today. The problem of crime is worse than ever in our nation's history. Colson is sure, and I believe he is right, that our government institutions are grossly inadequate for eradicating crime. He sees 75% of those released from prisons returning to our streets only to repeat their crimes. What is needed is a spiritual therapy that is vitally personal with marked social consequences. Colson and his ministry are on the right track. The underlying need is the spiritual rehabilitation of criminals. They must be remotivated from within, something iron bars and fences cannot bring about. As the chairman of Prison Fellowship Ministries Charles Colson leads others in what actually reduces crime as it remakes lives when the hearts of prisoners are inwardly changed. "A new heart will I put within you," said God through the prophets Ezekiel and Jeremiah. Colson understands this existentially, for he was formerly a counsel to President Nixon, who after his involvement in the scandalous Watergate affair, followed by imprisonment, was converted to Christ. He found "the new life" through a "new heart," which put away "the old things" of sinful self-gratification and artificial power. Since then he and his volunteers have introduced thousands of criminals to Christ, who thereby have found rehabilitation for themselves and their families with constructive lives offsetting their brokenness. Many have been freed from drugs and reborn to the new and higher life of inner peace and love.

Call it what we will, this is not something new but very much needed today. It is what leaders of the Evangelical Awakening like John Wesley and George Whitfield were involved in as they introduced thousands of people in England and Wales to the "new heart" based on faith commitments and which turned many people including children from low life styles, drunkenness and debauchery to the "new birth" and pursuit of holiness basic to true Christian discipleship.

Here is the basic answer to something strongly tributary to our cultural cancer. Leaders in the state of North Carolina, my son informs me, have recognized this and do not release prisoners until they have been similarly rehabilitated. Would that all churches would join together in promoting this kind of prison ministry. There is nothing else that approaches its effectiveness in aiding prisoners and their families while also making vivid the biblical principles essential to our judicial system at its best. Here we see what Dr. Peck basically meant by salvation for both our souls and our society. It is not too much to say that both Peck and Colson are pleading for what is *central* to the cure of our cultural cancer. They recognize that our materialistic biases and methods can save neither our souls nor our societies. What applies to criminals applies to all of us in government, business and education, for we need to be inwardly remotivated by the precepts and Grace of God. Nothing cleanses our cultural bacteria quite like that which regenerates human life from within. It is the basic key to curing our cultural cancer in its varied forms. Without the cure our civilization will collapse in time, for as explained above our basic "challenge" is moral and spiritual in nature. Materialistic ambitions and methods are not the answer to our social rickets and cultural anemia. Spiritual therapy is the basic answer linked with divine self-giving love.

Some time ago when I taught philosophical theology at Temple University, the noted psychiatrist, Dr. O. Spurgeon English, told me he was splitting a class which included medical and theological students. He said, "Your theology students far outdo our medical students. They understand much more the everyday problems of people." Though the sciences have an important place in our lives, including psychology, too often our educational leaders have become so specialized they have lost sight of the holistic view of the self. Mature psychiatry and theology have not done so. Not merely physical specimens, we are whole selves or no selves.

R.W. Sperry of Cal Tech has shown within his "emergent consciousness theory" that though human consciousness is a product of physical processes, consciousness, linked with "the brain traffic" of the nervous system can, in turn, affect the physical phenomena. This psycho-biological view enhances respect for psychosomatic medicine as related to the role of one's consciousness and the influence of a person's faith and attitude on one's health through more positive attitudes, good humor and hope.

But what our college teachers need most today is the mature critical or pro-scientific study of religion as related to ethics and philosophy. As one specialized in the philosophy of religion and the author of two books in the philosophy of science, I must reiterate that our schools of education ("teachers colleges") are literally betraying us because of their anemic curricula. Teachers steeped in methods fail to learn how to think dialectically so as to relate well what they know in one field to another. The result is poor teaching and weak cultural understanding. Being poor philosophers, they cannot think well and their students can't either. One serious consequence of this philosophical deficiency is the inability to correlate science and religion as teammates in the pursuit of truth. Even as a brain specialist, Dr. Sperry has conceded this.

A few years back Dr. Duane Sommerness, Superintendent of the Traverse City State Hospital in Michigan, invited me to address his classes in psychiatry on five occasions so as to foster a more holistic understanding of what they were specializing in by linking it with the total person. As a Christian he could see the need of this for broadening the therapeutic effects of their specialty. The noted Viennese psychoanalyst Dr. Viktor Frankl has seen the need for more than the Freudian "depth psychology," for we need what he calls the "height psychology" related to our philosophical and religious goals and purposes. Lacking in this, people of the West today are experiencing, says Frankl, a "new neurosis" due to the meaninglessness of their lives. Religion he sees to be a basic answer to this weakness. Much the same can be said of the views of another pro-religious psychiatrist, Dr. M. Scott Peck, the current writer referred to above.

Training, after all, is not necessarily education. Sound education "educes" insight into the whole of things — a profoundly philosophical issue all specialists need to learn. Slowly, the specialists in medicine and psychology are coming to see the need to address not only physical problems per se but their relation to the existential problems of the whole person, including the emotional, mental, intellectual, and spiritual perspectives. One major sign of this is that the M.D.'s of today are not so reluctant to learn things from Ph.D.'s. Segments of understanding are not enough. We need to interrelate our thinking in all fields. When they, including the religious perspective, are dealt with both critically and devoutly, John Greenleaf Whittier's words ring true: "And we are whole again." This is the recovery of true selfhood and a basic clue to overcoming our cultural cancer.

Chapter 17

The Creativity
of Consciousness

Consciousness is the seat of creative thought. It is the ability to coordinate one's sense perception with one's logic so as to interlace the inductive and empirical with the deductive and analytical. Consciousness is the mental creativity that centers about what Immanual Kant called "synthetic a priori judgments," or, better, it is what makes such thinking possible. However, in making this assertion the Kantian bifurcation of the knowing self is to be rejected. Dualism of the mind and body is overcome through a unified and holistic view of consciousness.

Consciousness is the coalescence of empirical bodily processes with the trans-empirical qualities of both logical and existential thinking. Not the separation of sense perception and logic, such as is essential to the modus operandi of positivism, it is rather the creative coalescence or integration of the two modes of thought. This coalescence and its - expanded inducements and deducements constitute the heart of what is meant by thought and the mental dimension of life.

Consciousness, though very much interrelated with the physical processes, is also trans-empirical or has the ability to transcend the very process to which it belongs. This is because it can introspect and reflect upon the processes and even investigate them scientifically. Yet, the scientific investigators themselves would not be possible without the existential involvement and creative thought of consciousness. In short, without bodily processes there would be no consciousness, and without consciousness there could be no scientific investigation, let alone the existential questionings: "Who am I?" and "What am I here for?" germane to the search for life's meaning.

Without consciousness the scientist could not formulate his hypotheses and theories. The great physicist Henri Poincare, for instance, saw how both scientific observation and hypotheses were dependent upon the knowing subject's mind, and, due to the mind's creative coordination, the observations and hypotheses implied each other. It takes more than separate moments of sense perception and logic to concoct a hypothesis. It involves the creative coordination of the two, combined with imagination and selection, even as it implies the correlations of what is inductive and deductive. There is also that sense in which prescientific and trans-scientific forms of cognition must be summoned before one can be scientific. As Aristotle said, the demonstrable rests upon the undemonstrable. In this case, the phenomenological level of epistemology is fundamental to the empirical just as the empirical is tributary to the phenomenological or what centers in consciousness. The empirical alone is totally irrelevant or inconsequential, because it presupposes the phenomenological, first, in cognition per se and, second, in the relevance or consequences of that cognition. It is this which is completely obviated in positivism.

Just as the behavioristic psychology of B.F. Skinner and others denies the reality of consciousness, so, too, it is obviated in positivistic thought. Though the logical positivist is either empirical or analytical in a given moment he loses sight of the coalescence of the two modes of thought on the part of consciousness. He loses sight of the human subject whose experience and logic they are or to whom they appertain. In doing so the positivist ignores what we mean by the creativity of consciousness, whose basic function it is to correlate experience and logic or the inductive and deductive. The positivist assumes that analytical thought, including mathematics, is a self-contained, objective methodology but in so doing neglects the phenomenological distinctiveness of the a priori principles, mental categories and/or intuitions, which comprise the foundations of logic and mathematics. This is a failure to recognize not only that consciousness is the seat of the first principles of logic but the creativity of its correlations of the different kinds of logic and their interrelationship with sense perception. To overlook the creative role of consciousness is to be oblivious to the human subject behind the scientific enterprise itself. It is the failure to acknowledge that logic and experience are *his* tributaries to knowledge and his instruments of interpretation. It is the failure to see the creative coalescence of logic and sense perception within a single experience of what Kant called "the synthetic a priori judgment." This so-called "judgment" is an interpretation on the part of the conscious subject; it is an appearance based on his combining of the empirical with the mental.

Consciousness, then, is essential to the knowing subject and what is deemed mental, while it draws upon the empirical bodily processes for its sustenance. Empirically grounded, consciousness is trans-empirical, subjective or mental, as well. In this respect it is an emergent level related to, yet distinctive from, the brain processes per se. Hence, it is inadequate to view reality as completely objective or mechanistic the way the biologist Jacque Monod sees it. The objective phenomena cannot be known or observed without the conscious subject-observer. Even the behavioristic psychologist, who tries to be completely objective in scientific methodology, has a functioning consciousness behind his work, even though he denies the reality of all consciousness as well as freedom. It was with good reason, then, that after B. F. Skinner came out with a book entitled *Beyond Freedom and Dignity* a philosopher should write an article entitled, 'Freedom and Dignity Beyond Skinner.'' To deny consciousness is surely to deny dignity, for it is to deny subjectivity.

Sheer mechanism or total objectivity in biology and psychology, while having a methodological place, is incomplete and is not symmetrical with the new physics, its quantum view of energy and its unpredictabilities. Furthermore, in a mechanistic system of molecules there is no place for truth or falsity. How can a machine-like creature function either truthfully or erroneously in relation to another? For that matter, how can one mechanism know another? Actually, the mechanist is unable to be consistently mechanistic, since he presupposes existentially the creative consciousness which he obviates or denies, theoretically.

Consciousness while drawing upon experience, even for its own sustenance, moves beyond it, functionally, i.e. transcends it by its capacity to examine, criticize and reflect upon it. This is something recognized also by the distinguished French philosopher Maurice Merleau-Ponty. Respectful of Edmund Husserl's phenomenological stress on the primacy of consciousness, Merleau-Ponty, I believe, improves upon him by his providing a link between consciousness and experience. This is to say that the psychology of consciousness cannot be separated from the psychology of experience, though they are distinguishable. This addresses the epistemological problem with balance while respectful of Husserl's emphasis upon the intuition of essences. Husserl saw how physicists like Galileo and Davy were not only inductive but eidetic in establishing a hypothesis and even a law based on a single observation.

What does this imply but the creativity of consciousness as it interrelates sense perception with intuition.

Merleau-Ponty sees that consciousness comes up with a "homogeneity" of the inductive and intuitive forms of knowledge. He states, "Any knowledge of fact always involves an a priori understanding of essence." Consciousness and experience are reciprocal and need each other. In fact, an empirical or inductive psychology cannot of itself penetrate or know consciousness from the inside, as it were, since its mode of understanding is strictly from the outside. The objective and subjective are interrelated, yet the objective methodology cannot probe the distinctively trans-empirical nature of the subjective. On the other hand, the more creative nature of the subjective level of consciousness is the source of the scientific methodology with its combinations of empirical data and analytical logic.

While consciousness depends upon empirical phenomena or process, even to exist or to be real, it supersedes the empirical, too. Thus, an objective methodology is no less than incomplete without presupposing the creative correlation of logic and sense perception that consciousness subjectively accounts for. The empirical psychology paves way for the phenomenological psychology, while the latter is trans-empirical in its reciprocal relation to the empirical and its holistic superseding of it. This parallels what the organismic theory of biology connotes, viz . . . that the whole is greater than the sum of its parts. In this case the objective phenomena are even irrelevant except for subjective phenomenon to which they are relevant. An objective induction without a subjective consciousness is incomplete, if not meaningless. Only consciousness can account for the reflection upon an unreflective experience. Experience alone is unreflective; only consciousness is reflective.

The phenomenological level of consciousness is more all-embracing than the empirical. Without it the empirical would have no significance. As Edmund Husserl recognized, it takes a creative, human subject to "assimilate natural data and logical meanings." Husserl shrewdly distinguished logical concepts of essences from their psychological representations in appearances. Something is known intuitively, viz. the essence of an object, which is not the same as the physical experiences or sense perceptions of an object. This eidetic feature of consciousness helps make the human subject trans-natural, holistic and existential. Even so, I must agree with Cornelius van Pearson when he says that Husserl's phenomenology is inadequately related to empirical psychology.

Apparently Merleau-Ponty has seen this, too. Be that as it may, logical thinking was rightly seen by Husserl to belong to a unique, conscious subject. At this point positivists are remiss for overlooking the matter and keeping logic merely a part of their methodology. Whose methodology is it, after all?

Cannot the two epistemological poles of empirical psychology and the phenomenology of consciousness be interrelated existentially? To me it appears that they can and should. Though the solution is not ontological in the form of a rational synthesis, it is holistic and existential belonging to the concrete self. Both conscious subjective and empirical psychology are essential to the knowing self. Neither sense perception, logic nor language would make sense or be pertinent, if there were no conscious subject to find them intelligible, meaningful and instrumental. At the same time there would be no conscious subject if it were not for the empirical processes beneath it. In short, the empirical level paves way for the phenomenological, while the latter is also trans-empirical. Each level is tributary to the other while belonging to a whole. Though the two levels are functionally different, they do not constitute a dualism but a balanced two-in-one existential interrelationship that is holistic.

Consciousness correlates induction and deduction, and in this respect it is distinctive. While this phenomenon per se is phenomenological, implying the necessity and uniqueness of consciousness, it is not removed from the empirical processes. Rather, as Merleau-Ponty suggests, "all consciousness is perceptual," it is consciousness "of something" and "directed toward the world." Yet consciousness is not reducible to sheer perception, for it is a higher, more enriched, creative and transcending level of life. Consequently, though persons are immersed in the natural world of perception, we are not limited to it. Better balanced than Husserl's autonomous view of consciousness, Merleau-Ponty improves upon it by acknowledging that the rational elements of knowledge are immanent, i.e. not independent of the empirical factors. "The perceiving mind is an incarnated mind," says Merleau-Ponty. The body and consciousness are thereby intermingled. The subjective and objective, though distinctive functionally, are vitally interrelated in a two-in-one relationship belonging to the whole self.

There is a profound sense in which perception is paradoxical in that, much like Heidegger's claim, the perceived object has existence only in so far as the conscious subject perceives it; the object is not alien to the perceiver. As Kant said, we think the world via our experiences of it. At the same time experience evokes the idea of being.

Ideational truth and perceived truth, or intellection and perception, while different, are related. Not two kinds of knowledge, here we have two degrees of clarification of the same knowledge. This blends with our thesis that consciousness is the coalescence of induction and deduction, the analytical and the empirical. Mind and body, while functionally distinctive, are linked or interrelated. Consciousness and perception, again, need each other while each is tributary to the whole self.

Consciousness or the conscious mind has a "direct and internal contact with itself" in a way usually ignored or denied by those sciences which keep it "externally conditioned." Consciousness, then, enables us to be aware that we are aware. Much like Husserl, Merleau-Ponty shrewdly sees that such a consciousness is essential to both philosophy and the social sciences. In fact, we must assert that the by-passing of this consciousness as in behavioristic psychology and positivistic thought is a definite threat to the humanities and the humanistic perspective. Positivism overtly states that moral values are merely emotive, hence meaningless.

Sensitive to what we regard as the creativity of consciousness, Merleau-Ponty accepts Husserl's idea of Wesenschau, the intuition of essences, and his idea of "intentionality" or the orientation of consciousness around "intentional objects" or the intuited essences of things. In this way consciousness is seen to transcend contingent phenomena or events while at the same time bound to them. As Merleau-Ponty states it, an "empirical psychology must be preceded by an eidetic psychology," which is to say that the perceptual needs the phenomenological to be organized and relevant. This supports our claim for the subjectivity beneath scientific objectivity and our appeal to the primacy of a holistic, existential perspective of consciousness.

Unlike positivism, phenomenology and existentialism take seriously the structure of consciousness brought to bear upon sense data and perception. Even scientific methodology is predicated on the understanding of the psychic content of thought. While sense perceptions impress the conscious mind, it is the conscious mind that recognizes the essence of objects and gives them meaning and order. Though consciousness is always intentional, i.e. "of something," it is superior to that of which it is conscious by transcending it.

Also, consciousness is a type of unity or unifying factor. It is what remembers, imagines and reconstructs the data of experience, even as it employs inductive and deductive logic in doing so. Basic to its cognition is intuition and the ability to analyze and synthesize. Intuition is the eidetic apprehension of the principles of being, providing the a priori structures of space, time and causality, which consciousness imposes on sense perception to organize them. Intuition is essential to the epistemic creativity of the human subject, for by it objective reality is filtered or conditioned and even selected. On this basis, consciousness provides the subjectivity fundamental to scientific objectivity. In addition, its memory provides what John Dewey called "a funded meaning," so that empirical elements of the past effect present perceptions. Similarly present perceptions arouse anticipations of future experiences. If this were not so a strain of music, for instance, would be reduced to staccato-like notes stretched apart without relationship, in which case there would be no music. Perceptions alone have no sense of time; only consciousness is time-conscious. Furthermore, the conjectures and imaginings basic to scientific hypotheses imply more than sense data per se. In fact, sense data without consciousness to organize and actualize their relevance would be fictitious or irrelevant. Thus, sense perceptions imply a consciousness existentially very much involved in what it observes. It is both caused and causal in a psychosomatic sense. Not a dualistic view, this implies a coalescent interrelationship of the physical and mental elements.

Also important to the role of consciousness is what Kierkegaard called "indirect communication," by which thoughts are evoked in a trans-empirical manner. Fundamental to humanistic and person-to-person forms of communication, it entails such things as imagery, allusion, metaphor, symbol, poetry, and paradox. As Paul Tillich has similarly shown, the very structure of being is involved in every sign, symbol and logical chain. To disregard this is to depreciate many elements pertinent to our concrete existence, especially the kinds of thinking involving humanistic values. Sir Arthur Eddington is one scientist who saw the significance of this kind of communication, conceding it to belong to what he called "the poetry of existence," and without which a philosophy will stand or fall. Aesthetic, moral and religious values demand the involvement of the transcending total-self with its creative interrelationships of intuition, logic, sense perception, imagination, and will. Values appertain to the whole conscious self, not part of him. Consciousness is the integrating factor of these capacities of the self. It is the core of the holistic self of concrete existence to which values are made subjectively pertinent. In short, consciousness is the seat of creative thought.

Does the philosophical interpretation herein set forth have scientific support? The answer is affirmative. Significant support for it is given by the noted psychobiologist, Roger W. Sperry of California Institute of Technology. Seeing how human acts follow patterns, not merely events of the brain excitation, Sperry takes issue with the psychological reductionists from Pavlov and Watson to B. F. Skinner. Their stress upon the conditioned reflex theory of behavior overlooks, Sperry contends, the important role of consciousness within the causal sequence of cerebral events. Taking issue with the behaviorists, we reiterate Sperry's claim: "Conscious mental forces do govern and direct the nerve impulse traffic and other biochemical and biophysical events in the brain and, hence, do have to be included as important features in the objective chain of control. . . ."

In view of Sperry's contentions consciousness can no longer be dismissed as a mere epiphenomenon of no consequence. Rather it is an integral aspect of brain activity. Accentuating the role of brain patterns, Sperry comes out on the side of mentalism, i.e. mental events even affect brain functions per se. Despite the less measurable nature of sensations, percepts and concepts, images and feelings, consciousness, to which they appertain, is observed to interact with the physical phenomena in a psychosomatic manner. Thus Sperry has an emergent theory of the mind in which both continuity and discontinuity between the physical and conscious functions are maintained in a two-in-one relationship. Though consciousness is dependent upon the cerebral mechanisms, it functions within them to the extent of actually influencing them, i.e. the conscious mind affects both the physicochemical and electronic processes as well as the patterns of the nerve impulses. This interactionary perspective makes Sperry's observations more holistic than most modern psychologies, and proexistential in that the "wholeness" of the knowing self is basic both to Sperry and the existentialist.

In asserting that the conscious mind influences the physical factors, with which it is related, Sperry contends that the emergent brain patterns of consciousness have a causal control power over the cellular, molecular and subnuclear particles of the brain. These patterns are mental forces which, as "causal determinants in brain functioning," govern the flow of "impulse traffic" over cerebral excitation. The holistic factor is that just as the lower functions contribute to the higher, the higher functions influence the lower. The conscious properties of the brain processes both involve and transcend "the nerve impulse traffic" of the brain. This makes consciousness transcendent of matter while at the same time linked with biophysical laws behind the nerve impulses. In short, Sperry's psychobiology gives support to the philosophical theory of consciousness set forth above. In so doing, it contributes to the cure of the materialistic cancer of our culture.

Chapter 18

The Creative Writer's Philosophical Responsibility

Today we are flooded with cheap literary realism. The few reactionaries are like the man who phoned the radio station, "If you're the station that gives us twice as much weather, turn it off. We're drowning!"

The creative writer has a much greater responsibility than sometimes recognized, much of which is philosophical in nature and scope. By the creative writer we mean the typical novelist, poet or essayist whether distinguished or less prominent. By a writer's philosophical responsibility we mean the direct and indirect cultural effectiveness of his work among the reading constituency and general public. There are a number of facets to this responsibility, which might well be underlined in question form for fresh consideration today.

The first question demands that we take a new look at the creative writer himself: Is the creative writer an artist of sorts? This, in turn, raises the immediate question: What do we mean by artist? Marshall McLuhan provocatively states, "The artist is the man in any field, scientific or humanistic who grasps the implications of his actions and of new knowledge in his own time. He is the man of integral awareness." This near-definition describes well the artist as a person of liberal learning, and upon accepting it we must assert that if the creative writer is not an artist he certainly should be. But, interestingly enough, what is here said of the artist can equally be said of the philosopher. Each must be persons of "integral awareness." There is a strong sense in which their paths cross vocationally: The writer is a philosopher-in-action, while as an artist he is perhaps one of a more persuasive caliber. At any rate, one of his chief functions is to articulate philosophical ideas in literary form. John-Paul Sartre is a contemporary case in point.

In large measure, as the artist goes, so goes contemporary culture. An artist of an especially persuasive type, the creative writer plays a stupendous role in the course of civilization. He conveys his ideas, which help steer a people's culture. As a set of beliefs and value judgments, a culture, in turn, steers a given civilization. Thus, as written ideas go, so in large measure the people will go. As the people come to assume more and more leisure time in the future, how can they manifest less apathy and more social consciousness unless the creative writer proves his art; he must jolt and jab them with his barbs and inspire and elevate them with his insight. This is no mean task. Aesthetic creativity without philosophical integrity, intellectual acuity and prophetic insight may be a banal drag on a culture rather than a boon or blessing. For the writer merely to echo his environment is both minimal creativity and minimal artistry. Such realism duplicates in its way what "progressive education" often is noted for, the pooling of ignorance. Such assumed artistry is more retrogressive than progressive to cultural resourcefulness.

Next we might ask: What should be the role of the creative writer in the age of the computer? In the face of the rising tides of mechanistic ways of doing things, is the future role of the creative writer jeopardized? Hardly. As movies and television and other media of the oral arts become more widespread, the creative writer's role, we suggest, may become more anonymous but also significant. Working more behind the scenes, his challenge may become more intense as his opportunities are enhanced. As the clamor for entertainment increases with more leisure time on the part of the public, the creative supply will have to meet the popular demand both in content and style. As the public's literacy and leisure become more characteristic of the American way of life, constructive entertainment will become even more of a premium than it is at present. Fresh ideas will become more the vogue while harder and harder to attain. Combined information and philosophical interpretation will constitute the creative writer's intensified art. Philosophical lucidity and clever style will become more of a creative team than ever before, as intellectual integrity joins forces with attention-getting techniques. Behind the scenes but in the forefront of artistic leadership in both the entertainment world and the new modes of educational endeavor through mass communication, the creative writer will loom larger than ever in importance.

But on the negative side, the creative writer will be under the serious temptation to compete with the oral artist as chief entertainer. If he capitulates to the temptation, his creativity is apt to spell degradation. Probably there is but one significant antidote to such a cultural disease: the creative writer must keep the philosophical content of his work uppermost while vibrant and alive with personal and social relevance to life situations. The already big order will be even bigger in the days ahead.

Similarly, the personally creative writer will be increasingly teased by the impersonal computer. The temptation will be to seek shortcuts to artistic achievement. Not as vulnerable as the perpetrator of "canned music," the writer is still apt to be caught up in the mechanistic whirlpool. Though the computer has its place, it is apt to deaden creative artistry and be as negligible as a quack's mechanical cure for cancer. Despite the strengths of the new modes of computation and communication, however, the creative writer will be involved in a "challenge and response" situation, since technology favors the oral word over the written. Despite McLuhan's doubts, the printed word will continue to be the strategic means of communication for a long time to come. In the United States, it will continue to be the "architect of nationalism" while it should increasingly become the architect of internationalism in our rapidly shrinking world. As literacy increases among our masses on every continent, the written word will continue to be the chief medium of propaganda. The political implications are quite marked, however, for according to a survey released by the University of Missouri the United States ranks but sixth in freedom of press.

A third question that needs to be asked is this: Should the creative writer regard literary style or aesthetic charm as an end in itself or should he employ it as a medium of truth? Should aesthetic taste override philosophical inspiration and content? In short, are artistic innovations to be seen as ends or means? Publisher Seth Richards makes his appraisal clear: "Innovation," he declares, "has too often been the signal for deterioration in the standards of prose composition." Not only does this apply to obscurantism in the use of language but to stylistic anarchy through the abandonment of traditional standards. I recall, for instance, when the novel, *Cry, The Beloved Country*, by Alan Paton first appeared. A provocative and creative work on race relations within a South African setting, its grammatical style was, nevertheless, utterly revolting. It was as though the author were in a state of adolescent rebellion against the use of classical grammar. This aspect of his style was so mechanically conspicuous that it detracted from the philosophical content by its impositions. Indeed, style should never be considered an end in itself, for it is always a medium that serves that which is superior to itself.

Should a piece of literature be deemed qualitatively superior unless it reflects not only a technique of beauty but the author's very *philosophy* of beauty as well? It would seem that a mature piece of creative literature should reflect an aesthetic form quite consistent with its content and especially the writer's interpretation of what beauty in general constitutes. A classical example would be Plato's dialogues in which the dialectical style of writing matches well the Socratic maieutics of thought and the author's aesthetic tastes. The same principle is reflected in Greek and Gothic architecture: the aesthetic forms reflect the aesthetic technique. Also, aesthetic interpretations are seen in "the stream of consciousness novels" of the early 1900's. The writer's aesthetic techniques and aesthetic perspectives are powerfully influenced by the Bergsonian philosophy of the period, since time-consciousness plays a major role in both content and structure. An authority on this, Dr. Shiv K. Kumar sees what we mean brilliantly expressed in the works of such artists as Dorothy Richardson, Virginia Woolf, and James Joyce.

In addition, T. S. Elliot's poem 'The Waste Land' is very much a combination of aesthetic style and philosophy. Even Faulkner's novels reflect a consistency here. As specialists remind us, his material in his greatest work appears on the surface as unrelated chunks of insight, but upon closer examination they are seen to interlock in one great whole. One of the most neglected literary geniuses is the Danish philosopher Soren Kierkegaard, whose powerful technique of "indirect communication" gets on the inside of his reader with remarkable ability to let him see things for himself. Kierkegaard's writing is a vivid example of how aesthetic technique and philosophical aesthetics can coalesce. Together they are the warp and woof of some of his most powerful passages. One can hardly appreciate his aesthetic technique, however, until one understands his philosophy, which is both existential and religious. Perhaps his book, *Stages On Life's Way*, illustrates this as clearly as any other single work.

One of the big prices we pay for overspecialized learning these days is the frequent neglect of the issue of how aesthetic form and aesthetic interpretation must coalesce. Sometimes specialists in literary technique completely ignore the meaning and content to an author's aesthetic views. At an eastern university a graduate student capable of taking his Ph.D. in either of several areas was considering a dissertation on T. S. Eliot. Learning of a teacher of literature who had recently written her dissertation on Eliot's aesthetics, he approached her about the possibility of taking her course on Eliot's works. When he questioned her about Eliot's philosophical aesthetics, she immediately begged off with, "I don't know anything about Eliot's philosophy — only his aesthetics."

"But," said the student, "a man's aesthetics is a part of his philosophy, and aesthetics is a long-standing branch of philosophical studies." The teacher's response was artificially cold, whereupon she went to the administrators to advise them that the student was ineligible to take her class! Perhaps it is obvious that the real problem was that the woman knew Eliot's stylistic techniques but not his interpretation of poetic beauty that gave birth to them. Her tragic error did open-faced violence not only to the student but the literary genius whom she herself admired. Eliot's aesthetics was given but mechanical treatment at the expense of its philosophical grounding. Little wonder, however, when today many departments of literature in our colleges and universities seldom encourage their students to study philosophy, despite the fact that all great literature must deal with it.

Fourth, should the creative writer reflect his social environment and intellectual climate or should he help modify them, so that contemporary culture might be redirected constructively? When a novel is historical in nature perhaps the matter is settled as in the case of Ole Rolvaag's *Giants in the Earth* and many others. But many novels of our time attempt to depict things the way they are seen to be, either popularly or through the writer's colored glasses by which he sees only what he looks for. There are bundles of the latter type from dime store novels to reputable works. A certain author entitled one of his novels *The Way We Live Today*. The novel's sex-suffused pages depict what that author sees realistically about contemporary sex life in certain quarters, but the "we" in his title is very much taken for granted. To say the least, such a book echoes the writer's selected environment and what he looks for, but little else. Is the height of literary creativity merely to duplicate what one sees and perhaps sees on a restricted level at that? I am reminded of a college teacher of creative writing for whom nothing rated an 'A' save romantic slush and slop. Implied here are the philosophical value judgments of both the writer and the appraiser. The writer's choice either to duplicate or to re-direct human tastes and practices demands consideration for what values are really worth writing about.

Is the creative writer responsible for the preservation of the higher moral and axiological aspects of a contemporary culture, or is he amoral or sterilely objective in the same way some scientists regard themselves in relation to their work? Is the author a conserver or possible transformer of values? And by the same token, is he possibly a disintegrator of values? Is he a prophetic critic, a constructive reactionist or a preserver of the status quo? Which is he to be? Can he be either or all perhaps? Whatever he now is, what should he be is the underlying question, especially with respect to the future course of events? In his book *Trousered Apes*, Duncan Williams attacks the moral relativism of much literature today, the extreme realism of which frequently echoes the worst on the double front of animalism and violence. Perhaps the time is overdue for such attacks. Writers need to see the philosophical responsibility of being reconditioners of our heavily conditioned existence. Humanistic freedom has been reduced to realistic license. What sociologist Pitirim Sorokin acknowledges to have become a sensate culture is now being glorified in the West to the exclusion of anything else by all too many writers. Meanwhile the bottom seems to be falling out of our civilization as men look into literary mirrors only to see themselves as little more than beasts. The supreme tragedy is that man is now demanned of his manhood. Needed today is a new vision of human possibilities based on new and higher incentives. Whose responsibility is it to clarify this for the people of this age if not the creative writer? A new set of ideational values must be articulated to offset the cheap realism expressed by four-letter words. New vision is needed to re-make literary tastes and ambitions. A firmer cultural footing must be found if we are to withstand the relativistic quicksands by which we are about to be swallowed.

Yet, critical realism is by no means altogether bad. Sometimes it has no substitute for shaking people out of their lethargy. As different as they are, Aldous Huxley's *Brave New World*, William S. Lederer's *A Nation of Sheep*, and Lederer and Burdick's *The Ugly American* are all of this type as they expose in down-to-earth terms some of the social and international issues of our day. Even so, more often than not today's realists are too atomistic. As creative writers they frequently analyze but do not synthesize. Should not the creative writer pull together as much as he takes apart? Should he not guide as much as he examines? But such is no mean task that calls for a philosophical sensitivity to what is unifying amidst the flux of things, what is permanent amidst change, what makes for wholeness amidst the parts. Overly atomistic, the extreme realist is much more superficial about these issues than were the romanticists spearheaded by Rousseau and Goethe, for instance. Rousseau tried to be as constructive as he was critical; Goethe's Faust at least posed deep-seated questions which implied a nostalgia for answers. Today there are some positive signs latent within the yearnings and feelings of the young dispossessed generation. Whether a neo-idealism will prove adequate, or even likely, remains to be seen, but it would be more holistic, should it materialize, than most twentieth-century realism.

Where do we go from here? is a related question. And how do we get there? is a subconscious concern. Assuming that the writer's role is not only to report what he observes but also to help lead men out of their cultural morass such questions are important. Both the fiction writer and the poet influence people profoundly, because they depict a human image by which men mould their lives. Iconoclasts of another day like Henry David Thoreau and Friedrich Nietzsche and those of our day like Albert Camus, Franz Kafka and Jean-Paul Sartre have helped pave the way for new points of view, but it is not enough merely to negatively attack "the establishment" of a given day. A positive and constructive role must surmount the negative turf-breaking. New values must replace those being debunked. After writing his pessimistic poetry T. S. Eliot turned to a positive kind. After negative exposures designed to move people to see themselves caught in a maelstrom of meaningless existence, he articulated a positive message designed to inspire a new outlook. For Eliot a naked temporal existence was eventually qualified by a faith-subsumed eternal dimension of life; glimmers of hope penetrated the gloom.

Similarly on the positive side stand some promising writers, who recognize that we are indeed drowning from literary weather reports. They are the kind who see that the creative writer's philosophical responsibility is to help change the climate. It is a herculean task but a challenging vocation. At Drew University a few years ago a number of young novelists and other writers participated in a summer seminar conducted by Dr. Stanley R. Hopper, then Dean of the Graduate School. They came together to study the implications of the creative writer's constructive role in contemporary culture. A literary critic of prominence and sensitive to the writer's important place in our society, Dr. Hopper is the author of *Spiritual Problems in Contemporary Literature* (Harper). Most of the young writers in the seminar were appreciative of what the said title implies and wanted to be among those who elevate their society rather than duplicate it. It is a wholesome sign.

It is our contention that much like the "ethics of creativeness" propounded by Nicholas Berdyaev, a fresh burst of constructive literary creativeness can be opened up philosophically only as talented writers become amenable to a re-conditioning from within; whereby spiritual values will be allowed to breathe with renewed relevance upon them and the reading public. The most promising such source today is the philosophy of religious existentialism whose creative impact has only begun to be felt through the poems of T. S. Eliot and the plays of Gabriel Marcel. The chief clue is the recovery of human dignity through a recovery of spiritual meaning. When this becomes more the vogue the creative writer will again prove himself not only an artist and connoisseur of the finer things of life but a diligent articulator of those human values that do more than echo one's environment but, rather, guide mankind to new heights of human possibility. Such a responsibility is indeed as awesome as it is timely. Those who accept it can make a great contribution to the cure of our cultural cancer.

Chapter 19

The Meaningful Life
and Self-Transcendence

Essential to the procurement of meaning in life is the phenomenon of self-transcendence. What is self-transcendence? It is basic to the fulfillment of one's potentialities and the overcoming of self-centeredness. It is that which makes human beings *sui generis*, i.e. more than closed systems or animals; it is what makes them aware of themselves as persons and keeps them open to the world of other selves as well as the need for a meaningful existence. Self-transcendence is what Viktor E. Frankl calls the "noological dimension," apart from which one is not fully human. It is what rounds-out a person as an existential whole not fully explainable by his or her parts.

It is because of this noological dimension of self-transcendence that any psychotherapy that merely seeks homeostasis or a relief of tensions falls short and betrays the characteristic of the human being as human. Though the Freudian and Adlerian perspectives in psychiatry have their place, they are in this respect too delimiting. Often patients need more than equilibrium or the reduction of tensions. Furthermore, such perspectives are too hedonistic, as psychologists like Allport and Maslow also have recognized. Such weaknesses in psychoanalysis and psychiatry are apt to neglect the need of persons to be creative, purposive, and value-oriented in the search for a meaning in life (Frankl, 1966, pp. 97 f.; cf. Frankl, 1967, pp. 18, 19).

Dr. Frankl argues provocatively that the pleasure principle beneath the homeostasis perspective in psychoanalysis is self-defeating. The more persons aim at pleasure or happiness the less they are apt to attain it. Pleasure is rather a side-effect or by-product of attaining a goal.

Both Freud and Adler missed this point. With Freud in mind, Frankl says, "Both orgasm and potency are impaired by being made the target of intention;" and with Adler in mind ". . . a person who displays and exhibits his status drive, will sooner or later be dismissed as a status-seeker" (1966, p. 98; 1967, pp. 37-40). Both are self-defeating forms of hedonism.

The will to meaning is a higher concern for self-transcendence, one that can envelop the lower drives by reorienting them. Yet, the drive for self-actualization stressed by Abraham H. Maslow and other psychologists today is not the highest intention: ". . . if made an end in itself," says Frankl, "it contradicts the self-transcending quality of human existence." Self-realization should be viewed as an effect, not an aim, of "meaning fulfillment," and unless this is the case it even loses its justification. Self-transcendence implies that being human is being directed to "meanings to fulfill or to other human beings lovingly to encounter" (Frankl 1966, p. 99; c. 1975, pp. 78 f. ; 1980, p. 6). It is to forget oneself by self-giving to a cause or person to love. Frankl underlines Aaron J. Ungersma's view that the Freudian pleasure principle is the infantile guide, the Adlerian power principle that of the adolescent and the will to meaning that of the adult. The three Viennese schools of psychoanalysis are to be seen with these respective emphases or perspectives; however, the first two appeal only to the unconscious levels of life. The third deals also with the conscious level; it does not supplant the other views but supplements them with a fuller, holistic, and existential picture of the human being.

The will to meaning is not a "drive" so much as a kind of "pull," since the human being ". . . is pushed by drives but pulled by meaning," and this implies decision. Were the search for meaning a drive, the homeostatic concern of the therapist would be sufficient, since it would be enough to settle for an equilibrium of tensions, but that is not always adequate. Furthermore, it is one thing to be driven toward something and quite another to strive for it. The decisive factor is that the individual must decide freely whether he or she wishes to fulfill his or her meaning. On the other hand, it is not enough simply to assert the preservation of freedom or willpower. "Meaning itself has to be elucidated" (Frankl, 1966, pp. 100, 127; cf. 1961).

Being distinctively human, Frankl believes, is being directed to something other than oneself. While subjectivity is basic there is also a "trans-subjectiveness," which is a person's involvement with other subjects as well as objects. There is a natural tension between object and subject. This tension goes with being human; even sports are invented to help people create and live with their tensions in a healthy way, even if somewhat ascetically. Also, a sound amount of polar tension between the reality of the "I am" and the ideal of "I ought" is favorable; the sense of ought helps make for self-transcendence and moves toward meaningfulness (Frankl, 1966, pp. 101-104, 136). All forms of reductionism, including that of Freud, compete with such meaningfulness, for they reduce ideals to mere defense mechanisms.

To overcome "existential vacuum," the feeling that life is blasé or absurd, one needs to develop a meaningful philosophy of life, which moves one toward possibilities, ideals and values (Frankl, 1965a, p.20). The self-transcendent search for meaning often implies "I ought." Now one's "being in the world" becomes "meaning in the world." This is more than self-expression or self-actualization and a mere use of things and people for the satisfaction of one's instinctual drives. A meaningful existence often implies creativity, loving relationships, and a sense of vocation about one's work. But, in addition, it implies a reckoning with "the tragic triad" of suffering, guilt, and life's transitoriness or fear of death. A therapist who only addresses the bodily or psychic factors and seeks only to tranquilize a patient's anxieties, say, about guilt or death, is remiss. Similarly, a person seldom despairs over suffering per se but whether it has any meaning in life. Such meaning cannot be grasped intellectually, for it supersedes human finitude; it is rooted in one's "total existence" and calls for an existential commitment to ontos or one's concrete Being. Logotherapy addresses itself to this matter in such a way as to help patients see meaning in their situation. Nothing is imposed from without so much as evoked or educed from within, and each patient is dealt with in ways peculiar to his or her existence. This often calls for a maieutic dialogue between the doctor and the patient about the basic issues of life (Frankl, 1967, pp. 52-53).

The frequent phenomenon of "emptiness" or "existential frustration," Frankl would have us understand, is due to a failure to find meaning in life. He states, "Even if this search is frustrated, it cannot be considered a sign of disease. It is spiritual distress, not mental disease." Why is it that? Existentially it is because the spirit of a person is the total self with special regard for what existentialists call "inwardness" and the Bible calls the "heart." How should clinicians view this? If in a reductionist way they address the existential distress as a sickness this "robs the patient of the potential fruits of his spiritual struggle" (Frankl, 1967, p. 72). Frankl thinks the psychiatrist needs a sound philosophy of life when treating a patient in despair. Instead of seeing everything in terms of alleged psychogenic roots, it is wiser to preserve the human phenomenon of the total person more in the phenomenological terms of the philosophers Husserl and Scheler. This preserves respect for the noological dimension of the human being, the quality that allows a person to be more than a biological and psychological specimen. It preserves the elements of self-transcendence and moral freedom so basic to what is distinctively human in the holistic, existential sense.

Psychiatrists who see the importance of the noological dimension of the patient will, for example, not only treat the feelings of guilt which a patient may have, but will respect the probability that the patient really is "existentially guilty." Thus they will not only consider the somagenic and psychogenic factors but also the noogenic factors. Problems of this kind are not merely pathological yet may eventuate in a neurotic condition, which Frankl calls "noogenic neurosis" (1967, pp. 43 f., 122; 1965a, p. xi). Logotherapy addresses such problems as a psychotherapy that respects the existential frustrations people may develop. Even in the case of hyperthyroidism (for which Frankl developed the first tranquilizer) and a patient's "anticipatory anxiety," the latter thrives on the existential vacuum. Frankl overtly states, "Filling this vacuum prevents the patient from having a relapse. Refocusing him on meaning and purpose and decentering him away from obsession and compulsion cause these symptoms to atrophy" (1967, p. 77; cf. p. 145). Here we see how the therapeutic factor is a noological supplement based on respect for a variety of psychotherapeutic approaches and techniques.

The psychiatrist should seek to enter into an I-thou relationship with the patient and never treat him or her as a mere means to any kind of end, lest the medical treatment become mechanized and the patient be overlooked as a person. The therapeutic relationship should be based on an I-thou encounter between persons. Contrary to Freud, a patient becomes an *ego* only in relation to a thou. This reminds us of the thesis of the existentialist Martin Buber. It implies that the doctor not only treat the patient's problem but also the patient's attitude toward it. Even one's suffering, aging, or dying can be ennobling rather than degrading. Much can depend upon the patient's religious outlook, says Frankl, when it comes to "the tragic triad" of pain, guilt and death (1967, pp. 87 ff.; cf. p. 143 ff; 1961, pp. 8 ff). These are the basic existential facts of life and should not be bypassed or obscured by the doctor. More than instinctual, they are spiritual concerns around which a growing amount of neurosis centers today. To reduce the fear of death to castration anxiety, for instance, is to deny an existential fact of life. A right attitude toward suffering, death and guilt can make all the difference in the world. As for the problem of guilt, Frankl states that a person ". . who has failed by a deed cannot change what happened, but by repentance he can change himself" (1967, p. 90). It is for reasons of this kind that Professor Farnsworth of Harvard has said, "Physicians must of necessity indulge in philosophy." Frankl similarly maintains that there should be no objection to the therapeutic effect of a patient's religious convictions. Here the words of Albert Einstein prove apropos, "What is the meaning of human life . . . ? To find a satisfying answer to this question means to be religious." (Frankl 1967, p. 93; cf. pp. 90-94, incl. note).

When Dr. Frankl differentiates the noological from the biological and psychological factors of existence, he is not thinking of different layers of personhood but so-called "dimensions." This preserves diversity but within the basic wholeness and unity of human nature in what Frankl calls "dimensional ontology." Soma and psyche do not exhaust humanness; we must be viewed holistically. While each perspective plays its part in psychotherapy, reductionism must be avoided, i.e. a closed "nothing but" interpretation should be dropped (Frankl, 1967, pp. 137-142; cf. 1965b). Every dimension should be respected within the whole human being. This is related to the fact that every cognition is based on a "polar tension between the objective and subjective. . . ." The dynamics involved is "noodynamics," which is more all embracing than psychodynamics alone (Frankl, 1967, p. 135). It is holistic and existential.

The self-transcendence or noological dimension of the human being involves elements of free will, reflection, self-detachment, humor, conscience, and the will to meaning. It implies that as people take an attitude toward themselves they can shape their character. We are not totally pawns of deterministic forces. Something as significant as conscience cannot be completely reduced to conditioning factors, lest the person be left on a sub-human level. In short, self-transcendence becomes a truly human phenomenon, which means that the human being is not a closed or reductionistic system (Frankl, 1961, pp. 15-30, 31 ff.; cf. 1965a, pp. 20, 188, 268-76). The latter kind of system is settled for in a homeostatic type of psychotherapy. Cultural creations become mere byproducts of the "drive for personal satisfaction," as Charlotte Buehler is said to suggest with Freud in mind. In contrast, Frankl believes that humans can live intentionally or with a purpose behind their striving, one that seeks to create values which foster mental health. Such intentional living is more than an aim at pleasure or happiness. Pleasure should be seen rather as an effect, much like Plato's view of happiness as an effect of contemplation. Fulfillment of meaning is more than self-actualization. The latter, again, is an effect of fulfilled meaning, the "unintentional effect of life's intentionality." Dr. Frankl illustrates this by the success of his first book, which was published anonymously; even unexpected effects followed meaningful intention (1961, pp. 32-38).

Similarly, Frankl employs the technique of "paradoxical intention" in which the patient is encouraged to exaggerate his or her fears and even wish the very thing that is feared, with tongue in cheek. Often this evokes humor, which becomes a coping device and relief measure.

Often to strive directly for a good conscience is to miss it, pharisaically. This is much like self-actualization as a goal. To make health one's chief aim is likewise to become a hypochondriac. These errors parallel the self-defeating pursuits of pleasure and self-actualization. It is to become childlike. Tension is not to be avoided at all costs. As seen above, a certain amount of tension belongs to being human and is indispensable for mental well-being. It has been observed, for instance, that when Berkeley students pleaded freedom of speech or picketed for a similar cause the number of psychiatric patients among them was greatly reduced. Thus, a goal amidst tensions of thought remedies the situation. Similarly when people have tasks to perform, mental health improves. Tasks combined with freedom to choose them is the best combination (Frankl, 1961, pp. 39-49).

Beneath the surface of the above discussion has bobbed a pertinent question: What is the meaning of a meaningful existence? This calls to mind the particular references to self-transcendence and the polar tension between object and subject; also "the tension between the 'I am' and the 'I ought,' or between reality and ideal, between being and meaning," as Frankl prefers to express it. Only in the "peak-experiences" of life do the 'ought' and the 'is' merge. Being human in the fullest sense implies there are meaning and values to fulfill. Authentic human existence demands respect for self-detachment and self-transcendence. All relativism of values falls short here. Though meanings differ from person to person they are unique as persons are unique. Basic is the matter of human existence transcending itself or being concerned about what is other than itself as well as itself. If there is no meaning, Frankl points out, other determinants have to be hypothesized to replace them, but, then, the humanness of behavior is lost. He states, "If psychology or, for that matter, psychotherapy is to be rehumanized, it has to remain cognizant of self-transcendence rather than scotomizing it." Escalating suicide figures in Sweden and Austria are directly related to a meaninglessness despite affluence; self-transcendence is obscured. As Frankl comments, "They have the means to live but no meaning to live for" (1961, pp. 50-54; 1980, pp. 6f).

One is restless, in the Augustinian sense, until one finds meaning in one's existence. Meanings, then, are unique to each individual. As Soren Kierkegaard said, "Truth is subjectivity." It is what is existentially relevant. There is no universal meaning, yet the existentially relevant meanings may have much in common. These are values of social significance. Socially, there even may be a hierarchy of values, but these do not relieve us from making decisions. The individual is free to accept or reject a value in the light of his or her conscience and situation. This is subjectivity but not sheer subjectivism; it is an interpretation of values, since meanings are discovered and not simply projected. Meanings are not arbitrarily given but found responsibly. Conscience plays an important role here. "Conscience," says Dr. Frankl, "could be defined as the intuitive capacity of man to find out the meaning of a situation" (1961, p. 63, cf. pp 55-63). Conscience may even find unique meanings, which contradict socially accepted values. Such had to be the case, Frankl believes, with the discovery of such values as "Thou shalt not kill" and "Thou shalt not commit adultery."

But today popular respect for these values is waning. This is the cause of increased noological neurosis based on the "existential vacuum." Therefore, if education cannot rely on traditional values it should at least refine the capacity which allows persons to find unique meanings or values based on authentic decisions of their own. Individuals will still have to resist bad effects of the existential vacuum, namely conformism and totalitarianism (1961, pp. 65, 83; cf. pp. 63 ff). Though our conscience may err, we must respect it if we are not to violate our own humanness. In agreement with existentialists, Frankl indicates that possible error does not relieve one from trial or commitment. Furthermore, since we might be wrong, we must respect the other person's belief or obedience to conscience. Except in an emergency like attempted suicide, the psychotherapist must not impose his or her values on patients but refer them to their own conscience. A person's conscience should neither be violated nor suppressed. Similarly, while a person needs to find a meaning it must not be imposed or prescribed by the doctor. Meaning may be fostered through creative work, by experiencing forms of beauty and goodness or by loving relationships with others. Dr. Frankl sees three types of values: creative, experiential, and attitudinal. Respectively, these imply what a person *gives* to the world; what they *take* from it; and the *stand* they take in their situation (1961, pp. 56-71). All are important to mental health.

As for attitudinal values, even helpless victims of hopeless situations can sometime rise above themselves and be changed. Bad predicaments can be greatly modified by attitudes that change predicaments into achievements. But what about inescapable suffering? It is not enough to be masochistic. Suffering must be accepted yet transmuted into something meaningful. This it does if it affects one for the better. Attitudinal values apply here, for ". . . there are no tragic and negative aspects which could not be by the stand one takes to them transmuted into positive accomplishments" (Frankl, 1961, p. 73; cf. 1980, pp. 7-9). Much the same applies to guilt, except that in the case of suffering one may accept one's fate, and in the case of guilt one reshapes oneself by an inner transmutation. Repentance in this respect is therapeutic.

As for the third aspect of "the tragic triad," viz. life's transitoriness, there is a responsible view also to be maintained not unlike Heidegger's "living toward death" to enhance one's authentic existence. One must see that one is responsible for using passing opportunities to actualize potentialities and realize values; one is responsible for how to suffer, how to regard oneself, and whom to love. Responsibility of this kind enhances the meaning of life. It also implies that attitudinal values are even more important than the others (Frankl, 1961, pp. 72-81).

As inferred, the existential vacuum of meaninglessness usually leads to social conformism or totalitarianism. Even Freudian psychologists admit that this phenomenon is growing. It centers much around boredom, apathy, and a feeling that life and the world are absurd or of no consequence. Scientific reductionism, relativism, and positivism contribute much to it among students today. The human being is reduced to a mere thing, a bored thing at that. Interest and initiative are stifled, and the suicide rate among students mounts. This pro-Freudian suspicion that the existential vacuum is pathological is due to keeping matters on the psychological plane and not opening up respect for the noological dimension of self-transcendence. The existential vacuum must not be left on the level of a psychogenic neurosis; it may be a cause of a noogenic neurosis based on a moral or spiritual problem (Frankl, 1961, pp. 83-93).

Sexual pleasure is often resorted to as an escape from one's existential frustration. The will to pleasure often becomes a substitute for the will to meaning. The will to power often does, too. It often assumes the form of gaining wealth, but commonly lacks purpose as one's means replace his ends. One thing people need more of today is leisure for contemplation and meditation, not just pleasure (Frankl, 1961, p. 93-98).

We have come to see that though Logotherapy does not invade the territory of theology, it does leave the door open to religion, leaving the patient to decide whether to pass through it or not. It is up to the patient to decide whether he/she is responsible to humanity, conscience, God, or perhaps all. As previously suggested, psychotherapy aims at mental health and religion at salvation; nevertheless, the two can be compatible and buttress each other. Though worship is to the glory of God, it can make for a meaning-giving composure in life. Logotherapy, which respects this fact, should be available to every patient regardless of what the doctor's own philosophy may be. Logotherapy can serve the religious perspective and the religious perspective can serve mental health. Psychotherapy and theology are not to be fused, Frankl recognizes, yet theology is the more inclusive discipline, since it can embrace all the anthropological dimensions.

Also, ultimate meaning or "supra-meaning," as Frankl expresses it, is more than an intellectual matter, since it is existentially grounded on one's whole being committed to God through faith. Kierkegaard spoke of this as total-self commitment and "the absolute relation to the Absolute." Frankl similarly sees it as trust. I see it as accepting God as the Absolute beyond all our relativisms and accepting the Absolute on His terms, not ours. Adapting a famous sentence from Ludwig Wittgenstein, Dr. Frankl translates it from agnostic to theistic terms, "To Him of Whom one cannot speak, to Him one must pray" (1961, p. 146; cf. pp. 142-150). Frankl refers to this in near-Kierkegaardian manner when he says, "What our patients need is unconditional faith in unconditional meaning" (1961, p. 156). When this is experienced no life is a total failure, for it is re-oriented around a meaning that supersedes life's transitoriness and finitude.

Frankl is very much aware that "biology is overarched by psychology, psychology by noology, and noology by theology" (1975, p. 13). The noological or self-transcendent dimension is uniquely human; it is the holistic seat of the existential self that seeks meaning. Religion is to Frankl our search for *ultimate* meaning. This is akin to Kierkegaard's view of faith's encounter with the Absolute and Tillich's respect for "the Ground of our being." Frankl's respect for the ultimate makes religion to him more than a matter of willful acquiescence to such virtues as faith, hope, and love. Symbols of God may be helpful, but for belief in God to be genuine it must be unconditional. It is, therefore, not an intellectual deduction but an existential commitment to the Unconditioned, which, as the infinite, supersedes all finite or conditional concepts. Here Frankl is very much in accord with theologians of an existential perspective, including Tillich, who see religion based psychologically on our Ultimate Concern.

Psychoanalysts since Freud and Adler have been prone to atomize human beings and reduce them to little more than the biological, whereas Logotherapy recognizes human beings in their full stature as human. It is not only "depth psychology" but "height psychology," since it is not only concerned with human problems based on the past but upon the possibilities for the future (Frankl, 1967, p. 18). The ego drives and energies of the lower dimensions are not denied, but seen as tributary to the whole self with the higher noological concerns and existential perspective. This implies that the human being is more than an "automaton of a psychic apparatus" and is seen to have the "autonomy of spiritual existence." The term "spiritual" here is meant to indicate the distinctively human, holistic, existential, and responsible elements of self-transcendence; it does not specify a certain brand of religion. To be responsible, however, is to face up to the question which life itself asks of a person: What is the meaning of my life? And it is to respond to it personally in the here and now of existence (Frankl, 1975, pp. 19-24). The religious response is one which seeks an ultimate meaning in life.

Frankl believes that the unconscious mind is not only instinctual but spiritual as well. Depth psychology was limited by Freud to the former, the instinctual id with its repressions. It should be understood that for Frankl the spiritual element is not only conscious, but unconscious. Existence itself is to a great extent unconscious in nature, since it can never be fully perceived. Even so, the conscious and unconscious cannot be sharply demarcated. However, the instinctual and spiritual are incommensurable. Far more important than the distinction between the conscious and the unconscious is that between the instinctual and the spiritual. Therefore, being a person is not just a matter of being driven by somagenic factors but being drawn to a meaningful end or, as Karl Jaspers puts it, "deciding what one is going to be." It is a case of being spiritual, i.e. having a reorientation around what one deems Ultimate, thus making one responsible for one's existence and destiny. This is what religious existentialists mean by "authentic existence," adapting the phrase from Heidegger. One chooses one's existence rather than being driven into it. For psychoanalysis not to come to grips with this element in life is for it to de-humanize the human being of humanness. It is to denigrate the unconscious by limiting it to the id or the instinctual and to overlook its spiritual quality. The psychotherapist who sees this will marshall this spiritual element of responsibility over against a "neurotic fatalism" (Frankl, 1975, pp. 25-29). To be human is to be a person or an existential spiritual center. One does not have a self but *is* a self. Such a self has a psychophysical dimension, however, identified as the "id." Yet there is a difference between "being" and "having." The human being *is* an individual but is also an integrated whole who *has* somatic, psychic, and spiritual aspects. The individual is a unity of the soma and psychic but is not a whole without the spiritual. The spiritual whole of existence is an *Urphenomenon*, i.e., it is not analyzable or reducible, since it belongs to the basic ontological nature of human existence with its freedom, responsibility and self-transcendence. The center of the whole person is the unconscious spirit. Like the eye that doesn't see that it sees, the unconscious, Frankl indicates, is what determines whether an experience will be conscious or unconscious (1975, pp. 29-32).

Conscience is not only conscious but is an important aspect of the unconscious spirit and the irreducible self in its wholeness of being. Belonging mainly to the unconscious, conscience is "irrational" or "prelogical," Frankl maintains, ostensibly contrary to Kant. Conscience belongs to the prescientific understanding and is even premoral in the sense that it precedes the understanding of moral and social values and is inscrutable in its judgments. The sense of "ought" is irrational, Frankl believes; it does not pertain to what *is* but what *ought to* be, something not real but "something to make real" and to be actualized. Implied here is an intuition of what is anticipated; hence Frankl regards it as "irrational" in the sense of being prerational or prelogical. He concedes a similar intuition and irrationality to love. No universal law of reason does justice to the individualistic nature of such intuitions, for it deals with concrete, personal cases. In both matters of conscience and love, choices are involved and instincts do not have the total say. Morals and love belong to the spiritual unconscious center of the person.

In this light the goal of psychotherapy is not to make everything conscious all the time. To do that to a violinist, for instance, would make him or her too self-conscious about playing, thus losing the creativity of the unconscious touch. Psychotherapy should bring the unconscious to the surface of the conscious only temporarily and then let it return to spiritual unconsciousness. It is the task of the therapist to reinstate the spontaneity of "the unreflected existential act." It is to respect what Blaise Pascal (*Pensees*) had in mind when he said, "The heart has reasons that reason knows not of" (see Frankl, 1975, pp. 32-39).

Conscience is not only unconscious psychologically but has a transcendent quality. People are masters of their will when they are not just driven but are responsible, or as they live by choice towards something and are not merely driven from or by something. People are similarly the servants of their conscience only as they realize that their conscience has a transcendent quality. This implies an inner dialogue, with the conscience mediating something higher. Conscience in this respect is the voice of the transcendent, spiritual quality or depth of a person. Frankl speaks of it as the "trans-human agent;" though personal it is also transpersonal. Frankl dares to speak of it as that "of which the human person is but the 'image'." It is what Frankl means by "the unconscious God." It implies that conscience is "a phenomenon pointing to its transcendent origin" (1975, pp. 52-55).

Without this transcendent quality of conscience a person would not be responsible, Frankl contends. In short the psychological fact of conscience is the immanent aspect of a transcendent phenomenon that supersedes it. As the voice of the transcendent, it is itself transcendent, belonging to the *imago dei*. This is something that irreligious people fail to recognize. Though responsible, they do not recognize that from which their conscience stems; they stop with the mere immanence of conscience, neglecting "the ultimate" or transcendent to which it is responsible. The religious person keeps the door open to the transcendent dimension or God. God is the ultimate reference or transcendent quality that gives conscience its categorical character or authority (Frankl, 1975, pp. 55-57).

Any attempt to reduce conscience to psychodynamics, says Frankl, fails. Conscience can be identified with neither the ego nor the superego. It is not a mere product of social conditioning or even psychosomatic drives, for it belongs to the whole existing self with its spiritual transcendence. Though the self may suppress the drives, conscience is not itself derived from them, for it belongs to the existential wholeness of a person, and this includes the spiritually transcendent or noological dimension, besides the somatic and psychic.

The spiritual unconscious is not reducible to the id, hence the existential description of the human being does not settle for the irrational and instinctual stages, as does psychoanalysis. The spiritual unconscious includes what Frankl calls "unconscious religiousness," which is a "latent relation to transcendence inherent in man." He speaks of it as "the transcendent unconscious," the intentional referent of which is the so-called "unconscious God." The spiritual unconscious implies that the human being has an unconscious relation to God that can become conscious. This does not mean that God is within the human being or that the unconscious is metaphysically divine or omniscient; nor does it mean an impersonal religious force or archetype in human beings, such as Carl G. Jung maintained. Though unconscious, it is very much personal and a matter of existential choice, not a collective unconscious drive or instinct (Frankl, 1975, pp. 58-72). When a matter of existential choice arises, the unconscious God becomes conscious to the person; it is then genuinely religious, because it is a matter of commitment, which proves most therapeutic when it is spontaneous.

Unconscious religiousness, much like the conscience, is "a latent relation to transcendence inherent in man." It is "a relationship between an immanent self and a transcendent thou" (or Self). The transcendent thou is the transcendent or "spiritual unconscious." This implies that the human being has an intentional relation to transcendence, even if only on the unconscious level. The referent here may be called God or what Frankl speaks of as "the unconscious God." Implied is an unconscious relation between the human being and God even if the transcendent element is identified as "the hidden God" of the psalmist. But Frankl is shrewd enough not to identify the unconscious as the divine itself but what relates to it. Some theologians would regard it as a point-of-contact or *Anknüpfungspunkt* between humans and God or that in humans which makes them susceptible and answerable to the transcendent. Even irreligious people reflect this latent relationship as manifested in ecstatic and blissful religious dreams, says Frankl. Contrary to Jung the spiritual unconscious is not an instinctual drive in the form of the religious archetype of the collective unconscious; it is rather a dimension of the "existential agent," viz. an inner sensitivity and susceptibility (Frankl, 1975, p. 61 ff.).

At times unconscious religiousness needs to become conscious. This is especially the case when it is repressed. Here the psychotherapist may be helpful. A noogenic neurosis can develop over such repression. St. Augustine spoke of it as an inner restlessness and said in a prayer in his *Confessions*, "We are restless, O Lord, until we rest in thee."

Critically speaking, though Dr. Frankl is amenable to a theological reference point for his view of conscience and the unconscious elements of the spiritual whole person, he is to be criticized for an inadequate differentiation between the human being's immanental sensitivity to the transcendent, on the one hand, and what to the theologian is the transcendence of God, on the other. The two are not the same, yet they are related in what we have referred to above as the point-of-contact between God and man centering in man's spiritual nature. Even so, Frankl does not slip into the immanental view of humanity and God, such as maintained by C.G. Jung throughout most of his career. Frankl's intention is to keep the mentally healthy person open to the God above all finite concepts of God, and this is wholesome, even as it is amenable to what most religious existentialists are sensitive to, viz. the Unconditioned Absolute which transcends our finite concepts even at their best. This need not imply an ontological dualism of a supernatural type but an ethical existential differentiation of a qualitative type.

In conclusion, Frankl's Logotherapy can help persons overcome the cultural cancer of our time, which competes with genuine self-fulfillment. The latter is realized at best when we find meaning in life. Who, then, can assist a person toward this discovery? Frankl concedes it is not only the psychotherapist, psychologist and philosopher but above all, he says, the pastor. His Logotherapy, then, is favorable to a religious outlook akin to the writer's book, "Discovering Your Real Self."

References

Frankl, V.E. *The Will to Meaning*. New York: World Publishing Co., 1961.

Frankl, V.E. *Man's Search for Meaning*. Boston: Beacon Press, 1962.

Frankl, V.E. *The Doctor and the Soul*. New York: A. A. Knopf, 1965a.

Frankl, V.E. The Peyton Lectures, Perkins School of Theology, Southern Methodist University, Dallas, TX, February 24, 1965b (on tape).

Frankl, V.E. Self-transcendence as a human phenomenon. *Journal of Humanistic Psychology*, 1966, 6(2), 97-106.

Frankl, V.E. *The Unconscious God*. Psychotherapy & Theology. New York: Simon & Schuster, 1975.

Conclusion

In this multi-faceted study, we have observed that our worst enemy is not the international threat of nuclear warfare but the cursed cancer within our culture. It is not from beyond us but within us.

Near the outset it was shown that our social malaise is based centrally on our academic weaknesses and our failure to reform our public schools and universities. Devices and techniques supported by more money, contrary to popular opinion among educational administrators and teachers, is not the basic answer. More mature curricula are much needed for our teachers, first, and their students, second. Fundamental is the need for philosophical acuity and dialectal thought, lest a type of barbarism continue to fester as material and sensuous interests mount up and as education limits itself to economic matters.

Without qualitative education our children and youth cannot be fully civilized. Fundamental to this is the clarification of traditional moral principles and values. Understanding problems and statistics of social errors will amount to little or nothing unless linked with studies of how human beings are a hindrance to one another mainly when moral principles are neglected and submerged by all sorts of materialistic and sensate drives. The practical ethical implications, however, must not be overlooked. Values must be linked with the social settings and personal situations of people. Genuine individualism cannot survive or be revived without them, nor our culture be stopped from slipping toward degradation and defeat. Most of the maladies of America today are due to the snubbing of traditional values. This, in turn, is related to a weak educational philosophy, which fails to give birth to curricula which warrant academic quality through discursive thought basic to intellectual maturity.

But our cultural condition is not hopeless. Our cultural cancer can be cured if we re-awaken to the needs and sources of our virtues and reckon seriously with the intellectual issues posed mainly in Part II. Both teachers and our public leaders as well as parents and serious-minded students must wrestle with them, so that hopes may be renewed and constructive redirection fulfilled through fresh reappraisals of what made our nation great in the first place and what will preserve and improve it.

If educators show a willingness to qualitatively improve all academia and if students show evidence of greater concern for our values at their best, there is hope. But this hope is conditional. It must be more than a matter of sentiment; it must grow with intellectual, moral and spiritual maturity, and this through hard work, higher standards and intense study of the qualitative philosophical matters essential thereto. Quality must redirect quantity; our ethical ends must control our empirical means.

As stated above, education must be designed for more than making a living in favor of what makes for living a life. Studies in the humanities must no longer be side-lined but interwoven with the scientific and technological studies and advancements, which will be future assets to our civilization only as guided by our ethical and spiritual principles at their best. When this relationship is kept uppermost in education and not peripheral or subsidiary, we can overcome our cultural cancer — from within. We can do so; yet to do so calls for remotivations akin to what Toynbee meant when he said, "We must pray for a reprieve." An inner illness demands an inner cure. I want to believe we can realize it if we wake up soon. Only then, to adapt the words in Isaiah 49:17, will "your builders outstrip your destroyers."

Index

R

Rafferty, Max, 20
Reichenbeck, Hans, 175
Richards, Seth, 189
Rolvaag, Ole, 191
Roof, Wade C., 154
Rousseau, J. Jacques, 55
Russell, Bertrand, 50, 77, 166, 167

S

Sartre, Jean-Paul, 11,14, 30, 57, 59, 60,
    188, 195
Schweitzer, Albert, 29, 46, 50, 77, 79
Schrödinger, Erwin, 109, 138
Skinner, B.F., 47, 53, 93, 113, 117, 120,
    124, 126, 135, 171, 179
Solzhenitsyn, Alexander, 3
Sommerness, M. Duane, 176
Sorokin, Peterim, 4, 50, 53, 63, 77,
    146, 192
Spengler, Arnold, 77
Sperry, R.W., vi, 29, 58, 94, 118, 120,
    122, 134, 136-138, 140, 141, 143-
    145, 168, 170

T

Thomas, Cal, 101, 102
Tillich, Paul, 48, 54, 58, 60, 146, 162-
    164, 183, 203-204
Tipler, Frank J., 129
Toynbee, Arnold, 3, 50, 53, 58, 63, 77,
    103, 146, 212

W

Washington, George, 97
Wesley, John, 26, 64, 67, 152, 153, 174
Whitehead, Alfred North, 4, 29, 49, 53,
    77, 107-108, 112, 121, 146, 160-
    161
Whitfield, George, 153, 174
Whittier, John Greenleaf, 176
Williams, Duncan, 192
Wittgenstein, Ludwig, 203